"This comprehensive collection of studies on networked citizenship covers changes in civic orientations, patterns of media use, modes of participation and organization, socialization and citizenship education, and the emergence of large scale protest. It is the new sourcebook for the field."
—**W. Lance Bennett,** *University of Washington, Seattle*

"The growing disconnect between young people and mainstream politics has been emerging as a central motif in the ongoing dilemmas of democracy, yet has all too often been framed by easy generalisations. This impressive volume charts a much more nuanced course; it rigorously probes the idea of 'the networked young citizen' both conceptually and empirically. The chapters explore the role of social media in relation to the other key factors that shape young people's evolving political horizons—and in so doing establish a new frontline in our understanding."
—**Peter Dahlgren,** *Lund University, Sweden*

# The Networked Young Citizen

The future engagement of young citizens from a wide range of socio-economic, ethnic and cultural backgrounds in democratic politics remains a crucial concern for academics, policy-makers, civics teachers and youth workers around the world. At a time when the negative relationship between socio-economic inequality and levels of political participation is compounded by high youth unemployment or precarious employment in many countries, it is not surprising that new social media communications may be seen as a means to re-engage young citizens. This edited collection explores the influence of social media, such as YouTube, Facebook and Twitter, upon the participatory culture of young citizens.

This collection, comprising contributions from a number of leading international scholars in this field, examines such themes as the possible effects of social media use upon patterns of political socialization; the potential of social media to ameliorate young people's political inequality; the role of social media communications for enhancing the civic education curriculum; and evidence for social media manifesting new forms of political engagement and participation by young citizens. These issues are considered from a number of theoretical and methodological approaches but all attempt to move beyond simplistic notions of young people as an undifferentiated category of 'the internet generation'.

**Brian D. Loader** is Associate-Director of the Science and Technology Studies Unit (SATSU) based at the University of York, UK. His academic interests are focused around the emergence of new information and communications technologies (ICTs), such as the internet, and the social, political and economic factors shaping their development and diffusion, and their implications for social, economic, governmental and cultural change. He is General Editor of the international journal *Information, Communication and Society* and has published extensively in this field. Recent books include *Cyberprotest: New Media, Citizens and Social Movements* (Routledge, 2004); *Young Citizens in the Digital Age* (Routledge, 2007); *Digital Welfare for the Third Age* (Routledge, 2008).

**Ariadne Vromen** is Associate Professor in the Department of Government and International Relations at the University of Sydney, in Australia. She has ongoing research interests in political participation, including on young people, politics and the internet.

**Michael A. Xenos** is Associate Professor of Communication Science at the University of Wisconsin-Madison, USA. His research focuses on how the context and content of political communication influences the quality of democratic deliberation, public opinion and civic engagement.

# Routledge Studies in Global Information, Politics and Society

Edited by Kenneth Rogerson, Duke University
and Laura Roselle, Elon University

International communication encompasses everything from one-to-one cross-cultural interactions to the global reach of a broad range of information and communications technologies and processes. *Routledge Studies in Global Information, Politics and Society* celebrates—and embraces—this depth and breadth. To completely understand communication, it must be studied in concert with many factors, since, most often, it is the foundational principle on which other subjects rest. This series provides a publishing space for scholarship in the expansive, yet intersecting, categories of communication and information processes and other disciplines.

# The Networked Young Citizen

Social Media, Political Participation and Civic Engagement

**Edited by Brian D. Loader,
Ariadne Vromen, and
Michael A. Xenos**

Routledge
Taylor & Francis Group

NEW YORK AND LONDON

First published 2014
by Routledge
711 Third Avenue, New York, NY 10017

and by Routledge
2 Park Square, Milton Park, Abingdon, Oxon OX14 4RN

*Routledge is an imprint of the Taylor & Francis Group,
an informa business*

*Library of Congress Cataloging-in-Publication Data*

The networked young citizen : social media, political participation
    and civic engagement / edited by Brian D. Loader (University of
    York, UK), Ariadne Vromen (University of Sydney, Australia) and
    Michael Xenos (University of Wisconsin at Madison, USA.
        pages cm. — (Routledge studies in global information, politics
    and society ; 5)
    1. Social media—Political aspects.    2. Online social networks—
Political aspects.    3. Young adults—Political activity.    4. Youth—
Political activity.    5. Internet—Political aspects.    6. Political
participation—Technological innovations.    7. Political socialization.
I. Loader, Brian, 1958– , author, editor of compilation.    II. Vromen,
Ariadne, author, editor of compilation.    III. Xenos, Michael Andrew,
author, editor of compilation.
    HM851.N4768 2014
    302.30285—dc23
    2013049207

ISBN: 978-1-138-78114-6 (pbk)
ISBN: 978-1-138-01999-7 (hbk)
ISBN: 978-1-315-77859-4 (ebk)


Typeset in Sabon
by Apex CoVantage, LLC

# Contents

# Contributors

**Leticia Bode** is an Assistant Professor in the Communication, Culture, and Technology master's program at Georgetown University. Her work lies at the intersection of communication, technology and political behaviour, emphasizing the role communication and information technologies may play in the acquisition and use of political information.

**Ian Davies** is Professor of Education at the University of York, UK. He is the author of numerous books (published by Routledge, Continuum, Sage and others) and many articles in academic journals, most of which explore issues related to teaching and learning about contemporary society (with a particular focus on citizenship education).

**Stephanie Edgerly** is an Assistant Professor in the Medill School of Journalism, Media, Integrated Marketing Communications at Northwestern University. Her research explores how changes in the new media landscape provide individuals with new opportunities for political engagement.

**Mats Ekström** is Professor in Media and Communication at the University of Gothenburg, Sweden. He did his PhD in Sociology at Uppsala University and was a Professor in Sociology (2001–2) and in Media and Communication (2002–11) at Örebro University.

**Brian D. Loader** is Associate-Director of the Science and Technology Studies Unit (SATSU) based at the University of York, UK. His academic interests are focused around the emergence of new information and communications technologies (ICTs), such as the internet, and the social, political and economic factors shaping their development and diffusion, and their implications for social, economic, governmental and cultural change. He is General Editor of the international journal *Information, Communication and Society*.

**Suzanne Mellor** is a Senior Research Fellow, joined the Australian Council for Educational Research (ACER) in 1990 and has worked on many policy and survey research projects, some of them evaluative of education policy and program implementation. She is currently Series Editor for ACER's major research journal: *Australian Education Review* and was co-author of the first of the renewed editions: *AER 47: The Case for Change: A review of contemporary research on Indigenous education outcomes,* first published in 2004.

**Tobias Olsson,** PhD, is Professor of Media and Communication Studies at Lund University, Sweden. He has extensive research experience within the areas of media and citizenship, Internet culture and mediated participation. Between 2009 and 2013 he coordinated the research project 'Organized Producers of Young Net Cultures' (funded by the Swedish Knowledge Foundation) and he is currently starting a research project on user-generated content within newspaper companies (Hamrin foundation, 2012–17).

**Edda Sant,** PhD, is a Social Studies Teacher and FPU Fellow from the Spanish Ministry of Education. She has published several papers in European and Latin-American journals and books in the area of citizenship and history education.

**Dhavan V. Shah** is the Louis A. and Mary E. Maier-Bascom Professor at the University of Wisconsin, where he is Director of the Mass Communication Research Center (MCRC) in the School of Journalism and Mass Communication. Shah's research focuses on communication influence on social judgments, civic and political engagement, and health support and behaviour.

**Adam Shehata,** PhD, is an Assistant Professor in media and communication at the Department of Information Technology and Media, Mid Sweden University.

**James Sloam** is Senior Lecturer in Politics at Royal Holloway, University of London, where he is also co-director of the Centre for European Politics. His recent research has focused on the civic and political engagement of young people in Europe and the United States.

**Yannis Theocharis** is Alexander von Humboldt Postdoctoral Fellow at the Mannheim Centre for European Social Research, University of Mannheim. His research interests include political behaviour, contentious politics, young people, social capital, internet and new media.

**Kjerstin Thorson** is an Assistant Professor in the Annenberg School for Communication and Journalism at the University of Southern California. Her research explores the effects of digital and social media on political engagement, activism and persuasion, especially among youth.

**Emily K. Vraga** is an Assistant Professor in the Department of Communication at George Mason University. Her research examines how political identity is socialized and its impact on the processing of media content, particularly disagreeable content, in the digital environment.

**Ariadne Vromen** is Associate Professor in the Department of Government and International Relations at the University of Sydney, in Australia. She has ongoing research interests in political participation, including on young people, politics and the internet.

**Chris Wells** is an Assistant Professor in the School of Journalism and Mass Communication at the University of Wisconsin-Madison. His research considers young citizens' styles of civic participation and expression in the digital age.

**Michael A. Xenos** is Associate Professor of Communication Science at the University of Wisconsin-Madison, USA. His research focuses on how the context and content of political communication influences the quality of democratic deliberation, public opinion, and civic engagement.

**Jung Hwan Yang** is a PhD student in the School of Journalism and Mass Communication at the University of Wisconsin-Madison. His research focuses on the implication of information technology in politics and social interaction.

# Preface

This collection of essays arose from an International Communications Association (ICA) preconference held in London, June 2013. It brought together some of the leading international scholars in the field of political communication, young people, citizenship education and social media. The focus for the event was a critical exploration of the potential influence of social media communications technologies upon the participatory culture of young citizens. This was not simply an idle curiosity. It was conducted against a backdrop of several significant factors, all of which might have serious ramifications for the future of democratic politics. Combined with the now well-rehearsed refrain about the disillusionment of young people with modern politics, we had also recently witnessed a variety of high-profile political protests and campaigns around the world primarily involving young people and orchestrated in large measure through social media such as YouTube, Facebook and Twitter. Moreover, many of these demonstrations were taking place in the context of, and in opposition to, a world financial crisis that was directly affecting the lived experience of many young people.

The future engagement of young citizens from a wide range of socio-economic, ethnic and cultural backgrounds in democratic politics remains a crucial concern for political commentators, scholars, policy-makers, civics teachers and youth workers around the world. At a time when the negative relationship between socio-economic inequality and levels of political participation is compounded by high youth unemployment or precarious employment in many countries, it is not surprising that the political class and others are concerned to re-engage young citizens. Some have been optimistic in hoping that wide availability of the Internet and social media might act to stimulate a stronger participatory culture among people. The contributions to this edited collection, however, reveal a more complex relationship between contemporary youth norms, social media and a reconfiguration of democratic politics in the shape of the *networked young citizen*.

All the presentations given at the original event have been extensively revised as a result of the discussions and continuing debates. It is structured to examine such issues as the possible effects of social media use upon patterns of political socialization; the potential of social media to ameliorate young people's political inequality; the role of social media communications for enhancing the civic education curriculum; and evidence for social media manifesting new forms of political engagement and participation by young citizens.

Our thanks go to all the participants who attended the conference and contributed to making the occasion such an intellectually rewarding one. Many have been friends for several years, sharing our interest in young citizens, new media and democratic politics. But of course it is always enjoyable and stimulating to meet and hear from new entrants to this important area of academic enquiry. We would like to thank the Spencer Foundation, which provided valuable financial support without which the event would not have been possible in the first place. The World Universities Network (WUN) study group on Networking Young Citizens has been and continues to be a valuable source of support for enabling us to meet with and remain in touch with a critical mass of scholars in this area. Special thanks go to Sarah Shrive-Morrison for organizing the conference administration and without whom we would not have been able to enjoy such a gathering nearly so much.

Finally, we would like to thank our respective partners, Kim Loader, Diarmuid Maguire and Jenel Johnson, for their constant support and encouragement.

Brian D. Loader, Ingleby Arncliffe, North Yorkshire, UK
Ariadne Vromen, Sydney, Australia
Michael A. Xenos, Madison, Wisconsin, USA
2013

# Series Editors' Foreword

In every generation, younger citizens tend to experiment with political activism—ranging from apathy and indifference to violent protests—in ways that may be different from their older, more experienced compatriots. Tackling this generational tension head on, Loader, Vromen and Xenos examine how technologies have had an impact on this social/political experimentation.

In the past, one way of looking at the digital divide was to say that older people have not adopted technologies to the extent younger people had. Most scholars agreed that this "divide" would eventually work itself out, as younger people comfortable with technology grow older with it. But, it is not simply the existence of new technologies that matters here. It is the innovation in how they are used, adapted and used again in situations that vary by politics, economics and culture. The authors provide engaging narratives and convincing evidence to demonstrate both how and why young people take—or don't take—risks in their political participation and civic engagement and the integral role that technologies have in those decision-making processes and activities.

This volume shows how this divide can still be an interesting and valuable part of an IT research agenda and is an extremely strong addition to the research on technology and political process.

Ken Rogerson

# Acknowledgements

The material in Chapter 2 is based upon work supported by the Spencer Foundation. Any opinions, findings, and conclusions or recommendations expressed in this material are those of the authors and do not necessarily reflect the views of the Spencer Foundation.

# 1 Introduction: The Networked Young Citizen

## Social Media, Political Participation and Civic Engagement

*Brian D. Loader, Ariadne Vromen and Michael A. Xenos*

The accusation that young people are politically apathetic and somehow failing in their duty to participate in many democratic societies worldwide has been refuted by a growing number of academics in recent years (Loader, 2007; Marsh, O'Toole, & Jones, 2007). Undoubtedly many young citizens have indeed become disenchanted with mainstream political parties and with those who claim to speak on their behalf. But this should not be misinterpreted as a lack of interest on the part of youth with the political issues that influence their everyday lived experience and their normative concerns for the planet and its inhabitants. As the recent waves of protest demonstrations by young people in all their different forms and contexts testify, the suggestion that the next generation of citizens is any less politically engaged than previous ones seems at least premature. How, then, are we to understand the actions and political values of the future custodians of our polities and what are their implications for democratic governance?

There can be little doubt that the institutions and practices of modern representative government have been subject to growing disillusionment from young citizens. A reluctance to vote at elections, join political parties or have a high regard for their politicians all suggest that many young people are turning away from mainstream politics in many countries (Fieldhouse, Tranmer, & Russell, 2007; Van Biezen, Mair, & Poguntke, 2012). Instead, participation in social movements, rallies, protests, consumer boycotts all point to the possible displacement of traditional models of representative democracy as the dominant cultural form of engagement by alternative approaches increasingly characterized through networking practices. The political identity and attitudes of young citizens are thereby seen to be increasingly shaped less by their social ties to family, neighbourhood, school or work but, rather, by the manner in which they participate and interact through the social networks which they themselves have had a significant part in constructing. Central to this model of 'networked individualism' (Rainie & Wellman, 2012) is the role played by the Internet and network communication technologies. Of particular relevance, and the primary focus of this edited collection, is the potential of social media platforms such as Facebook, Twitter and YouTube for influencing the political deportment and civic engagement of what we describe as the *networked young citizen*.

## ASSEMBLING THE NETWORKED YOUNG CITIZEN

The debate on citizenship is replete with discourses that exhort young people to adopt the dutiful practices of participation that correspond to the regulatory norms established by earlier generations. Thus, active citizens should vote at elections, respect their representatives, join political groups and engage in voluntary activities in their civic communities. It is a model of the citizen as someone who should be *seen* to support the representative system through their dutiful actions but whose *voice* should not be heard. Indeed, the very future prospects for democracy are seen to depend upon the support of the electorate as performed and reproduced through these acts of citizenship. Small wonder, then, that the political class in many democracies is so concerned about the disaffection of so many young people with these norms of participation (Putnam, 2000; Stoker, 2006).

This emergent disjuncture between conventional representative government and the everyday concerns of young people was vividly captured in a television discussion between the forthright BBC interviewer Jeremy Paxman and the charismatic, and opinionated celebrity actor and comic, Russell Brand in the autumn of 2013. Brand had been invited by the *New Statesman* political magazine to be a guest editor for one of its issues and so was asked to discuss his political views on the late-night current affairs programme *Newsnight*. Whilst he is a sometimes controversial figure, this was the first time that Brand had entered the world of 'celebrity politics' (Street, 2004). Often condescending in his style of interrogation, Paxman on this occasion appeared to be genuinely engaged by Brand's arguments. What seemed to surprise Paxman in particular was Brand's admission that he had never voted and that he exhorted young people to follow his example. In this excerpt Brand justifies his view.

> I'm not voting out of apathy, I'm not voting out of absolute indifference, and weariness and exhaustion from the lies, treachery, deceit of the political class that has been going on for generations and which has reached fever pitch where we have a disenfranchised, disillusioned, despondent underclass that are not being represented by that political system so voting for it is tacit complicity with that system. And that is not something I'm offering up.

In many respects, through this intervention in print and on television, Brand is following a familiar path taken by other popular celebrities entering the political sphere. As John Street has described it, 'celebrity politics is a code for the performance of representations through the gestures and media available to those who wish to claim "representativeness"' (Street, 2004:445). Thus, despite the fact that Brand does not explicitly claim to speak on behalf of younger people, his accomplished use of the media to challenge the conventional perspectives of democratic engagement can be interpreted as just such an attempt to speak more legitimately than politicians for young citizens whose voice is seldom heard (Coleman, 2002). In this sense his performance, as seen on television and more widely through YouTube, can be regarded as an act intended to disrupt the normative repetitive depictions of the dutiful citizen. Instead, when asked by Paxman to give an alternative to a model of democracy as voting, he gave a response which foregrounds an emerging contemporary political aesthetic through which young citizens can engage.

> The time is now, change is occurring, we are at a time when communication is instantaneous and there are communities all over the world. The Occupy movement made a difference, even if only that it introduced to the popular public lexicon the idea of the 1% versus the 99%. People for the first time in a generation are aware of massive corporate and economic exploitation. These things are not nonsense and these are subjects which are not being addressed . . . Until they are taken seriously . . . why would I encourage a constituency of young people who are indifferent to vote?

The 'representativeness' of Brand is here expressed as an attempt to claim that the political class is failing to address some of the most important challenges confronting young citizens. Instead, alternative communication channels and modes of action, such as those enacted during the Arab Spring, or the Occupy movement, express the voice of young citizens around the world.

Whilst less dramatic or entertaining than Brand's narrative, a groundswell of academic opinion has also suggested that the political attitudes of many young people in many parts of the world can increasingly be characterised by a less deferential and more individualised (Beck, 1992; Giddens, 1991; Inglehart, 1990), self-actualizing (Bennett, Wells, & Rank, 2009) and critical disposition (Norris, 2002) which marks a departure from the dutiful norms of citizenship (Dalton, 2008). Such cultural changes in political participation are shaped of course by wider economic and social forces and they do not happen overnight. Moreover, the decline in mainstream engagement has been on-going for some time in many countries (Norris, 2002). Instead of regarding them as the death knell of western models of democracy, however, it may be more useful to see them as potentially heralding a recalibration of modern political institutions and practices in ways that are more sensitive to the dissatisfaction felt by many young people with their political systems. Young citizens may, as a consequence, be finding new ways to voice their opinions and garnering new agents of representativeness, such as Russell Brand, to envision their views.

What, then, does our emerging networked young citizen look like? How can we recognise these actors? Drawing from the literature (Bang, 2004; Beck, 1994; Bennett, Wells, & Freelon, 2011; Giddens, 1991) it is helpful to take a number of key features to assemble what we call the *networked young citizen*. Networking young citizens are far less likely to become members of political or civic organizations such as parties or trades unions; they are more likely to participate in horizontal or non-hierarchical networks; they are more project orientated; they reflexively engage in life-style politics; they are not dutiful but self-actualizing; their historical reference points are less likely to be those of modern welfare capitalism but, rather, global information networked capitalism; and their social relations are increasingly enacted through a social media networked environment.

This is of course an ideal type construction and is not intended to represent all young citizens in every respect. Its value is as a framework against which we may assess the normative political dispositions of young people. So the networked young citizen is not necessarily typical of all young people in every society. Our objective is not to provide yet another generalization about all young people being characterised as a type. Rather, we believe that it is a useful analytical device by which to assess the evidence for cultural change. Some further clarifications need to be made to our assemblage. First, this does not represent an all-encompassing discontinuity with previous dutiful models. Networked young citizens may live conterminously with other dutiful citizens and, indeed, share some of each other's attributes on occasions. Second, networked citizenship can be seen as fluid and always under construction within regulatory norms and structuring processes. A model of citizenship that is fluid and constituent of lived experience does not suggest apathy but, rather, an identity whose realisation has to be performed and enacted. Part of that performance may surely include disrupting dominant discourses and repeated citations resonant of dutiful models of citizenship (Loader, 2012). Third, networking young citizens are shaped by different individual lived experiences that will not be the same for everyone. Consequently issues of inequality and power come into play. Networks and networking do not imply a power vacuum where all are equal. Instead, the benefits accrued by access to social and cultural capital through particular networks foreground the need to differentiate between social networks. Networks exhibit new regulatory norms of exclusion as well as inclusion. They also require us to consider what kinds of capacities are required by young people for effective networked citizenship.

## ARE ALL YOUNG CITIZENS NETWORKED EQUALLY?

The competitive advantages to be accrued through membership of the most resource-rich networks have become particularly pronounced as a consequence of the world financial crisis since 2007. Whilst young people as a whole have been disproportionately hit harder by these events as compared with other age groups, the burdens have not been evenly distributed across all young people. Educational and employment opportunities for young people have been significantly influenced by social and cultural factors such as class, ethnicity, gender, sexuality and location. Consequently, the economic recession has both compounded the alienation of many young citizens and threatens to produce further personal insecurity for millions of individuals as they join the ranks of the emerging *precariat* (Standing, 2011).

A danger therefore exists of a growing mass of disenchanted young people subject to unemployment, insecure job prospects and without voice or representation in the public domain. In August 2013 approximately one quarter of young European citizens were unemployed (Eurostat). A more accurate indicator is that providing figures for those 'not in employment, education or training' (NEETs), which is still alarmingly high, with 14 million aged 15–29 recorded in 2011. This situation is not uniform across European Union member states, with NEET figures being significantly higher in the east (e.g. Romania, Bulgaria) and south (e.g. Portugal, Spain, Greece), as compared with those in the north (e.g. Germany, Netherlands, UK, Nordic countries). In the USA the figure for those out of work or education was almost 16 per cent of 18–29 year olds in October 2013. The transition from youth to adulthood in the twenty-first century is therefore beset by growing social inequality, structural unemployment and a disaffection with politics which, when combined, are shaping the opportunities for social inclusion and security of many young citizens.

How, then, does the networked young citizen relate to this picture of global social and economic inequality? Recent developments suggest a strong relationship between social media use and political engagement that raises questions about the potential for social media to help to stem or even reverse patterns of political inequality that have troubled scholars for years. Michael Xenos, Ariadne Vromen and Brian D. Loader explore this contention in Chapter 2 of this volume, where they articulate a model of social media and political engagement among young people and test it using data from representative samples of young citizens in Australia, the United States and the United Kingdom. Their results suggest a strong, positive relationship between social media use and political engagement among young people across all three countries, and provide additional insights regarding the role played by social media use in the processes by which young people become politically engaged. Notably, the results also provide reasons to be cautiously optimistic concerning the overall influence of this popular new form of social networking on long-standing patterns of political inequality.

For some time a number of academics have believed that the interactive, collaborative and user-generated content capacities of social media technologies themselves offer the prospect of facilitating new modes of

political communication which are more commensurate with those contemporary youth cultures associated with the networked young citizen.
They point to an electoral affinity between what are perceived as the
inherent democratic features of social media and its potential for enhancing the participative and deliberative skills of young citizens (Jenkins,
2006; Benkler, 2006; Leadbeater, 2008). This notion of *participatory
culture* has quickly managed to gain a strong foothold in contemporary debates about social media and user engagement. The concept's
primary advocate, Henry Jenkins, uses it to describe a cultural situation
in which established relations between media producers and users have
been disrupted to the point at which 'we might now see them as participants who interact with each other' (Jenkins, 2006:3). Hence, studies of, for instance, Facebook, blogging and YouTube have looked into
what participatory practices these environments offer and are capable
of fostering. Overall, these studies have often looked for, and found,
engaged online users and inspiring participatory practices—especially
among young people.

But what is the impact of engagement, and participation, within participatory cultures of social media on the public orientation of young people?
On this connection, the existing literature is rather unclear. The third chapter in this collection, written by Mats Ekström, Tobias Olsson, and Adam
Shehata, addresses this question by drawing upon longitudinal survey data
from a sample of Swedish 13- to 18-year-olds. The concept of public orientation is measured by three indicators: young people's values, interests and
everyday peer talk. These indicators are analysed with reference to respondents' Internet orientations, which are conceptualised as four separate but
interrelated spaces (a news space, a space for social interaction, a game
space and a creative space). The results primarily emphasise the importance
of orientations towards news space and space for social interaction. Overall, the findings strongly suggest that orientations towards these spaces are
related to adolescents' public orientation. The findings confirm the centrality of news and information in political socialisation, but they also challenge the idea that social media platforms—such as Facebook, Twitter and
blogging—enable forms of social interaction and creative production that
have an overall positive impact on young people's public orientation.

## TRANSITIONS FROM CHILDHOOD TO ADULTHOOD

As one might expect from a period when dutiful conceptions of citizenship
were *de rigueur,* scholars exploring how young people were socialised into
their political attitudes regarded the role of parents as paramount. Values
and political orientations were seen as transmitted from parent to child
in a linear learning mode. The networking young citizen model, constituent of self-actualising, reflexive and interactive attributes, would suggest,

however, a more complex and critical learning path in which the young person plays a more co-constructive role. In Chapter 4 Emily Vraga, Leticia Bode, Jung Hwan Yang, Stephanie Edgerly, Kjerstin Thorson, Chris Wells, and Dhavan V. Shah draw upon contemporary theories of political socialisation which move away from tradition-transmission perspectives to consider the diverse ways in which parents and children can develop discrete political orientations. In their study made during a competitive US presidential campaign they examine various pathways through which influence occurs across generations in terms of partisanship and candidate evaluations. There results suggest that while harmonious attitudes remain the norm, there are substantial opportunities for young citizens to demonstrate their independence, particularly when gaining different perspectives from schools and social media sources. Their findings are an important contribution to our understanding of how young networking citizens and their parents come to understand politics and the factors that shape youth socialisation. Of particular influence in this new socialisation perspective is the role played by social media as a means of facilitating mutual understanding between parents and young people.

How, then, do these social networking environments influence political talk and understanding among young citizens? Do they make it easier for young citizens to chat about the public issues which affect their lived experience? Are they more likely to share political opinions and views? In Chapter 5 Kjerstin Thorson provides a microanalysis of political talk and interaction by young citizens networking on Facebook. Her investigation leads her to propose that participatory culture is shaped through social networking sites by social ambiguities that can actually increase the risk and uncertainties associated with talking politics, rather than reduce them. She reports on two sets of in-depth interviews conducted to explore the ways that uncertainties about audience reception of posts on Facebook inspire strategies for 'inventing' modes of political interaction, for some, and, for others, to suppress opinion expression by creating the sense that talking politics on the site is a high-risk endeavour.

## EDUCATING THE NETWORKED YOUNG CITIZEN?

Concern over the perceived disengagement of young citizens from mainstream politics has led to the adoption of civic or citizenship education as a means to combat these trends in many democracies. In the UK, for example, following the publication of the Crick Report, citizenship education became a compulsory feature of the England and Wales National Curriculum after 2002. Citizenship education is now internationally accepted and included in national curricula in many parts of the world. Although it remains a broad field there has recently been a growing acceptance of its essential elements and aims regarding the need to promote understanding and the potential for involvement in contemporary society. Whatever particular form it takes in the respective curriculum there is frequently a growing emphasis upon the development of *active citizenship* and community cohesion (Smith, Lister, Middleton, & Cox, 2005). Whilst the concept of 'active citizenship' might be thought to have resonance with the more fluid and diverse forms of social participation associated with our networked young citizen, the notion can instead be regarded as a reworking of our familiar friend the dutiful citizen. In this new guise of constructive social participation, citizenship includes, as one might expect, participation by young people in conventional political activities such as voting and party membership; but it also increasingly includes volunteering, community cohesion and the development of 'social capital' (Putnam, 2000). Consequently, whilst emphasising the duty of citizens to engage in voluntary activities and 'give something back' to their communities, such curricula do not yet seem to encompass self-actualising democratic engagement with unconventional political activity associated with protest and social movements and repertoires of participation through consumer boycotts, wearing emblems, protesting or signing petitions. As such, they raise questions about the potential disjuncture between what young people are learning in formal education classes and what they might experience as networking young citizens.

To date little attention has been given to the role of social media in connection with citizenship or civic education. What, for example, is its current usage by teachers and learners; is there a necessary fundamental link between what is supposedly a more democratic means of communication and education that aims at promoting democratic understanding and involvement; and, if such a link exists, what pedagogical developments would be expected to emerge in the future? Suzanne Mellor addresses these questions in Chapter 6 by reporting on an Australian research project which examined the ways in which social media was integrated in the teaching and learning of mid-secondary students in three different schools in Melbourne. This approach was further developed by Ian Davies and Edda Sant in a small-scale project in England which is reported on here in Chapter 7. Specifically, all the authors wanted to know in what ways school students use social media in their social or informal community-based networks; what the similarities and significant differences are in young people's use of social media in their schooling and personal settings; how young people perceive their personal use of social media in supporting enhanced citizenship participation and engagement; and, in what ways social media was effectively used in school-based citizenship education programmes to support citizenship. As with Mellor's investigation, Davies and Sant used questionnaire and interview data gathered from students and teachers in three schools for their analysis. Their findings suggest that students frequently use social media for personal and social reasons and that some of them consider that this technology may also be of some help educationally. More precisely, students and teachers felt that social media could enhance citizenship engagement, knowledge and participation insofar as people can be informed and updated; everybody has the right to give their opinion and to be listened to on an equal basis, and posted opinions can be discussed; people may organise and may inform others about their actions; and people can engage in global citizenship by knowing people from other cultures. Such attributes and perspectives can again be seen as consistent with the model of the networked young citizen.

The reflexive nature of many young people is again borne out by their critical adoption of social media. Many of the students in both studies exhibited reservations. They felt that the content of information presented through social media cannot be easily verified; that these forms of technology may be harmfully addictive; that any benefits of social media can be achieved face to face; that it may merely help those who are already engaged; and that there would be specific gaps in young people's knowledge as a result of too great a reliance on social media.

Nonetheless, the challenges of introducing social media into the classroom and embracing new modes of citizenship beyond the dutiful were still in evidence. The authors found, for example, that teachers used social media much less frequently than students, whilst also acknowledging its general educational potential. This conflict between teachers' recognition of the possible pedagogic benefits of incorporating social media in the future and its current low usage could be explained by the need to preserve professional independence; to maintain barriers between teachers' private and professional lives; and is connected with uncertainty about their own expertise with technology. Yet, despite these important considerations, the authors conclude that social media may indeed enhance citizenship education through engagement in relation to identity (generating a sense of belonging, global citizenship and forming new groups); promoting knowledge about citizenship (searching sources, commenting, discussing); and facilitating participation (informing people; organising social movements; being democratic as opinions are developed).

## ALTERNATIVE NETWORKING YOUNG CITIZENS?

The final part in this edited collection turns to the alternative forms of political engagement as expressions of emerging political norms characteristic of the networked young citizen. In chapter 7 James Sloam examines the role that social media has played in the development of protest movements across the continent of Europe. Networking young citizens have mobilised through mass demonstrations such as the *indignados,* outraged against political corruption and unemployment in Spain, and the Occupy movement, voicing its anger against what it sees as the social inequality arising from global capitalism. Rejecting traditional political elites and organisations, young citizens have also been involved in the development of new political parties such as the German Pirate Party and the Italian Five-Star Movement. As commentators have observed, a defining characteristic of these developments has been the manner in which young people have used networks to spread and share their protests across continents and national borders (Bennett & Segerberg, 2012). Sloam seeks to demonstrate how 'digitally networked action' has enabled a 'quickening' of youth participation—an intensification of political participation amongst young, highly educated citizens in search of a mouthpiece for their 'indignation'.

In Chapter 9 Yannis Theocharis takes a microanalysis of one specific protest to explore in detail the use of websites and blogs during the 2010 UK anti-cuts protests, where students across the UK occupied more than thirty-five universities in a symbolic act of opposition to government plans to cut education funding and increase tuition fees. Theocharis draws our attention to an important distinction between the social media platforms, which have been a primary focus, and other networking channels that play an important role for networking young citizens. Although social media have largely monopolised the debate on online political activism in recent years, the students in his study did not limit their online e-tactics to the use of social media, but also used websites and blogs extensively to describe and contextualise their views, demands, protest experiences and actions.

## CONCLUDING REMARKS

The engagement of each new generation of young people with the practices and institutions of democratic governance in a society is an essential means by which such a political system retains its legitimacy. Without their consent and commitment, the authority of politicians and policymakers to represent the values and interests of future citizens is called into question. The attitudes and political values of young people are therefore often seen as foretelling the future. Socialisation is important here, as it is assumed that attitudes developed in youth are likely to remain. This has been disputed and may be more mixed. But they are nonetheless important agents of social and political change. Increasingly shaped by wider forces of globalisation, the digital revolution and reflexive individualism, the concept of the networked young citizen may become a compelling one that is gaining currency through empirical investigation. It suggests an emerging generational cohort that is more sceptical of politicians and mainstream conventional political institutions. But it also raises the possibility of the networking young citizen playing a more significant role in reconfiguring our democratic practices.

Opponents of such an approach will no doubt both reject the notion of emerging political norms associated with the networked young citizen and contend that any move away from the dutiful or active citizen model will undermine liberal representative democracy. Fearful of the 'personalisation' of politics as a means to undermine serious rational deliberation and even encourage populist rhetoric of the sort expressed by Russell Brand, such critics can only see these developments as evidence for the trivialisation of democracy. Yet, in the face of growing evidence to the contrary, these commentators seem bereft of ideas to address the growing estrangement between young citizens and mainstream political parties, politicians and electoral engagement. The scepticism expressed by young people towards those who represent them, rather than being taken as a measure of apathy, could instead be seen as a perfectly legitimate democratic attitude of reflexively engaged citizens conscious of their personal circumstances.

Here the distinction between scepticism and cynicism is crucial. The former positive democratic attitude, derived from a more educated population and with critical sensibilities, can act to strengthen participatory models of democracy previously considered impractical due to the perceived poor quality of the electorate (Schumpeter, 1943). Through effective networking young citizens have demonstrated a capacity to increasingly hold representatives to account and critically monitor their policies and actions. Social media combined with other networking opportunities enables the networked young citizen to reflexively consider a wider range of political discourses and share these with friends or engage in connective repertoires of political action (Bennett & Segerberg, 2012). Such processes of reconfiguration do not require representative systems to disappear but they do demand that our democratic systems need to be more culturally receptive to the lived experiences of those they serve. Stephen Coleman (2013) provides an excellent exploration of just how a central democratic act such as voting, when seen as a cultural activity, raises essential questions about its relevance to the emotional experience of those citizens expected to participate. It is an intellectual approach that is both compatible with Russell Brand's clarion call and pragmatic in its desire to reconnect voting with the electorate's everyday concerns and changing norms.

Yet it is also important that such reconfigurations do not disguise differential capabilities and relations of power that are also a constituent feature of networking. As Bourdieu (1984) reminds us, access to social and cultural capital is often used to ensure unequal social distinctions between citizens. In the context of growing social inequality, social networking may thus reinforce divisions that are detrimental to democracy (Schlozman *et al.*, 2012). Whilst the present academic debate continues to be divided between those who maintain an adherence to dutiful citizenship, the contributions to this book have all been prepared to recognise that new forms of networked young citizenship, more compatible to the times and contemporary youth culture, may be more fruitful both for understanding contemporary developments and also for future democratic governance.

## REFERENCES

Bang, H. P. (2004). Culture Governance: Governing Self-Reflexive Modernity. *Public Administration, 82*(1), 157–190. doi: 10.1111/j.0033-3298.2004.00389.x.

Beck, U. (1992). *Risk Society: Towards a New Modernity.* London: Sage.

Beck, U. (1994). The Reinvention of Politics: Towards a Theory of Reflexive Modernization. In U. Beck, A. Giddens, & S. Lash (Eds.), *Reflexive Modernization: Politics, Tradition and Aesthetics in Modern Social Order* (pp. 1–55). Stanford, CA: Stanford University Press.

Benkler, Y. (2006). *The Wealth of Networks: How Social Production Transforms Markets and Freedom.* New Haven, CT: Yale University Press.

Bennett, W. L., & Segerberg, A. (2012). The Logic of Connective Action. *Information, Communication & Society, 15*(5), 739–768. doi: 10.1080/1369118X.2012.670661.

Bennett, W. L., Wells, C., & Freelon, D. (2011). Communicating Civic Engagement: Contrasting Models of Citizenship in the Youth Web Sphere. *Journal of Communication, 61*(5), 835–856. doi: 10.1111/j.1460-2466.2011.01588.x.

Bennett, W. L., Wells, C., & Rank, A. (2009). Young Citizens and Civic Learning: Two Paradigms of Citizenship in the Digital Age. *Citizenship Studies, 13*(2), 105–120. doi: 10.1080/13621020902731116.

Bourdieu, P. (1984). *Distinction: A Social Critique of the Judgement of Taste.* London: Routledge.

Coleman, S. (2002). The People's Voice. In J. Bartle (Ed.) *Political Communication* (pp 246–258). London: Frank Cass

Coleman, S. (2013). *How Voters Feel.* Cambridge: Cambridge University Press.

Dalton, R. J. (2008). Citizenship Norms and the Expansion of Political Participation. *Political Studies, 56*(1), 76–98. Retrieved from http://doi.wiley.com/10.1111/j.1467-9248.2007.00718.x.

Fieldhouse, E., Tranmer, M., & Russell, A. (2007). Something about Young People or Something about Elections? Electoral Participation of Young People in Europe: Evidence from a Multilevel Analysis of the European Social Survey. *European Journal of Political Research, 46*(6), 797–822. doi: 10.1111/j.1475-6765.2007.00713.x.

Giddens, A. (1991). *Modernity and Self Identity.* Cambridge: Polity.

Inglehart, R. (1990). *Culture Shift in Advanced Industrial Society.* Princeton, NJ: Princeton University Press.

Jenkins, H. (2006) *Convergence Culture: Where Old and New Media Collide.* New York: New York University Press.

Leadbeater, C. (2008). *We-Think: Mass Innovation, Not Mass Production.* London: Profile Books.

Loader, B. D. (2007). *Young Citizens in the Digital Age: Political Engagement, Young People and New Media.* London: Routledge.

Loader, B. D. (2012). Digital Democracy: Towards User-Generated Politics? In B. Isakhan and S. Stockwell (Eds.) *The Edinburgh Companion to the History of Democracy.* Edinburgh: Edinburgh University Press.

Marsh, D., O'Toole, T., & Jones, S. (2007). *Young People and Politics in the UK.* Basingstoke: Palgrave.

Norris, P. (2002). *Democratic Pheonix: Reinventing Democratic Activism.* Cambridge: Cambridge University Press.

Putnam, R. (2000). *Bowling Alone: The Collapse and Revival of American Community.* New York: Simon & Schuster.

Rainie, L., & Wellman, B. (2012). *Networked: The New Social Operating System.* Cambridge, MA: MIT Press.

Schlozman, K. L., Verba, S., & Brady, H. E. (2012). *The Unheavenly Chorus: Unequal Political Voice and the Broken Promise of American Democracy.* Princeton, NJ: Princeton University Press.

Schumpeter, J. A. (1943). *Capitalism, Socialism and Democracy.* London: Routledge.

Smith, N., Lister, R., Middleton, S., & Cox, L. (2005). Young People as 'Active Citizens': Towards and Inclusionary View of Citizenship and Constructive Participation. In C. Pole, J. Pilcher, & J. Williams (Eds.), *Young People in Transition: Becoming Citizens?* Basingstoke: Palgrave.

Standing, G. (2011). *The Precariat: The New Dangerous Class.* London: Bloomsbury.

Stoker, G. (2006). *Why Politics Matters: Making Democracy Work.* Basingstoke: Palgrave.

Street, J. (2004). Celebrity Politicians?: Popular Culture and Political Representation. *The British Journal of Politics & International Relations.* Retrieved from http://onlinelibrary.wiley.com/doi/10.1111/j.1467-856X.2004.00149.x/full.

Van Biezen, I., Mair, P., & Poguntke, T. (2012). Going, going, . . . Gone? The Decline of Party Membership in Contemporary Europe. *European Journal of Political Research, 51*(1), 24–56. doi: 10.1111/j.1475-6765.2011.01995.x.

Part I

# Political Culture, Socialization and Social Media Adoption

# 2   The Great Equalizer?

## Patterns of Social Media Use and Youth Political Engagement in Three Advanced Democracies

*Michael A. Xenos, Ariadne Vromen and Brian D. Loader*[1]

From the events of the Arab Spring to the occupation of Zuccotti Park, stories of mass protests saturated with the aura of young people's savvy use of social media platforms have produced headlines with growing regularity. It has also become conventional wisdom to attribute US President Barack Obama's initial and later re-election victories to his campaign's deft deployment of social media to mobilize the youth vote. In the United States and other democracies, social media activity is disproportionately concentrated among young people (Australian Communications and Media Authority 2013; Brenner 2013; Woollaston 2013). As a result, there has been an explosive growth in studies examining relationships between social media use and political engagement, sometimes with a specific focus on young people (e.g. Bode 2012; Conroy, Feezell, & Guerrero 2012; Gil de Zúñiga, Jung, & Valenzuela 2012; Vitak *et al.* 2011). These developments contribute to a growing popular understanding of social media as a potent tool for moving young people to political engagement.

Such developments are particularly significant for political communication research because they raise questions about the potential for social media to help stem or reverse patterns of political inequality that have troubled scholars for years (Brady, Verba, & Schlozman 1995; Carlisle & Patton 2013; Morris & Morris 2013; Schlozman, Verba, & Brady 2010). Underlying these studies is a belief that by lowering the costs of many different forms of engagement and providing new ways to discover and get involved with issues, social media may have great potential for not just mobilizing but also broadening political participation. The optimistic tone of these studies echoes earlier waves of enthusiasm surrounding the potential impact of general internet use on political engagement and political equality. Indeed, after summarizing such scholarship, the authors of a recent study explain that their work "see[s] social media as having the same influence but taking it one step further to provide the individual greater flexibility to actively engage in the public sphere" (Carlisle & Patton 2013, p. 3). Just as first-generation studies of internet use and participation quickly seized on questions of whether that new technology would alter fundamental dynamics of political voice, contemporary political communication scholars have begun to ask similar questions regarding social media.

Prospects for significant progress on these questions, however, are limited by a number of factors. As we will explain in our review of the existing literature, these include a number of empirical, conceptual, and theoretical issues. In this chapter we seek to overcome limitations in this literature by articulating a model of social media and political engagement among young people that draws on contemporary scholarship concerning the processes by which contemporary young people actively construct their roles as citizens. We test hypotheses derived from this model using data from nationally representative surveys of young people (aged 16–29) in three advanced democracies: Australia, the United States, and the United Kingdom. Our results suggest a strong, positive relationship between social media use and political engagement across all three countries, and suggest that social media may be helping to soften traditional patterns of political inequality.

## SOCIAL MEDIA AND POLITICAL ENGAGEMENT

Social media and political engagement are both concepts that are subject to a variety of interpretations. We consider "social media" to include a variety of internet-based tools that users engage with by maintaining an individual profile and interacting with others based on a network of connections. In an effort to better synthesize general patterns of relationships between social media use and political participation, we also adopt an expansive conception of "political engagement."

The rapidly growing literature on social media use and political engagement has so far produced mixed results. On the optimistic side, a number of studies have suggested a positive relationship between social media use and various indicators of political engagement (Bode 2012; Valenzuela, Park, & Kee 2009; Zhang, Seltzer, & Bichard 2013). Other studies report positive relationships between social media use and political engagement, but delimit those relationships to specific kinds of social media use, or a circumscribed set of engagement outcomes (Gil de Zúñiga, Jung, & Valenzuela 2012; Vitak *et al.* 2011). These studies suggest that the spread of social media among young people and the broader public has had salutary effects on political engagement, but at the same time suggest that the relationship between social media use and engagement may be limited to individuals who would likely be relatively engaged without social media. Still other studies suggest a very weak relationship between social media use and political engagement, or none at all (Baumgartner & Morris 2009; Dimitrova & Bystrom 2013). Baumgartner and Morris (2009), for instance, found small and inconsistent effects of social networking site use on a range of engagement outcomes in their study of social networking site use surrounding the 2008 Iowa caucuses, ultimately concluding that "the hyperbole surrounding new Web developments . . . as they relate to citizenship may be just that—hype" (p. 38).

Despite this mixed pattern of results, a few scholars have recently started to explore whether the mobilizing potential of social media is powerful enough to directly affect classic patterns of stratification by socioeconomic status (SES) and other factors in political engagement behaviors. Here too, however, results have not been consistent. On the one hand, the venerable scholars of stratification and participation Schlozman, Verba, and Brady (2010) found little evidence of "counter-stratificational effects" with respect to social networking site use and socioeconomic status in their analysis of nationally representative Pew Internet and American Life Project survey data. They did, however, find that social networking site use was associated with countertrends to traditional disparities in participation based on age (Schlozman *et al.* 2010). In a similar study, however, Morris and Morris (2013) found patterns implicating internet use in the closing of traditional socioeconomic status gaps in participation, using a measure of internet use in which social media figured quite prominently. Thus, in the emerging literature on the implications of social media use for patterns of stratification in political engagement, we find a much smaller but similarly mixed set of results.

A number of factors may explain the elusiveness of clear patterns of findings within the emerging literature on social media and political engagement. First, as is understandable in early exploratory research, many existing studies have been relatively limited in empirical scope. Many rely on samples of college students, collected with varying degrees of sophistication (Baumgartner & Morris 2009; Bode 2012; Valenzuela *et al.* 2009; Vitak *et al.* 2011). Others have used nationally representative samples of adults, of varying sizes (Gil de Zúñiga, Jung, & Valenzuela 2012; Zhang, Seltzer, & Bichard 2013). Most are centered on a particular focusing event, such as the Iowa caucuses (e.g. Baumgartner & Morris 2009; Bode 2012; Dimitrova & Bystrom 2013; Zhang *et al.* 2013). A consistent pattern within the sets' findings reported in this literature, based on these variations, could point the way toward an orderly synthesis of the mixed picture of results reported so far. Unfortunately, however, these methodological variations cut across the range of results found within this growing literature. A similar set of observations can be made regarding variations in conceptualization of the primary independent and dependent variables of social media use and political engagement. As noted earlier, both of these concepts enjoy a multifaceted existence within the broader literature. Once again, there appear to be no clear patterns based on these kinds of differences among existing findings on social media and political engagement. Indeed, while some studies suggest a direct relationship between the sheer time spent with social media and political engagement (e.g. Bode 2012; Zhang *et al.* 2013), others suggest that such a relationship should be expected only with politically oriented activities in social media (e.g. Gil de Zúñiga *et al.* 2012; Vitak *et al.* 2011). A few studies suggest a slight relationship between the kinds of political engagement examined and the strength of the relationship with social media use, such that mobilizing effects appear stronger for civic as opposed to political engagement, and so-called "lightweight" or online forms of involvement versus their more complicated offline cousins (Baumgartner & Morris 2009; Valenzuela *et al.*; Vitak *et al.* 2011). For each of these examples, however, there are studies in which such patterns are not readily apparent (e.g. Bode 2012; Zhang *et al.* 2013). Thus, as with the methodological differences, it appears that variations in the conceptualization of independent and dependent variables mainly contribute to a general shortage of clear and definitive patterns with respect to the relationship between social media use and political engagement.

In addition to these issues within the current literature on social media and political engagement, we would further identify an important sub-stantive limitation. Specifically, given the well-known skew of social media use toward younger cohorts, and the veritable tradition of attend-ing to issues related to youth in research on digital media and politics, it is surprising that the connection between social media use and youth has rarely been explicitly theorized in research focused on social media use and political engagement. To be sure, it is often mentioned that social media use is concentrated among young people; but typically this is dis-cussed in passing or, more often, simply as a justification for using readily available samples of college students. This overlooks an important oppor-tunity to directly incorporate valuable insights about a core element of the principal user base of social media into efforts aimed at understand-ing its implications for patterns of political engagement. For example, a large amount of research on "digital natives" and related concepts documents the sense in which contemporary young people have a unique relationship with digital media, particularly its newer features that are the heart of social media (Tapscott 2008). Additionally, scholarship on youth and politics has shown that young people also have a distinct set of political interests and interactions with politics (Levine 2007). More-over, scholarship on political socialization and related concepts reminds us that many of the most avid users of social media have recently under-gone, or are in the process of undergoing, important experiences that will powerfully shape their political engagement over time (Amnå *et al.* 2009; Lee, Shah, & McLeod 2012; McLeod & Shah 2009; Sapiro 2004; Shah, McLeod, & Lee 2009; Torney-Purta 2000). As we will discuss in more detail shortly, attention to these youth-focused factors offers a useful set of concepts for understanding how social media use may be initiating new patterns of political engagement in the digital age.

## THEORETICAL MODEL, HYPOTHESES, AND RESEARCH QUESTIONS

In constructing a theoretical model of social media use and political engagement among young people, we draw from previous research on general internet use and political engagement. In concrete terms, we expect a mix of direct and differential relationships, with the latter conditioned by predispositions and individual characteristics independently associated with political engagement activities (Xenos & Moy 2007). Along these lines, we expect that social media should be directly associated with political engagement, but we also assume that the mobilizing power of social media will not affect all young people in the same way. To elaborate on these expectations, we first consider the mobilizing properties of social media, and then explore how key characteristics and predispositions of social media users may interact with social media use to produce specific patterns of differential relationships between social media use and political engagement.

Perhaps the most basic argument for the mobilizing potential of social media use follows the sentiment expressed by Carlisle and Patton (2013) and cited in the introduction to this chapter. By this logic, social media possesses the same mobilizing features of the internet as a whole, but takes them all "one step further" by overcoming one of the key limitations of the Web 1.0 world. Moreover, as a quintessential example of Web 2.0 functionalities, social media has the added qualities of making it much easier for individuals to engage in online versions of a number of traditional and nontraditional acts of political involvement, such as participating in political discussions, persuading others how to vote, as well as engaging in a variety of forms of online activism. In addition, we expect that the unique properties of social media could also directly stimulate political engagement through other pathways. Perhaps the most discussed in existing research literature flows through social media's fostering of social capital and informal discussions about politics, which have long been associated with higher levels of political engagement (Bode 2012; Chong *et al.* 2011; Conroy *et al.* 2012; Ellison, Steinfield, & Lampe 2007; Gil de Zúñiga *et al.* 2012). Another possible pathway stems from the unique sense in which social media departs from most other web experiences. Through habitual reviews of their "news feeds," users are often presented with information that they may not have been particularly seeking, creating rare opportunities for incidental exposure. This kind of dynamic has already been documented for likelihood of exposure to political content that runs counter to users' existing political ideologies (Messing & Westwood 2012), and others have applied a similar logic to incidental exposure across lines of general interest in politics (Morris & Morris 2013). Individuals who may be relatively uninterested or unengaged in politics need only "know" a handful of interested and engaged others in order to be regularly presented with incidental cues and information about political issues that could result in greater engagement, especially during times of high political activity such as a national election. Based on these considerations, we offer our first hypothesis.

*H1*: Social media use will be positively related to political engagement.

Such considerations, however, focus mainly on attributes of social media that might be equally experienced by any and all users. Young people, however, are the heaviest users of social media, and are also in the process of forming norms and habits of citizen engagement that are typically stable across the life course (Amnå *et al.* 2009; Sapiro 2004). These factors are likely independently related to political engagement, but are also of additional theoretical interest based on their possible interactions with social media use in patterns of youth engagement. We now turn to two such factors: political socialization, and newly emerging norms of citizenship believed to be concentrated among young people in advanced post-industrial democracies. Research on political socialization suggests that young people who come from homes in which politics are regularly discussed among family members are significantly more likely to engage in a variety of political behaviors (Andolina & Jenkins 2003; Lee *et al.* 2012). In addition, research has also highlighted the positive influence that school-based civic learning experiences can have on later patterns of political engagement (Galston 2004; Kahne & Westheimer 2006; Torney-Purta & Amadeo 2003). Socialization is also likely to have effects on the relationship between social media and political engagement. Specifically, we posit that young people who might be stimulated to political involvement through incidental exposure or other political interactions facilitated by social media may be significantly more apt to express that involvement through various political activities, if they have already developed civic competencies through family and school experiences. Based on these considerations we thus offer two related hypotheses about social media use, political socialization, and political engagement.

$H2_a$: Political socialization experiences will be positively related to political engagement.

And

$H2_b$: Positive political socialization experiences will significantly enhance the relationship between social media use and political engagement.

An additional factor that is vitally important for understanding the relationship between social media use and political engagement is the emergence of distinctly new norms of citizenship. Citing a variety of broader social and economic currents commonly experienced within advanced democracies, some have argued that contemporary youth are beginning to relate to politics and public life in ways that are distinctly different from the dutiful conception of political involvement dominant among previous generations (Bennett 2012; Dalton 2008). Work in this vein has suggested that young people may be abandoning traditional modes of so-called "dutiful" citizen participation (voting, party membership, reading the newspaper), in favor of a more personalized politics of self-actualization and expressive engagement with greater emphasis on nontraditional modes of engagement such as digital networking, volunteering, and consumer activism (Bennett, Wells, & Freelon 2011; Loader 2007). Though this "norm set for the next era" (Bennett 2012, p. 30) involves both a turn away from more traditional forms of political engagement such as voting, as well as a turn toward newer forms of political action such as political consumerism, we believe it is reasonable to treat "actualizing citizenship" norms (Bennett 2008) as a general predictor of political engagement for contemporary youth, all else equal.

As with political socialization, we further expect actualizing citizenship norms to be implicated in a set of contingent relationships involving social media use and political engagement among young people. Because such norms reflect a distinct expression of contemporary interest in politics among young people, we expect social media use to serve as a moderator for the relationship between norms and political engagement. Here, we emphasize the affordances and capabilities of social media for the particular kinds of political engagement that scholars such as Bennett (2008, 2012) suggest are a natural outgrowth of the adoption of actualizing citizenship norms. We thus offer the following hypotheses concerning actualizing citizenship norms, social media use, and political engagement.

$H3_a$: Actualizing norms of citizenship will be positively related to political engagement.

And

$H3_b$: Social media use will significantly enhance the relationship between actualizing norms of citizenship and political engagement.

Our general theoretical model encompassing each of these predictions is summarized in Figure 2.1.

As noted earlier, our project of constructing a model explaining youth political engagement as a function of social media use and other factors is in many ways but a means to an end. Our primary interest is exploring the extent to which relationships between social media use and youth engagement may have implications for patterns of unequal political voice,

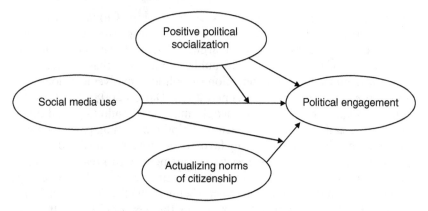

*Figure 2.1* Model of social media and political engagement (control variables
        omitted)

primarily along the lines of socioeconomic status, but also along other
dimensions such as age and race or ethnicity. There are at least two ways
in which social media use could affect such patterns of inequality. First,
as discussed earlier, social media use could result in direct "counterstratificational" effects by raising political engagement among the previously
uninvolved to levels that are much closer to those exhibited by the more
involved. Another possibility is that the direct influence of widespread
social media use on political engagement could serve to broaden the overall pool of young people engaged in politics, contributing to a less rapid,
but no less significant, softening of political inequality patterns over time,
through generational replacement. Given the relative dearth of clear patterns in this literature, and an absence of strong theoretical expectations
on this question, rather than formulating a clear hypothesis regarding patterns of political inequality, we simply offer the following research question to guide our anlysis.

RQ1: To what extent does social media use among young people
affect patterns of political inequality?

As noted earlier, another impetus for our study is that existing research in
this area includes few large-scale empirical investigations. It is thus important to explore the extent to which relationships between social media
use and political engagement are stable or generalizable across a broad
array of advanced democracies. Though many factors in our model are
believed to be consistent across advanced democracies, political socialization experiences and the institutional arrangements within which political
engagement is practiced vary distinctly from country to country (Hahn
1998; Torney-Purta 2000; Torney-Purta & Amadeo 2003). Our focus on
these issues is expressed in our second research question.

RQ2: To what extent do patterns of social media use and youth political engagement vary based on differences in national and political contexts among advanced democracies?

## DATA

To test our model and shed light on our research questions we analyze survey data collected in three advanced democracies: Australia, the United States, and the United Kingdom. These countries represent an excellent set of cases for study, in that they are all subject to the kinds of social and economic trends identified earlier as particularly salient to understanding contemporary patterns of youth engagement. They also share a common language and many cultural references, while offering a reasonable amount of variation in civic education contexts, political institutions, and other factors. As noted earlier, we chose to limit our survey populations to individuals aged 16–29, which includes the range of ages typically associated with contemporary individuals' experience of "emerging adulthood" (Arnett 2000), as well as those age groups routinely identified as the heaviest users of social media. We contracted with a social research firm to administer our survey to nationally representative samples of young people in each country. The surveys were identical, with the exception of minor modifications of some items to reflect differences in language usage or, in some cases, relevant options (e.g. educational levels). Participants were systematically recruited from online panels to create samples that mirrored census data in each country on key dimensions such as gender and age. Across all three countries, 3,685 young people completed our surveys, between late March and early May of 2013, including 1,216 in Australia, 1,228 in the United Kingdom, and 1,241 in the United States.

We constructed two distinct measures of our dependent variable, political engagement. The first, *individual engagement,* was based on questions involving 12 individual acts of civic or political engagement, modeled on items used by Zukin *et al.* (2006). Given the age range of our sample and compulsory voting in Australia, we did not ask about voting. The otherwise inclusive list featured conventional political activities such as trying to influence how others might vote in an election, as well as more civic-oriented acts like raising money for charitable causes, and nontraditional political activities such as buying (or not buying) goods or services, based on political or ethical reasons. Participants were asked whether they engaged in these activities in the past year, either online, offline, or in some combination of online or offline forms ($M = 4.10$, $SD = 3.88$). Our second political engagement variable, *collective political engagement,* was designed to capture activities that specifically involved working with others in organizations. Again, we sought to capture a wide array of different kinds of engagement, so we included items related to "political groups or causes," "nonpolitical or charitable groups," and groups associated with political candidates or parties. In all, we asked participants whether they joined, worked, or volunteered, with five different kinds of groups, allowing them to count activities that may or may not have involved the internet to varying degrees ($M = 1.00$, $SD = 1.34$).

To capture social media use, we created an index of social media use based on the frequency with which participants used nine popular social media platforms. Respondents specified usage on an 8-point scale ranging from "Never" (0) to "Multiple times per day" (7). We combined responses to these items into a single scale of social media use ($M = 1.83$, $SD = 1.12$). Our index of frequency of use across the 10 platform options enjoys reasonable validity (Cronbach's $\alpha = .76$).

To represent the other major factors in our theoretical model—political socialization and actualizing citizenship norms—we created four distinct independent variables. Three of these were related to socialization. Political talk in the home was measured using responses to a series of survey items that asked participants to indicate the frequency with which their early family experiences included talking about news and political affairs, using a 5-point frequency scale ranging from "Never" (0) to "All the time" (4). Across the full sample this variable has a mean of 1.64 and a standard deviation of .89. We also created two measures of civic education experiences. Given the significant differences in the ways that civic education is handled in each of the study countries, our civic education items focused on general experiences involving teachers and political material. The first of these was intended to tap "traditional" or "general" civic education experiences and was based on three items that asked students to reflect on their secondary or high-school experiences and express agreement or disagreement (on a standard 5-point scale) with statements like "When people had different opinions on political or social issues, teachers encouraged us to discuss things" (Cronbach's $\alpha = .80$, $M = 3.41$, $SD = 0.91$). We also created a variable that captured digital literacy as part of civics education. This variable was based on three items similar to those just described, but focused on the internet (e.g. "Teachers provided instruction on how to assess the trustworthiness of information found on the internet" and "Students were required to use the internet to learn about politics or political issues"). This variable allows us to distinguish between ordinary civic education experiences and those that might reasonably be expected to be particularly relevant to social media and political engagement (Cronbach's $\alpha = .76$, $M = 2.99$, $SD = 0.97$).

Finally, to capture actualizing norms of citizenship we used a series of items that asked participants to indicate the extent to which various kinds of political activities were personally important to them, using a 4-point scale ranging from "Not important at all" (1) to "Extremely important" (4). Items used here were constructed based on the explanations of actualizing citizenship norms elaborated in earlier theoretical work by

Bennett (2008), which emphasize a personal as opposed to dutiful orientation toward politics, as well as a relatively broad conception of politics and a "networked" view of social relations. They included the following statements: "Volunteering your time or donating money to community organizations," "Taking moral, ethical, or political considerations into account when buying products or services," and "Communicating with others about social issues of personal concern" ($M = 2.45, SD = 0.76$).

We also included a number of additional variables in our analysis, including a range of demographic variables and other control variables that were selected based on their demonstrated relationships with political engagement in previous studies. In terms of demographics, we included measures of age ($M = 23, SD = 3.88$), gender (female = 1, 52% across the three samples), race (nonwhite = 1, 24% across the three samples), and a measure of parents' education. Parents' education was selected as our best proxy for socioeconomic status, given that our age range included minor children, individuals at various stages of the normal course of educational attainment, and the difficulty of obtaining reliable estimates of household income from the youngest members of our target populations. Since educational levels are different across the three countries, we converted the raw measures of parental education to a zero-to-one scale and then mean-centered these within each country, creating a measure of parents' education across the comparative data set that ranges from $-.47$ to $0.48$ and has a standard deviation of .20. Additional control variables included a measure of attention to political news, which was based on standard 4-point scales of attention paid to local, national, political, and international news (Cronbach's $\alpha = .80, M = 1.79, SD = 0.67$), a two-item measure of internal political efficacy ($r = .92, M = 3.10, SD = 1.00$), and a binary measure of whether participants identified with, or considered themselves members of, an identifiable political party (61.4% across the full data set).

## METHODS

Our analytic approach involved testing a series of hierarchical ordinary least squares (OLS) regression models, in which we entered blocks of variables based on their assumed causal order. Blocks were entered in the following order: demographics, media attention, efficacy, and partisanship, followed by a block including our socialization and norms variables (to test $H2_a$ and $H3_a$), a block for social media use (to test $H1$), and finally a block including interactions between social media use and demographic variables, as well as interactions between social media use and socialization experiences (to test $H2_b$), and between social media use and actualizing citizenship norms (to test $H3_b$). Whereas we report upon-entry coefficient estimates for the first four blocks, we report before-entry coefficient estimates in the final block to limit the effects of multicollinearity on our evaluation of the interaction effects. The total adjusted $R^2$ reported in each column, however, is derived from a fully specified version of each model. To simplify our analysis, we estimated models separately for each country. Cases were deleted listwise in the event of missing data. Finally, where relevant, we used the Clarify package in STATA to create plots of significant interactions, reflecting expected values on the dependent variables (and 95 percent confidence intervals) for various combinations of relevant independent variables (typically one standard deviation above or below each variable's appropriate country mean).

## FINDINGS

The results from our regression analyses across each of the three countries in which we collected data, and across our two indicators of political engagement, are reported in Tables 2.1 and 2.2. Overall, the models perform quite well, producing $F$ values well within acceptable significance levels (in all cases $p < .000$), and explaining roughly one-third of the variation in individual political engagement, and just over one-fifth of the variation in collective political engagement, across the three countries.

The clearest pattern in our data is unambiguous support for *H1* across all three countries and for both indicators of political engagement. The results reported in Table 2.1 indicate that social media use is significantly related to individual political engagement in Australia ($\beta = .28, p < .000$), the United States ($\beta = .30, p < .000$), and the United Kingdom ($\beta = .33, p < .000$). Similarly, the results summarized in Table 2.2 reflect the same pattern (Australia: $\beta = .21, p < .000$, US: $\beta = .21, p < .000$, UK: $\beta = .20, p < .000$). To provide a more real-world sense of these results, on the basis of the unstandardized regression coefficients (not reported), movement of one standard deviation on the social media use scale is generally associated with one additional act of individual participation, and nearly a third of an act of collective participation, all else equal. These estimates hold equally across the advanced democracies included in our analysis. Considering that the mean number of individual acts of participation is four, and the mean number of collective acts is one, we interpret this as substantial demonstration of a direct relationship between social media use and political engagement.

Recall that $H2_a$ and $H2_b$ concerned the relationship between civic education experiences and interactions between these experiences and social media use. Results here were somewhat mixed, but ultimately fairly consistent with our expectations. Specifically, we found political talk in the home to be significantly associated with individual political engagement across the three country cases (Australia: $\beta = .08, p < .05$, US: $\beta = .07, p < .000$, UK: $\beta = .08, p < .05$), and the corresponding results for collective political engagement were marginally or statistically significant (Australia: $\beta = .07, p < .10$, US: $\beta = .08, p < .05$, UK: $\beta = .06, p < .10$).

*Table 2.1* Individual political engagement as explained by social media use, political socialization, and actualizing norms of citizenship

|  | Australia | USA | UK |
|---|---|---|---|
| *Demographics* | | | |
| Age | .04 | .00 | .09** |
| Gender (female) | −.05 | −.13*** | −.10** |
| Race (non-white) | .17*** | .04 | .12 |
| Parents' education | .20*** | .13*** | .15*** |
| Incremental adjusted $R^2$ | .08 | .04 | .05 |
| *Media use, efficacy, and partisanship* | | | |
| Attention to political news | .08* | .25*** | −.04 |
| Internal political efficacy | .31*** | .24*** | .30*** |
| Party identification/membership | .12*** | .04 | .09 |
| Incremental adjusted $R^2$ | .23 | .21 | .18 |
| *Political socialization and norms* | | | |
| Political talk in home | .08* | .07*** | .08* |
| Civic education (traditional) | −.02 | −.05 | −.04 |
| Civic education (digital) | .13*** | .05 | .09* |
| Actualizing norms of citizenship | .20*** | .25*** | .25*** |
| Incremental adjusted $R^2$ | .29 | .27 | .23 |
| *Social media use* | | | |
| Time spent with social media platforms | .28*** | .30*** | .33*** |
| Incremental adjusted $R^2$ | .36 | .34 | .32 |
| *Interactions* | | | |
| Social media × Age | .27 | .17 | −.03 |
| Social media × Parents' education | .00 | .04 | −.03 |
| Social media × Race (non-white) | .09 | .00 | −.03 |
| Social media × Political talk in home | .05 | .07 | −.06 |
| Social media × Civic education (traditional) | .04 | .15 | −.02 |
| Social media × Civic education (digital) | .11 | .16 | .17 |
| Social media × Actualizing norms | .01 | −.02 | .01 |
| Total adjusted $R^2$ | .36 | .34 | .33 |
| N | 924 | 972 | 897 |

*Note*: Cell entries are standardized regression coefficients. $p < .10$, *: $p < .05$, **: $p < .01$, ***: $p < .000$

*Table 2.2* Group political engagement as explained by social media use, political socialization, and actualizing norms of citizenship

|  | Australia | USA | UK |
|---|---|---|---|
| *Demographics* | | | |
| Age | –.04 | –.10** | –.05 |
| Gender (female) | –.01 | –.10** | –.05 |
| Race (non-white) | .09** | .06# | .13*** |
| Parents' education | .16*** | .13*** | .18*** |
| Incremental adjusted $R^2$ | .04 | .04 | .06 |
| *Media use, efficacy, and partisanship* | | | |
| Attention to political news | .14*** | .25*** | .09* |
| Internal political efficacy | .17*** | .10** | .15*** |
| Party identification/membership | .07* | .04 | .11** |
| Incremental adjusted $R^2$ | .11 | .14 | .12 |
| *Political socialization and norms* | | | |
| Political talk in home | .07# | .08* | .06# |
| Civic education (traditional) | –.06 | –.01 | –.03 |
| Civic education (digital) | .11** | .07# | .04 |
| Actualizing norms of citizenship | .19*** | .22*** | .22*** |
| Incremental adjusted $R^2$ | .15 | .19 | .16 |
| *Social media use* | | | |
| Time spent with social media platforms | .21*** | .21*** | .20*** |
| Incremental adjusted $R^2$ | .19 | .23 | .20 |
| *Interactions* | | | |
| Social media × Age | .27 | .11 | –.10 |
| Social media × Parents' education | .16** | .05 | .03 |
| Social media × Race (non-white) | –.01 | .14* | .02 |
| Social media × Political talk in home | .22* | .18* | .24* |
| Social media × Civic education (traditional) | .41** | .22 | .16 |
| Social media × Civic education (digital) | .50*** | .27* | .28* |
| Social media × Actualizing norms | .16 | .17 | .50*** |
| Total adjusted $R^2$ | .21 | .23 | .21 |
| N | 924 | 972 | 897 |

*Note:* Cell entries are standardized regression coefficients. $p < .10$, *: $p < .05$, **: $p < .01$, ***: $p < .000$

Traditional civic education experiences were not significantly associated with either form of political engagement. However, "digital" civic education experiences, which mix digital media literacy with civic or political discussion topics, were found to be significantly and positively related to individual political engagement in Australia ($\beta = .13$, $p < .000$) and the United Kingdom ($\beta = .09$, $p < .05$), significantly and positively related to collective political engagement in Australia ($\beta = .11$, $p < .01$) and marginally and positively related to collective political engagement in the United States ($\beta = .07$, $p < .10$). Taken as a whole, we interpret these results as moderate support for $H2_a$.

With respect to the conditioning of the relationship between social media use and political engagement by political socialization ($H2_b$), we found little support with respect to individual political engagement, but considerable support when we turn to collective acts of political engagement. Specifically, we find robust positive and significant results for the interactive term "Social media × Political talk in home" (Australia: $\beta = .22$, $p < .05$, US: $\beta = .18$, $p < .05$, UK: $\beta = .24$, $p < .05$). We also find a similar result for the traditional civics education and social media use interaction in the Australian case ($\beta = .41$, $p < .01$). The strongest results here, however, concern the interaction between "digital" civic education experiences and social media use, which again are positive and statistically significant across all three countries (Australia: $\beta = .50$, $p < .000$, US: $\beta = .27$, $p < .05$, UK: $\beta = .28$, $p < .05$). Figure 2.2 illustrates this interaction within the Australian data.

Our remaining hypotheses, $H3_a$ and $H3_b$, pursue a similar set of predictions with respect to "actualizing" norms of citizenship. Overall, our

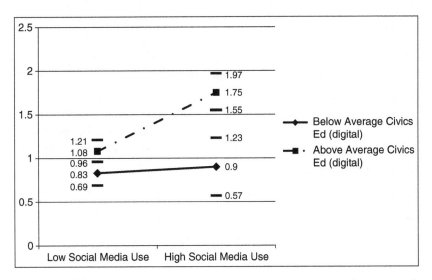

*Figure 2.2* Collective political engagement as a function of civics education and social media use (Australia)

results lend considerable support to the notion that such norms are of critical importance to understanding contemporary youth engagement. The clearest pattern of findings here is robust support for $H3_a$. As seen in Table 2.1, the results here are positive, significant, and strikingly consistent across the country cases for individual political engagement (Australia: $\beta = .20$, $p < .000$, US: $\beta = .25$, $p < .000$, UK: $\beta = .25$, $p < .000$).

A similar pattern of findings for collective political engagement is clearly visible in Table 2.2 (Australia: $\beta = .19$, $p < .000$, US: $\beta = .22$, $p < .000$, UK: $\beta = .22$, $p < .000$). Results associated with the interaction term between actualizing norms and social media use, however, lent little support for $H3_b$, except with respect to collective political engagement among British youth ($\beta = .50$, $p < .000$). We plot this interaction in Figure 2.3.

In addition to providing a comprehensive series of tests of our hypotheses, our results also shed considerable light on our central research questions. With respect to our primary research question, we identified two plausible outcomes. The interaction terms between social media use and demographic characteristics in each of the regression models provide direct leverage over the first, that of counterstratificational effects. These interaction terms enable us to explore the possibility that social media use may be directly associated with political inequality, either increasing or decreasing stratification. As a careful examination of the coefficients for the interaction terms reveals, in 16 out of 18 trials relevant to this question, we find no significant results. Aside from the two significant results, the overall pattern presents no clear implication regarding a direct relationship between social media use and political inequality.

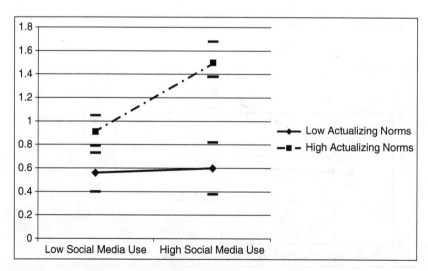

*Figure 2.3* Collective political engagement as a function of actualizing norms and social media use (UK)

The second plausible scenario related to *RQ1* was that reasonably strong and direct relationships between social media use and indicators of political engagement could signal the possibility of a generational softening of stratification in political engagement. Taken as a whole, our results are much more suggestive of this state of affairs. To be sure, consistent with the findings of Schlozman *et al.*'s analysis (2010), our models reveal a persistent, positive, and significant relationship between SES and political engagement, whether the dependent variable is individual (Australia: $\beta = .20, p < .000$, US: $\beta = .13, p < .000$, UK: $\beta = .15, p < .000$) or collective (Australia: $\beta = .16, p < .000$, US: $\beta = .13, p < .000$, UK: $\beta = .18, p < .000$) political activity. At the same time, however, a number of additional factors suggest that social media use may indeed be softening patterns of political inequality. First, as noted earlier, we find a strong, significant, and robust positive relationship between social media use and political engagement. Perhaps more telling, however, is the pattern of explained variance across the various blocks in the six models. Though SES remains a significant predictor of political engagement, for instance, it is worth noting that the entire block of demographic variables explains no more than roughly 30 percent of the total explained variance in any of the models, and generally explains between 15 and 20 percent of the total explained variance across most of the models. Additionally, in four of the six models, social media use alone explains as much or more total variance as the combined block of demographic variables. In two models, those for individual political engagement in the United States and the United Kingdom, the social media use variable explains nearly twice as much variance in the dependent variable as compared to demographic factors. Stated plainly, our results suggest that if one were seeking an efficient single indicator of political engagement among young people in the countries studied here, social media use would appear to be as good as, or better than, SES.

In terms of our second research question, concerning the extent to which our findings are consistent across the three advanced democracies in which we collected our survey data, the foregoing presentation of results has already revealed many of the relevant patterns. In addition to the pattern of support for *H1*, findings were also consistent across the three countries in terms of support for *H3$_a$*, concerning actualizing norms of citizenship, and the persistent relationship between SES and political engagement just discussed. Though a number of variables performed differently across the models, two patterns of country-based variations are worth explicit discussion here. The first is civic education, particularly in "digital" form, which, overall, appears to have the most explanatory power in Australia. The second is actualizing norms, which, as mentioned, earlier appears to exhibit the kind of contingent relationship with social media use with respect to collective political engagement only in the British case.

## DISCUSSION

In this chapter we have advanced a theoretical model of social media use and political engagement, in an effort to understand the possible implications of increasingly widespread use of internet services with social media functionality for longstanding patterns of political inequality. Paying particular attention to the fact that social media is largely dominated by younger users, we have focused on theoretical concepts that are particularly relevant to contemporary youth in advanced democracies, and we have deliberately narrowed our empirical focus to users between the ages of 16 and 29. In search of broadly applicable findings and a parsimonious model, we have used particularly inclusive measures of our primary variables of interest. Our results lend strong support to our hypothesis that social media is positively related to political engagement, and suggest a number of patterns consistent with a flattening out of social asymmetries in political engagement over time, via a process of generational replacement. Though our principal findings are relatively consistent across the advanced democracies in which we conducted our research, we also identified a number of areas in which country-specific variations on these findings may deserve further inquiry.

Before discussing the implications of these findings for future research in the area of digital media use and political engagement, it is important to first acknowledge and discuss some limitations of the present study. First, as a cross-sectional design, the present study is inherently unable to provide any definitive conclusions regarding causal relationships. Even without clear leverage over causal questions, however, the present investigation still offers the most comprehensive study of social media use and political engagement among contemporary youth to date. Whereas previous work has focused on convenience or otherwise limited samples of college students, or perhaps representative samples of a single country, the analyses presented here provide an unprecedented level of reach in terms of examining patterns of social media use, political engagement, and political equality across contemporary advanced democracies. Even with considerable support and advances in research infrastructure, conducting research in this area still involves a fundamental dilemma between an emphasis on internal versus external validity. Given the current state of research in this area, we made a calculated choice to emphasize the latter.

Additional limitations stem from issues related to the specific variables and measures included in our study. For example, while the best available proxy, our measure of SES, is somewhat rough. Ultimately, we take our finding of a significant relationship between this indicator and political engagement as an indication that it nonetheless provides a useful measure of SES that behaves similarly to other measures used in the literature. Finally, it is undoubtedly a further limitation that our principal independent and dependent variables are more broadly cast than most others used in the literature. Prior studies in this area have demonstrated the value of attending to distinctions between various social media platforms (e.g. Pasek *et al.* 2009), types of social media use (e.g. Gil de Zúñiga *et al.* 2012), or forms of what we consider political engagement (e.g. Dalton 2008; Zukin *et al.* 2006). As useful as the insights that flow from such distinctions may be, however, we believe there is also value in establishing a set of basic relationships between general versions of the variables explored in our analysis. Moreover, in the case of opting for a general (as opposed to a more politically focused) approach to social media use, such a tack preserves an important separation between independent and dependent variables. In a world in which most acts of political engagement can be and are carried out within social media, a focus on general use behaviors as independent variables may be the only way to avoid measuring the same activity on both sides of the regression equation (Morris & Morris 2013).

The aforementioned limitations of the present study notwithstanding, we believe the findings reported here offer a number of significant implications and questions for future research. Most important, the results of our inquiry offer a clear signal regarding the fundamental relationship between social media use and political engagement that is not provided by the existing body of research on these questions. On the basis of these findings, future studies can more confidently explore causal relationships between key variables of interest. Additionally, it is hoped that our results also contribute to research in this area by further demonstrating the importance of attending to variables particularly relevant to young people, such as political socialization and newly emerging norms of citizenship, in all areas of research on digital media and citizenship. Differences in their experiences with socialization, and their norms and attitudes toward politics and public affairs, are clearly relevant to understanding how young citizens interact with social media and the political world. Future research in this area should explore these contingent relationships in more detail.

A number of additional questions for future research are suggested by the country-specific findings we report on the roles played by "digital" civic education experiences and actualizing norms of citizenship. Clearly, the results reported here suggest that there may be something particularly interesting happening with civics education in Australia. Indeed, readers familiar with comparative studies of civics education should find our results particularly interesting, given that, unlike the other two countries in our study, Australia lacks explicit and consistent civics curricula across all of its schools. At the same time, scholars interested in actualizing norms and forms of political engagement and organizing may take particular interest in British politics, based on our findings.

As a final reflection, we believe the present study provides an important and unprecedented empirical validation of many claims regarding social media use and youth political engagement, while pointing the way toward critical areas for future scholarship. We hope that future studies will be able to build upon these findings to not only identify hyperbole and hype where appropriate, but move us ever closer to a comprehensive understanding of how new information technologies affect our youngest political actors, and thus the shape of political engagement overall.

## NOTE

1  This material is based upon work supported by the Spencer Foundation. Any opinions, findings, and conclusions or recommendations expressed in this material are those of the authors and do not necessarily reflect the views of the Spencer Foundation.

## REFERENCES

Amnå, E., Ekström, M., Kerr, M. & Stattin, H. (2009). Political Socialization and Human Agency. The Development of Civic Engagement from Adolescence to Adulthood. *Statsvetenskaplig Tidskrift, 111*(1): 27–40.

Andolina, M., & Jenkins, K. (2003). Habits from Home, Lessons from School: Influences on Youth Civic Engagement. *PS: Political Science & Politics, 36*(2), 275–280. Retrieved from http://journals.cambridge.org/production/action/cjo GetFulltext?fulltextid=147396.

Arnett, J. J. (2000). Emerging Adulthood: A Theory of Development from the Late Teens through the Twenties. *American Psychologist, 55*(5), 469–480. doi: 10. 1037//0003-066X.55.5.469.

Australian Communications and Media Authority. (2013). *Like, Post, Share: Young Australians' Experience of Social Media*. Retrieved from www.acma. gov.au/~/media/mediacomms/Report/pdf/Like post share Young Australians experience of social media Quantitative research report.pdf.

Baumgartner, J. C., & Morris, J. S. (2009). MyFaceTube Politics: Social Networking Web Sites and Political Engagement of Young Adults. *Social Science Computer Review, 28*(1), 24–44. doi: 10.1177/0894439309334325.

Bennett, W. L. (2008). Changing Citizenship in the Digital Age. In W. L. Bennett (Ed.), *Civic Life Online: Learning how Digital Media Can Engage Youth* (pp. 1–24). Cambridge, MA: MIT Press.

Bennett, W. L. (2012). The Personalization of Politics: Political Identity, Social Media, and Changing Patterns of Participation. *The Annals of the American Academy of Political and Social Science, 644*(1), 20–39. doi: 10.1177/000271 6212451428.

Bennett, W. L., Wells, C., & and Freelon, D. (2011). Communicating Civic Engagement: Contrasting Models of Citizenship in the Youth Web Sphere. *Journal of Communication, 61*(5): 835–856.

Bode, L. (2012). Facebooking It to the Polls: A Study in Online Social Networking and Political Behavior. *Journal of Information Technology & Politics, 9*(4), 352–369. doi: 10.1080/19331681.2012.709045.

Brady, H., Verba, S., & Schlozman, K. (1995). Beyond SES: A Resource Model of Political Participation. *American Political Science Review, 89*(2), 271–294. Retrieved from www.jstor.org/stable/10.2307/2082425.

Brenner, J. (2013). Pew Internet: Social Networking (full detail). *Pew Internet and American Life Project*. Retrieved from http://pewinternet.org/Commen tary/2012/March/Pew-Internet-Social-Networking-full-detail.aspx.

Carlisle, J. E., & Patton, R. C. (2013). Is Social Media Changing how We Understand Political Engagement? An Analysis of Facebook and the 2008 Presidential Election. *Political Research Quarterly*. doi: 10.1177/10659129134 82758.

Chong, S., Farquharson, K., Choy, E. A., Lukman, Z. M., & Mokhtar, M. K. (2011). Enhancing Youth Civic Engagement and Generalized Trust through Bonding Social Capital among Friends. *Pertanika Journal of Social Sciences and Humanities, 19,* 57–64.

Conroy, M., Feezell, J. T., & Guerrero, M. (2012). Facebook and Political Engagement: A Study of Online Political Group Membership and Offline Political Engagement. *Computers in Human Behavior, 28*(5), 1535–1546. doi: 10.1016/j.chb.2012.03.012.

Dalton, R. J. (2008). *The Good Citizen: How a Younger Generation Is Reshaping American Politics, Revised Edition* (p. 200). Thousand Oaks, CA: CQ Press. Retrieved from www.amazon.com/The-Good-Citizen-Generation-Reshaping/dp/1604265566.

Dimitrova, D. V., & Bystrom, D. (2013). The Effects of Social Media on Political Participation and Candidate Image Evaluations in the 2012 Iowa Caucuses. *American Behavioral Scientist*. doi: 10.1177/0002764213489011.

Ellison, N. B., Steinfield, C., & Lampe, C. (2007). The Benefits of Facebook "Friends": Social Capital and College Students' Use of Online Social Network Sites. *Journal of Computer-Mediated Communication, 12*(4), 1143–1168. doi: 10.1111/j.1083-6101.2007.00367.x.

Galston, W. A. (2004). Civic Education and Political Participation. *PS: Political Science & Politics, 37*(2): 263–266.

Gil de Zúñiga, H., Jung, N., & Valenzuela, S. (2012). Social Media Use for News and Individuals' Social Capital, Civic Engagement and Political Participation. *Journal of Computer-Mediated Communication, 17*(3), 319–336. doi: 10.1111/j.1083-6101.2012.01574.x.

Hahn, C. (1998). *Becoming Political: Comparative Perspectives on Citizenship Education*. Albany, NY: SUNY Press.

Kahne, J., & Westheimer, J. (2006). The Limits of Political Efficacy: Educating Citizens for a Democratic Society. *PS: Political Science & Politics, 39*(2), 289–296.

Lee, N.-J., Shah, D. V., & McLeod, J. M. (2012). Processes of Political Socialization: A Communication Mediation Approach to Youth Civic Engagement. *Communication Research*. doi: 10.1177/0093650212436712.

Levine, P. (2007). *The Future of Democracy: Developing the Next Generation of American Citizens (Civil Society: Historical and Contemporary Perspectives)* (p. 308). Lebanon, NH: Tufts University Press. Retrieved from www.amazon.com/The-Future-Democracy-Contemporary-Perspectives/dp/1584656484.

Loader, B. D. (2007). Introduction: Young Citizens in the Digital Age: Disaffected or Displaced? In B. Loader (Ed.), *Young Citizens in the Digital Age: Political Engagement, Young People and New Media* (pp. 1–18). New York: Routledge.

McLeod, J. M., & Shah, D. V. (2009). Communication and Political Socialization: Challenges and Opportunities for Research. *Political Communication, 26*(1), 1–10. doi: 10.1080/10584600802686105.

Messing, S., & Westwood, S. J. (2012). Selective Exposure in the Age of Social Media: Endorsements Trump Partisan Source Affiliation when Selecting News Online. *Communication Research*. doi: 10.1177/0093650212466406.

Morris, D. S., & Morris, J. S. (2013). Digital Inequality and Participation in the Political Process: Real or Imagined? *Social Science Computer Review*. doi: 10.1177/0894439313489259.

Pasek, J., More, E., & Romer, D. (2009). Realizing the Social Internet? Online Social Networking Meets Offline Civic Engagement. *Journal of Information Technology & Politics, 6*(3–4), 197–215. doi: 10.1080/19331680902996403.

Sapiro, V. (2004). Not Your Parents' Political Socialization: Introduction for a New Generation. *Annual Review of Political Science, 7*(1), 1–23. doi: 10.1146/annurev.polisci.7.012003.104840.

Schlozman, K. L., Verba, S., & Brady, H. E. (2010). Weapon of the Strong? Participatory Inequality and the Internet. *Perspectives on Politics, 8*(02), 487–509. Retrieved from http://journals.cambridge.org/abstract_S1537592710001210.

Shah, D. V., McLeod, J. M., & Lee, N. (2009). Communication Competence as a Foundation for Civic Competence: Processes of Socialization into Citizenship. *Political Communication, 26*(1), 102–117. doi: 10.1080/105846008027 10384.

Tapscott, D. (2008). *Grown Up Digital: How the Net Generation is Changing Your World* (p. 384). New York: McGraw-Hill. Retrieved from www.amazon.com/Grown-Up-Digital-Generation-Changing/dp/0071508635.

Torney-Purta, J. (2000). Comparative Perspectives on Political Socialization and Civic Education. *Comparative Education Review, 44*(1), 88–95. Retrieved from www.jstor.org/stable/10.2307/1189228.

Torney-Purta, J., & Amadeo, J. A. 2003. A Cross-National Analysis of Political and Civic Involvement Among Adolescents. *PS: Political Science & Politics, 36*(2): 269–274.

Valenzuela, S., Park, N., & Kee, K. F. (2009). Is There Social Capital in a Social Network Site? Facebook Use and College Students' Life Satisfaction, Trust, and Participation. *Journal of Computer-Mediated Communication, 14*(4), 875–901. doi: 10.1111/j.1083-6101.2009.01474.x.

Vitak, J., Zube, P., Smock, A., Carr, C. T., Ellison, N., & Lampe, C. (2011). It's Complicated: Facebook Users' Political Participation in the 2008 Election. *Cyberpsychology, Behavior and Social Networking, 14*(3), 107–14. doi: 10.1089/cyber.2009.0226.

Woollaston, V. (2013). Britons Are the Second Most Prolific Facebook and Twitter Users in Europe with a Fifth now Aged over 65. *Daily Mail Online*. Retrieved from www.dailymail.co.uk/sciencetech/article-2340893/Britons-second-prolific-Facebook-Twitter-users-EUROPE-fifth-aged-65.html.

Xenos, M., & Moy, P. (2007). Direct and Differential Effects of the Internet on Political and Civic Engagement. *Journal of Communication, 57*(4): 704–718.

Zhang, W., Seltzer, T., & Bichard, S. L. (2013). Two Sides of the Coin: Assessing the Influence of Social Network Site Use during the 2012 U.S. Presidential Campaign. *Social Science Computer Review*. doi: 10.1177/0894439313489962.

Zukin, C., Keeter, S., Andolina, M., Jenkins, K., & Carpini, M. X. D. (2006). *A New Engagement? Political Participation, Civic Life, and the Changing American Citizen* (p. 272). New York: Oxford University Press. Retrieved from www.amazon.com/New-Engagement-Political-Participation-Changing/dp/0195183177.

# 3 Spaces for Public Orientation?

## Longitudinal Effects of Internet Use in Adolescence

*Mats Ekström, Tobias Olsson and Adam Shehata*

Adolescence is a critical time for identity construction and the development of values and social relationships, with implications also for individuals' public orientations and democratic engagement (Arnett, 2004; Buckingham, 2008; Flanagan, 2013; Jennings & Stoker, 2004; Mazur & Kozarian, 2010; Romer, Jamieson & Pasek, 2009; Stattin & Kerr, 2002). As Flanagan (2013) argues, this is a time in life when individuals tend to develop an understanding of themselves as citizens, commit to more self-transcendent values, learn about the public domain and form ideas about how social and political institutions work. However, this also means that adolescence is a period of differentiation, when some people's political interest and engagement increase, while those of others remain weak (Amnå, Kim & Miklikowska, 2013). These are differences that might have long-term implications (Jennings & Stoker, 2004). Some research into political socialization has explained such differences in relation to aspects of family life, school, peer networks and media use (Flanagan, 2013; Lee, Shah & McLeod, 2013; McLeod, 2000). The integration of Internet and social media in adolescents' daily lives has created new challenges for this research. This inspires the chapter's overall research question: How does young people's engagement in different *Internet spaces* affect the development of their *public orientation* during adolescence?

The potential of the Internet to promote young people's democratic engagement is a key issue in contemporary political socialization research (Bakker & de Vreese, 2011; Bennett, 2008; Buckingham, 2008; Ekström & Östman, 2013a; Harris, Wyn & Younes, 2010; Lee, Shah & McLeod, 2013; Livingstone, Bober & Helsper, 2005; Loader, 2007; Pasek, More & Romer, 2009; Shah, McLeod & Lee, 2009; Vromen, 2007). Our knowledge of the Internet as a context for changing forms of civic engagement (Bennett, Wells & Rank, 2009; Loader, 2007; Vromen, 2011; Wells, 2013), as well as for the mechanisms of political socialization (Ekström & Östman, 2013a; Lee, Shah & McLeod, 2013), has increased significantly. With a few exceptions (Lee, Shah & McLeod, 2013), this research has, however, focused primarily on young people as a group and how the Internet might promote their civic engagement, rather than the *developments and socialization processes that occur during adolescence.*

The studies are mainly based on cross-sectional rather than longitudinal designs. Despite there being a huge scholarly interest in young people's political socialization, so far we know little about the longitudinal impact of different forms of Internet use during adolescence.

In this study we make use of the advantages of longitudinal panel data in order to explore how young people's *public orientation* develops during a phase in life (age 13–20) described as being critical for political socialization. More specifically, we investigate the main longitudinal effects of young people's engagement in four different *Internet spaces* (a news space, a space for social interaction, a game space and a creative space). Before describing the methods and results, in the next section we will discuss the two key concepts of the study: public orientation and Internet spaces.

## PUBLIC ORIENTATION AND INTERNET SPACES: THEORETICAL POSITIONS AND EMPIRICAL DEMARCATIONS

### Public Orientation

Previous research has investigated different aspects of young people's demo-cratic engagement; political knowledge, values, participation in traditional political institutions, and a variety of different off- and online political activi-ties, protests, political consumerism etc. Democratic engagement and politi-cal participation are best understood as multidimensional concepts, and there is a broad scholarly consensus today on the importance of inclusive concep-tualization that includes both evolving and also less institutionalized forms of engagement (Amnå *et al.*, 2009; Bakker & de Vreese, 2011; Dahlgren, 2009; Lee, Shah & McLeod, 2013; Vromen, 2011). Meanwhile, research clearly shows that effects observed on one dimension of engagement cannot be generalized to other dimensions, as the mechanisms are partly distinct (Ekström & Östman, 2013a), and of course also because some forms of engagement are more demanding and less frequent than others.

In this study we focus on what we would prefer to call *public orienta-tion*. The concept refers to a general orientation—in values, interests and everyday practices—towards what Couldry, Livingstone and Markham (2007: xv) describe as 'a world of public issues beyond what is private interest'. Such an orientation to common concerns, an understanding of oneself as interrelated to wider communities, is a basic precondition for a democratic engagement. Without in any way questioning the importance of active and demanding forms of participation, we follow researchers who have questioned a too-strong focus on either traditional political participation or alternative and spectacular activism (Harris, Wyn & Younes, 2010), as this makes *important differences in democratic engage-ment* among large groups of 'ordinary' young people invisible. We under-stand public orientation as a form of involvement in society and politics which does not require, but sometimes manifests itself in, more active participation (Ekman & Amnå, 2012). As argued by Ekman and Amnå (2012), it is important not to neglect the 'standbyers', i.e. those young people who have an interest in politics, are connected to the public and perceive themselves as being potentially active in the future.

We focus here on three dimensions of public orientation. *Values* are recognized as an important aspect of youth identity which also guides their actions in different contexts (Flanagan, 2013: 27; Knafo & Schwartz, 2004). In adolescence, individuals in general tend to develop more self-transcendent values related to a concern for the common good, for justice and for the welfare of all people as well as for nature (Datler, Jagodzinski & Schmidt, 2013; Flanagan, 2013; Stattin & Kerr, 2002). We investigate how young people's involvement in different Internet spaces may affect the development of such self-transcendent values that are expected to be approved in general socialization.

*Political interest* is among the most commonly used concepts in political socialization research (Delli Carpini & Keeter, 1996; Prior, 2010; van Deth, 2000). It is understood as a dimension of a democratic involvement and is known as a powerful predictor of political participation (Ekman & Amnå, 2012). Interest is an important dimension of our concept of public orientation, as it captures people's attention to and positive curiosity about politics. In order to avoid a too-narrow understanding of politics (related mainly to institutional politics) we have broadened this dimension to include interest in both political and societal questions.

*Talking with peers* is an important way for young people to become engaged in politics and public concerns on an everyday basis (Ekström & Östman, 2013b). Talking about politics and societal questions allows people to express their values and opinions and to enrich their understanding of the larger world. The most promising theoretical contributions in current political socialization research have also ascribed great explanatory power to interpersonal communication (McDevitt 2005; Lee, Shah & McLeod, 2013; Shah, McLeod & Lee, 2009). Empirical studies clearly show that the orientation of talk in family and with peers— the opportunities to discuss societal and political questions—matters for young people's democratic engagement (Ekström & Östman, 2013b). Interpersonal communication has also proved to be an important mediator of influences from media use to political participation (Lee, Shah & McLeod, 2013). There are thus good reasons to integrate talking about politics and societal questions as a dimension of public orientation.

## Internet Spaces

An important challenge in research on Internet and political socialization involves developing approaches in which the diversity of Internet practices is taken into account. In analytical terms, what does it actually mean to be 'using the Internet'? This challenge has triggered a debate among scholars regarding how to best make sense of people's Internet usage. In this context, Pasek, More and Romer (2009) have argued—convincingly—for the need to refine existing categories of use in a way that makes research on Internet effects sensitive to the fact that 'we must establish a more informed understanding of the differences among Web site users' (p. 201). Following this vein, we have developed a notion of Internet *space* in order to capture a middle ground; we conceive of Internet spaces as an empirical intermediate ground in-between overarching conceptualizations (and measures) of 'Internet usage' and very specific analyses of use of individual platforms or even websites.

Our notion of Internet spaces has been informed by initial analyses of data on young people's Internet use. This analysis revealed four key factors: Internet usage oriented towards news and information outlets, Internet practices related to social interaction, game-oriented Internet use and Internet use focused on creative practices. These four factors subsume a variety of Internet practices in a manner that makes it relevant to conceptualize them as separate but interrelated Internet *spaces* within which users move. As a consequence, we have conceptualized them as *news space, space for social interaction, game space* and *creative space*. These will be explored in more detail below and related to previous studies and hypotheses about possible implications of Internet use for the development of public orientation during adolescence.

Theoretically, the notion of Internet space is inspired by Henri Lefebvre's theory of space (Lefebvre, 1974/1991), as this makes it possible to account for how the Internet offers a great variety of infrastructures, facilities and related affordances. According to Lefebvre, spaces are social products, made by and made use of in social practice—and this is equally true for online and offline spaces. These socially produced spaces differ from one another in terms of their physical presence, their infrastructure and in the way in which they stimulate some forms of action while impeding others. Following Lefebvre's argument, we perceive Internet spaces to correspond to specific uses of spaces, i.e. to certain practices 'that they express and constitute' (Lefebvre, 1974/1991: 16). This notion of space also relates to recent theoretical developments within research that argue for the need to problematize what sort of spaces are actually being engendered by the Internet. In the light of a study of different online social networks, Zizi Papacharissi (2009) has argued for the need to discriminate between online spaces with regard to their architecture. She notes that 'online spaces function architecturally, suggesting particular uses or highlighting technological affordances' (p. 216). In a similar vein, Olsson (2014) critically analyses how the Internet's so-called 'architecture of participation' (Web 2.0) becomes shaped into very diverse participatory spaces, depending on what social logic informs their production.

## News Space

Accessing online news venues is one of the most popular practices among Internet users and has been ever since the Internet started to reach the mass market in the early 1990s. New facilities for news and freely available information are constantly developed on the Internet and people have the opportunity to obtain knowledge from a broad range of sources. Previous empirical research on online news spaces indicates an overall positive correlation between online news consumption and public orientation. When including the use of online news into the overarching concept of 'information', Pasek *et al.* (2009) show that '[i]ndividuals who frequently use the Internet for information are more likely to participate in offline clubs and groups and to demonstrate high levels of political knowledge' (p. 207). Focusing on online news more specifically, but not exclusively on sites aimed at young people, Gil De Zúñiga, Puig-I-Abril and Rojas (2009) argue that online news consumption matters for overall public engagement. Similarly, Lee, Shah and McLeod (2013) have very recently indicated that news consumption via digital media is a 'strong online pathway' to civic participation. Thus, movements within Internet news space tend to have a positive impact on public orientation.

## Space for Social Interaction

The advent of the term Web 2.0, which among other things has evolved into the notion of 'social media', has underscored the Internet's social capabilities, which are manifested in a wide range of facilities for the formation of networks, communities and relations. Applications such as Facebook, Twitter, YouTube and online message services are perhaps the most renowned, but by no means the only examples from this space. In the theoretical literature, this space for social interaction has often been interpreted as a participatory space (Burgess & Green, 2009), with a potential to stimulate participation both online and within society (and culture) at large (Jenkins, 2006). Although we know that young people's contacts in social media are often concentrated on the peers they meet offline, social media also enables a widening of their networks and social circles (Mesch, 2012). The possibilities and chances of coming in contact with people from various backgrounds and identities are recognized as important in terms of political socialization (Flanagan, 2013: 232). The idea is that an awareness of differences in life situations, experiences and opinions is significant for the development of public orientations, helping youth to see themselves as being interrelated to wider communities, and also provoking them to take a stance on questions of common concern.

So far, however, empirical research has offered shifting assessments regarding how people's movements within online spaces for social interaction impact on public orientation. When separating civic participation from political participation, and studying both young and old users, Zhang, Johnson, Seltzer and Bichard, (2010) found that 'reliance on social networking sites [. . .] was positively related to civic participation but not to political participation or confidence in government' (pp. 86–87). This somewhat fluctuating character of the impact of the space for social interaction has also been confirmed in further studies. Drawing on an analysis of varying uses of this space, Valenzuela, Arriagada and Scherman (2012) claim that the results of their study are consistent with previous studies, as their study underscores how 'informational and social interactive uses of media can lead to participatory forms of behaviour, while entertainment uses can drive people away from collective action' (ibid.: 310).

## Game Space

According to our data, various gaming activities are salient components in young people's Internet practices, while also significantly contributing to differences in youth Internet habits. Playing games online of course also involves, for example, social interaction, but this set of social environments, practices and experiences is sufficiently distinguished to make up a space of its own. The literature on how online gaming relates to public orientation suggests, for instance, that gaming experiences such as helping other players, interacting with a social issue within a game and organizing multiplayer games (Lenhart, Kahne, Middaugh, Evans & Vitak, 2008) have a positive impact. Drawing on a large empirical study, Kahne, Middaugh and Evans (2009) summarize some key points concerning video games and public orientation (or, rather, civic engagement). They state, for instance, that 'the overall amount of game play is unrelated to civic engagement' (p. 40), but that civic 'gaming experiences are strongly related to civic engagement' (p. 42).

## Creative Space

The Internet's interactive features offer a plethora of relatively easily accessible opportunities for content production and creative activities among users (cf. Jenkins, 2006). This includes practices for public distribution of one's own ideas, texts and images; collaborative production, sharing and publishing of online content in blogging, YouTube postings, music/videos, etc. We perceive this as a relatively coherent space which encourages active agency, creativity and public expressivity, and there are good reasons to assume that young people's engagement in this creative space promotes a public orientation. The learning involved and the encouragement provided for self-expression and making their voices heard in public are central processes in youth political socialization.

Recent empirical research into the effects of young people's movements within this Internet space reveals interesting results. Based on their panel study, Ekström and Östman (2013a) argue for the need for research to further attend to the potential for public orientation in 'creative forms of Internet use' (p. 17), as they seem have a positive impact on young people's civic participation. The development and use of a creative Internet space is also the core of what Wells (2013: 15) describes as a general transformation of 'the communication dynamics of civic engagement' towards more actualizing and participatory forms (see also Bennett, Wells & Rank, 2009). Wells (2013: 5) seems to suggest that young people's possibilities to participate in the production and sharing of information have become at least as important for their civic orientation as for the receiving and reading of information from news sources.

There are thus reasons to believe that an engagement in different Internet spaces has positive implications for the development of public orientation during adolescence. What distinguishes the research we have related to so far, however, is that it has focused on political socialization. Research in other areas has explored other aspects of young people's socialization and activities in different Internet spaces that also have to be taken into account. Several studies, for example, indicate that 'social media' and what we conceptualize as interactional and creative Internet spaces are used by adolescents primarily for the maintenance and development of friendships, close and romantic relationships and self-presentations (Mazur & Kozarian, 2010; Mesch, 2012). There are no clear connections between such activities and a public orientation. On the contrary, it is reasonable to suppose that social media and blogs also promote self-focused values to some extent as well as a general orientation to personal life-styles and success. What is actualized in participatory forms of media use might be self-presentations and self-affirmation as much as an orientation towards a common good.

The aim of this study, however, is not to investigate these different processes or mechanisms in any detail. We are instead examining the main effects of young people's engagement in Internet spaces. In this sense we provide a test of the more general ideas of Internet spaces as supportive contexts in political socialization during adolescence.

## METHODS

### Participants and Data Collection

The study uses data from three waves in a longitudinal study conducted among youths who were aged between 13 and 17 years at the time of the first data collection. There was approximately one year between the data collections. The study was performed in Örebro, a region with a population of approximately 275,000. This region is representative of the national averages in terms of demographics such as unemployment rate, family income, population density and political leanings. However, the proportion of people with immigrant backgrounds is somewhat higher among 5- to 24-year-olds, as compared with the Swedish average (33 per cent vs 20 per cent; Statistics Sweden, 2010). The sample included all 13- to 14-year-old students (junior high school) and 16- to 17-year-old students (senior high school) at 13 different schools in the region. This represents 13 of 26 schools and approximately 50 per cent of all students in the target groups. The schools were selected so that the sample comprised both vocational and theoretical programmes and schools in areas representative of differences in the distribution of social and ethnic backgrounds. The data collection was conducted during scheduled school hours and was managed by trained research assistants.

*Cohort 1*

2010: Selection = 960; N = 904; Part. rate = 94%

2011: Selection = 987; N = 883; Part. rate = 89%

2012: Selection = 954; N = 843; Part. rate = 88%

*Cohort 2*

2010: Selection = 1052; N = 892; Part. rate = 85%

2011: Selection = 996; N = 807; Part. rate = 81%

2012: Selection = 914; N = 740; Part. rate = 81%

The study is thus based not on a random national sample but on a regional one, and the strategic sampling ensured the representativeness of significant background variables. The design, based on the respondents filling out questionnaires in the classroom during ordinary school hours, made a random national sample almost impossible. However, the strength of the design is in the rather exceptional response rate across the three waves of data collection, and not least the quality of the data related to the on-site administration and monitoring of questionnaire completion.

## Measuring Public Orientations

As noted above, we use three indicators of adolescents' public orientation: values, interests and everyday peer talk.

Inspired by Stattin and Kerr (2002) (cf. Flanagan 2013), we constructed a relative index based on adolescents' self-focused and self-transcendent values based on the importance attached to a range of lower-order values measured by the survey question: *How important is the following to you?*

Self-focused values included the following five items: (1) 'Having fun', (2) 'Having a lot of free time', (3) 'Having a lot of money', (4) 'Looking good', and (5) 'Freedom to do whatever I please' (Wave 1 Cronbach's $\alpha$ = .65, M = .76, SD = .15). Self-transcendent values included (1) 'Equality, equal opportunities for all people', (2) 'A peaceful world free from war and conflicts', (3) 'Helping other people', (4) 'Working together with others for a better society', and (5) 'Developing close relations to other people' (Wave 1 Cronbach's $\alpha$ = .76, M = .80, SD = .15). The participants were able to rate the importance they attached to these items on a scale from 1 ('Not at all important') to 5 ('Very important'), but all items were recoded to range between 0 and 1 before summation. Finally, the index of self-focused values was subtracted from the index of self-transcendent values in order to create a measure of the relative importance of self-transcendent values rather than self-focused values.

Our second indicator of public orientation is political interest, which can be measured by using the following three items: *People differ in how they feel about politics. What are your feelings?* with response categories ranging from (1) 'Really fun' to (6) 'Extremely boring'; *How interested are you in politics?* ranging from (1) 'Very interested' to (5) 'Not at all interested'; *How interested are you in what is happening in society?* ranging from (1) 'Very interested' to (5) 'Not at all interested'. These three items were reversed and recoded to range between 0 and 1 before being summed into an additive political interest index (Wave 1 Cronbach's $\alpha$ = .82, M = .46, SD = .23).

The third indicator of public orientation is peer talk. Following Ekström and Östman (2013b), we distinguish between public- and private-oriented peer talk. Peer talk was measured using several items following the survey question: *How often do you and your friends talk about the following?* Public-oriented peer talk is based on the following three items: (1) 'What you have heard on the news about what is happening in Sweden and around the world' (2) Environmental issues, and (3) Politics or societal issues (Wave 1 Cronbach's $\alpha$ = .74, M = .33, SD = .22). Private-oriented peer talk consists of the following two items: (1) Films, music and TV series; (2) 'What you will do at the weekend' (Wave 1 Pearson's $r$ = .30, M = .805, SD = .16). The response categories for these items ranged from (1) 'Very often' to (4) 'Never', but all items were recoded to range between 0 and 1 before summation. As for values, we subtracted the private peer-talk index from the public peer-talk index to create an index of relative public-orientation talk.

## Measuring Internet Space Orientation

The respondents' involvement in different Internet spaces was measured by asking them to report the frequency of a number of activities on a scale ranging from 'Never' (1), through 'A few times a week' (3), to 'Daily' (5).

Orientation towards *news space* comprised the following four items (1) 'Reading the newspaper', (2) 'Visiting sites to get information about some of my interests', (3) 'Searching for information' and (4) 'Visiting websites to get information about one of my interests' (Wave 1 Cronbach's $\alpha$ = .73, M = .45, SD = .23).

An orientation towards *space for social interaction* was captured by the following three items: (1) 'Talking to friends using MSN, ICQ, or instant messaging service', (2) 'Keeping in touch with or up to date with my friends through Facebook or something similar', and (3) Publish information about myself using Facebook, an online picture diary, Twitter or similar websites' (Wave 1 Cronbach's $\alpha$ = .77, M = .65, SD = .26).

A *creative space orientation* included the following four items: (1) 'Writing my own blog', (2) 'Producing music/videos', (3) 'Sharing music, films, or videos', (4) 'Uploading my own music or films at e.g., MySpace, YouTube' (Wave 1 Cronbach's $\alpha$ = .80, M = .19, SD = .23).

Finally, an orientation towards *game space* was measured using the following item: 'Playing games' (Wave 1 M = .51, SD = .36).

## Control Variables

In the models we controlled for gender (51 per cent girls), age, immigrant status and socioeconomic background. The immigrant variable measured whether the respondents' parents were born outside the EU (18.7 per cent of the sample). Subjective socioeconomic status was measured with five items such as 'If you compare your family with other families, do you think you have more or less money to buy things with?' Finally, we controlled for adolescents' perceptions of their parents' political interest, tapped by the following two items: (1) 'My parents are interested in what happens in the world' and (2) 'My parents follow the news'.

## Data Analysis

To address our research question we rely on both cross-sectional and longitudinal analysis. In addition to the cross-sectional regression models focusing on the relationship between space orientations and each outcome variable measured in the first panel wave, two panel models using information from all three waves are estimated.

First, we use a *lagged dependent variable model (LDV)* to analyse how the changes in each outcome variable between successive waves are related to orientations towards different Internet spaces. More specifically, the dependent variable is regressed on its lagged value from the previous panel wave, along with the space orientations also measured in the previous wave. By so doing, the regression coefficients for our focal independent variables indicate how orientation towards different Internet spaces is related to changes in the three indicators of public orientation over time. To account for differences in socio-demographic background, the LDV model also includes sex, age, family socioeconomic status and parents' country of origin as control variables.

Second, to utilize the fact that we have each variable measured at three points in time, we also estimate a *fixed effects model (FE)*. By focusing only on individual-level variation in both independent and dependent variables between panel waves, the FE estimator accounts for unobserved heterogeneity between units, i.e. differences between individuals that influence the outcome but that do not vary over time (Allison, 2009; Finkel, 2008; Kennedy, 2008). Therefore, the FE estimator basically controls for omitted variables by using 'each individual as his or her own control' (Allison, 2009: 1). As a consequence, these models can only estimate the effects of factors that change over time. The fact that all focal independent and dependent variables were measured at each panel wave provides this opportunity to analyse how changes in Internet space orientations are related to changes in each outcome variable, controlling for unobserved (stable) heterogeneity at the individual level.

## RESULTS AND ANALYSIS

Before we focus on the effects of space orientations on our indicators of public orientation, Table 3.1 displays the bivariate correlation between orientations toward different Internet spaces using cross-sectional data from the first panel wave.

These correlations indicate that adolescents with a news orientation are also more involved in all the other Internet spaces being analysed here. However, a news space orientation is most strongly related to a creative space ($r = 0.32$, $p < 0.01$) orientation, and less so to the game space dimension ($r = 0.15$, $p < 0.01$). Furthermore, adolescents with a strong orientation towards space for social interaction tend also to be active in creative spaces ($r = 0.42$, $p < 0.01$). It is also worth noting that game space seems to be somewhat of an outlier in the sense of its being more weakly correlated with the other orientations. While game activity is unrelated to social interaction, it is modestly but positively related to news ($r = 0.15$, $p < 0.01$) and creative ($r = 0.16$, $p < 0.01$) space orientation.

*Table 3.1* Bivariate correlations between orientation towards Internet spaces (Pearson's $r$)

|                   | News    | Social Interaction | Creative | Political |
|-------------------|---------|--------------------|----------|-----------|
| News              | 1.00    |                    |          |           |
| Social interaction| .26***  | 1.00               |          |           |
| Creative          | .32***  | .42***             | 1.00     |           |
| Game              | .15***  | .04                | .16***   | .02       |

*$p < .05$. **$p < .01$. ***$p < .001$

Thus, adolescents who are active in one type of Internet space also tend be active in others, but there also seem to be certain clusters of orientations that are more closely related to one another—for instance a (1) news orientation, a (2) creative/social interaction space as well as a (3) game space orientation.

To further explore the effects we estimated a series of cross-sectional and panel data regression models for each of the three public orientation variables—values, political interest and peer talk. As outlined above, we estimated two different panel models: an *LDV* that captures how orientation towards specific Internet spaces is related to changes in each outcome variable over time, and an *FE* that primarily accounts for unobserved heterogeneity at the individual level.

Starting with values, Table 3.2 provides substantial evidence that an orientation toward space for social interaction, in particular, matters. The cross-sectional model reveals that all socio-demographic background variables have statistically significant effects on self-transcendent values.

*Table 3.2* Cross-sectional and longitudinal effects on self-transcendent values

|  | Cross-Sectional Model | Lagged Dependent Variable (LDV) Model | Fixed Effects (FE) Model |
|---|---|---|---|
| Sex (1 = man) | .08*** (.02) | .04*** (.01) | — |
| Age | −.02* (.01) | .00** (.00) | — |
| Foreign | .05** (.01) | .02* (.01) | — |
| SES | −.15*** (.02) | −.03 (.02) | — |
| Parents' political interest | .10** (.02) | .05* (.02) | |
| News space | .12** (.03) | .03 (.02) | .05* (.02) |
| Social space | −.10*** (.02) | −.03* (.01) | −.07*** (.02) |
| Creative space | −.02 (.03) | .00 (.02) | −.04 (.02) |
| Game space | −.07*** (.01) | −.00 (.01) | .01 (.01) |
| Self-trans. values$_{t-1}$ | — | .60*** (.02) | — |
| Wave 2 | — | — | −.01* (.00) |
| Wave 3 | — | — | −.06*** (.01) |
| $R^2$ | .16 | .42 | .06 |
| N | 1680 | 1432 | 1964 |

*Note*: Robust standard errors in parentheses are clustered on the school level (cross-sectional model) and respondent level (LDV and FE). R-squared within presented for the three-wave fixed effects regression.

\*$p < .05$. \*\*$p < .01$. \*\*\*$p < .001$.

Boys, adolescents with at least one parent from a non-European country, as well as those whose with politically interested parents tend to possess stronger self-transcendent values, while both age and family socio-economic status is negatively related to such values. More importantly, however, although news space orientation is positively related to the possession of self-transcendent values, adolescents whose orientations are directed towards the social interactive and game space dimensions tend to possess more self-focused values. No such associations are found with respect to the creative space dimension.

Turning to the longitudinal models, there is substantial evidence that an orientation towards the space for social interaction is related to a decrease (increase) in self-transcendent (self-focused) values over time. The LDV yields a negative longitudinal effect ($b = -0.03$, $p < 0.05$) of the space for social interaction—suggesting that a stronger orientation at time 1 is related to lower self-transcendent values at time 2. The FE also suggests a negative effect of the space for social interaction ($b = -0.07$, $p < 0.001$), but this also indicates a positive effect of news space orientation ($b = 0.05$, $p < 0.05$).

The findings thus suggest that adolescents' public orientation values are most consistently influenced by an orientation towards the space for social interaction, but there is also some evidence that news space orientations also matter.

Table 3.3 similarly presents the results of three regression models predicting political interest. In the cross-sectional case, orientations toward news, social interaction and game spaces are all related to interest in politics. However, while the news space ($b = 0.39$, $p < 0.00$) is positively related to interest, both the space for social interaction ($b = -0.11$, $p < 0.01$) and game space ($b = -0.10$, $p < 0.01$) have negative effects on adolescents' interest in politics. Both the news space and space for social interaction effects also apply to the FE, suggesting that changes in these variables are related to changes in political interest. While individual-level increases in news orientation are related to higher levels of interest ($b = 0.17$, $p < 0.001$), the opposite is true for increases in social interaction orientation ($b = -0.05$, $p < 0.01$). At the same time, only the news space orientation effect reaches levels of statistical significance in the LDV. Overall, the findings are most consistent when it comes to orientation towards news spaces and somewhat less so when it comes to the space for social interaction. While news space is related to increases in adolescents' interest in politics, orientation towards the space for social interaction seems to have the opposite effect.

Finally, Table 3.4 focuses on the effects of Internet space orientation in the content of adolescents' interpersonal communication with their friends. Again, orientations toward the news and social interaction spaces seem to have the most consistent influence on adolescents' public orientation, irrespective of model specification. The effect of news space

Table 3.3 Cross-sectional and longitudinal effects on political interest

| | Cross-Sectional Model | Lagged Dependent Variable (LDV) Model | Fixed Effects (FE) Model |
|---|---|---|---|
| Sex (1 = man) | .00 (.02) | −.00 (.01) | — |
| Age | .00 (.01) | .01* (.00) | — |
| Foreign | .01 (.02) | −.02* (.01) | — |
| SES | −.05* (.02) | .04* (.02) | — |
| Parents' political interest | .32*** (.03) | .09*** (.02) | .10*** (.02) |
| News space | .39*** (.04) | .07*** (.02) | .17*** (.02) |
| Social space | −.11** (.03) | −.00 (.01) | −.05** (.02) |
| Creative space | −.03 (.03) | −.03 (.02) | −.01 (.02) |
| Game space | −.10** (.02) | −.01 (.01) | −.01 (.02) |
| Political interest$_{t-1}$ | — | .67*** (.02) | — |
| Wave 2 | — | — | .02*** (.00) |
| Wave 3 | — | — | .02*** (.01) |
| $R^2$ | .28 | .53 | .07 |
| N | 1662 | 1400 | 1954 |

Note: Robust standard errors in parentheses are clustered on the school level (cross-sectional model) and respondent level (LDV and FE). R-squared within presented for the three-wave fixed effects regression.
*$p < .05$. **$p < .01$. ***$p < .001$.

orientation is positive and statistically significant in the cross-sectional ($b = 0.31$, $p < 0.001$) as well as the LDV ($b = 0.11$, $p < 0.001$) and the FE ($b = 0.20$, $p < 0.001$) models. That is, not only do adolescents active in news spaces discuss public issues more frequently with their friends, but this orientation also seems to increase such conversations over time. Similarly, not only is an orientation toward the space for social interaction negatively related to peer conversations regarding public issues in the cross-sectional case ($b = −0.26$, $p < 0.001$), but also the LDV ($b = −0.06$, $p < 0.01$) and FE ($b = −0.14$, $p < 0.001$) indicates that there is also some longitudinal evidence.

While both an orientation towards the creative space ($b = 0.09$, $p < 0.05$) and towards the game space ($b = −0.06$, $p < 0.001$) spaces are cross-sectionally related to peer talk, none of these effects holds in the longitudinal models.

In sum up, the results presented here primarily emphasize the importance of orientations towards news space and space for social interaction. Overall, the findings strongly suggest that orientations towards these spaces are related to adolescents' public orientation—regardless of the

Table 3.4 Cross-sectional and longitudinal effects on public-oriented peer talk

| | Cross-Sectional Model | Lagged Dependent Variable (LDV) Model | Fixed Effects (FE) Model |
|---|---|---|---|
| Sex (1 = man) | −.03 (.02) | −.02 (.01) | — |
| Age | .01 (.01) | .01*** (.00) | — |
| Foreign | .04 (.03) | .01 (.01) | — |
| SES | −.13** (.03) | −.05* (.02) | — |
| Parents' political interest | .14** (.04) | .07** (.02) | .05 (.03) |
| News space | .31*** (.04) | .11*** (.02) | .20*** (.03) |
| Social space | −.26*** (.02) | −.06** (.02) | −.14*** (.02) |
| Creative space | .09* (.03) | −.03 (.02) | .04 (.03) |
| Game space | −.06*** (.01) | −.01 (.01) | −.03 (.02) |
| Peer talk$_{-1}$ | — | .42*** (.02) | — |
| Wave 2 | — | — | .01 (.01) |
| Wave 3 | — | — | .0 (.01) |
| $R^2$ | .16 | .27 | .04 |
| N | 1677 | 1426 | 1964 |

*Note:* Robust standard errors in parentheses are clustered on the school-level (cross-sectional model) and respondent-level (LDV and FE). R-squared within presented for the three-wave fixed effects regression.

*p < .05. **p < .01. ***p < .001.

indicators used to analyse their public orientation. At the same time, both the creative and the game spaces seem to be less important for adolescents' development of a public orientation.

## DISCUSSION

This study confirms that the Internet provides contexts with significantly different implications for political socialization in adolescence. We have examined the development of three basic aspects of public orientation: values, interests and conversations. Based on previous socialization research we can expect a general increase in such orientations in adolescence (e.g. Flanagan, 2013). Our longitudinal study, however, clearly indicates that this development is affected, supported and countered by young people's involvement in different Internet spaces. More specifically, four implications of the study are important to emphasize.

Firstly, the study offers a strong theoretical and empirical argument for theoretical approaches in which different Internet spaces and activities are separated. We have developed a notion of *Internet spaces* that covers contexts and practices in analytical middle ground in between analyses of *either* Internet use as such *or* specific websites and Internet application. The suggested distinction between news space, space for social interaction, game space and creative space is closely related to infrastructures and social practices on the Internet. Based on this conceptualization, we have observed consistent differences in longitudinal influences with regard to all three aspects of public orientation. Such a conceptualization is obviously not able to capture all the differences in social practices on the Internet that may have implications for young people's public orientations. Finding ways of developing our concepts of the Internet in more depth is an important challenge for political socialization research. However, we believe that this study demonstrates the benefits of understanding the Internet as consisting of rather distinct spaces.

Secondly, the study confirms the centrality of news and information in political socialization. The study demonstrates the positive longitudinal effects of young people's involvement in the online news space. This is not in itself a surprising result. The positive effects of news media use on youth civic engagement and political participation are well documented in previous research (Bakker & de Vreese, 2011; Buckingham, 2000; Lee, Shah & McLeod, 2013; Pasek *et al.*, 2006). However, the consistent longitudinal effects not only on political interest and political talk but also on self-transcendent values, a development recognized as a general aspect of socialization in adolescence, are particularly important in our study (Datler, Jagodzinski & Schmidt, 2013; Flanagan, 2013; Stattin & Kerr, 2002). The clear contrast between news and the engagement in other Internet spaces is also notable.

Thirdly, the empirical results challenge the idea that Internet facilities such as Facebook, Twitter and blogging enable forms of social interaction and creative production that have an overall positive impact on young people's public orientation. Interactional and creative Internet spaces of course involve a variety of practices with different implications. There is no doubt that the Internet supports both old and evolving forms of democratic engagement. In this study, however, we have focused on the main effects of young people's priorities and orientations towards specific Internet spaces. The question is whether a frequent engagement in interactional and creative Internet spaces in general promotes a development of public orientations in adolescence. The answer is no. Such engagement has negative longitudinal effects on self-transcendent values, political interest and talk about politics and societal questions. This study thus clearly indicates that the facilities on the Internet often described as 'social' media offer environments which mainly draw young people's attention away from common concerns. Thus, self-transcendent values are countered rather than strengthened. Within the literature on Web 2.0 and social networking media, there has been a tendency to presuppose

the value of participatory online practices—not only for political participation, but also for orientations to society and culture more generally
(Anderson, 2009; Benkler, 2006; Shirky, 2008). While the literature on
participatory culture emphasizes the opportunities for young people to
engage in public concerns (Jenkins, 2006), social media is also a context
for self-presentations, leisure and life-styles. These are not necessarily in
conflict. This study, however, clearly indicates that social media has an
overall tendency to promote self-focused values, interests and talking
about personal rather than public life.

The Internet has obviously partly changed the ways in which people
keep themselves informed about public concerns. More specifically,
researchers have suggested that traditional forms of news consumption or reading have become less important when people participate to
a greater extent in the sharing and production of information in social
networks, and by using digital media (see e.g. Wells, 2013). Our study
suggests that this is anything but a clear-cut process. The Internet is
obviously an important news context for young people, with significant implications for their public orientation. What is crucial is thus
not necessarily traditional forms of news reading (paper) and viewing
(television). However, the measures of Internet news used in this study
capture a relationship to news which is partly similar to traditional
forms (e.g. reading news on the web). It involves a reading of news in
new forms and is associated with extended opportunities to share news
with others. However, it still involves engagement in a news space,
and with the information offered mainly by centralized news provid-
ers that is of crucial significance for young people's development of a
general public orientation in terms of values and everyday practices.
Nothing in this study suggests that the space for social interaction
and creative space on the Internet are about to replace the news space
as a crucial context for public connections (Couldry, Livingstone &
Markham, 2007) and the development of a broader public orientation
in adolescence.

This is not to say that online discussions and expressions are irrelevant as driving forces in the development of political engagement. In
previous studies (Ekström & Östman, 2013a) we have, for example,
shown that expressive on-line activities have the potential to promote
offline political participation. Based on the 'communication mediation
approach' to political socialization, Lee, Shah and McLeod (2013: 18)
also show that 'informational use of media stimulates discussion and
expression, which in turn boosts civic and political participation'. In
this article we have focused not on specific mechanisms but on the main
effects of young people's everyday involvement in different Internet
spaces. The study confirms that news media use inspires talk about
public concerns. More importantly, however, the study suggests that the
different patterns of everyday Internet use created in early adolescence

are of significant importance for the more general public orientation developed during adolescence. We believe that the study raises at least three significant questions to be explored in future research. Firstly, given that patterns of Internet use have significant implications for political socialization in adolescence, it is important to explore how such patterns develop in the first place, in relation to patterns in the family, influences from peers and also young people's own explorations and experiences of different Internet spaces. Secondly, we have analysed how Internet use at a specific time in life influences public orientation over a few years. However, another question is how young people's movements between Internet spaces over time matter for their public orientations. Thirdly, previous research indicates that adolescence is a formative period with long-term implications for civic and political engagement (Jennings & Stoker, 2004). Whether this applies to the aspects of political socialization analysed in this chapter is a question for future research to explore.

## REFERENCES

Allison, P. (2009). *Fixed effects regression*. Thousand Oaks, CA: Sage Publications.

Amnå, E., Ekström, M., Kerr, M., & Stattin, H. (2009). Political socialization and human agency: The development of civic engagement from adolescence to adulthood. *Statsvetenskaplig tidskrift 111*, 27–40. Retrieved from: http://journals.lub.lu.se/index.php/st/article/view/8141/7243.

Amnå, E., Kim, Y., & Miklikowska, M. (2013, September). Diversity, latency, and change: Moving beyond stereotyped notions of youths' civic engagement. Paper presented at the General Conference of the European Consortium for Political Research, Bordeaux.

Anderson, C. (2009). *The longer tail: How endless choice is creating unlimited demand*. London: Random House Business Books.

Arnett, J. J. (2004). *Emerging adulthood: The winding road from the late teens through the twenties*. New York: Oxford University Press.

Bakker, T. & de Vreese, C. H. (2011). Good news for the future? Young people, internet use, and political participation. *Communication Research 38*(4), 51–70. doi: 10.1177/0093650210381738.

Benkler, Y. (2006). *The wealth of networks*. New Haven, CT: Yale University Press.

Bennett, L. (2008). Changing citizenship in the digital age. In L. Bennett (Ed.), *Civic life online* (pp. 1–24). Cambridge, MA: MIT Press.

Bennett W. L., Wells, C., & Rank, A. (2009). Young citizens and civic learning: Two paradigms of citizenship in the digital age. *Citizenship Studies 13*, 105–120. doi: 10.1080/13621020902731116.

Buckingham, D. (2000). *The making of citizens: Young people, news and citizenship*. New York: Routledge.

Buckingham, D. (2008). Introducing identity. In D. Buckingham (Ed.), *Youth, identity and digital media* (pp. 1–24). Cambridge, MA: MIT Press.

Burgess, J., & Green, J. (2009). *YouTube: Online video and participatory culture*. Cambridge, MA: Polity.

Couldry, N., Livingstone, S., & Markham, T. (2007). *Media consumption and public engagement*. Basingstoke: Palgrave Macmillan.

Dahlgren, P. (2009). *Media and political engagement: Citizens, communication and democracy.* Cambridge: Cambridge University Press.

Datler, G., Jagodzinski, W., & Schmidt, P. (2013). Two theories on the test bench: Internal and external validity of the theories of Ronald Inglehart and Shalom Schwartz. *Social Science Research 42*, 906–925.

Delli Carpini, M. X., & Keeter, S. (1996). *What Americans know about politics and why it matters*. New Haven, CT: Yale University Press.

Ekman, J., & Amnå, E. (2012). Political participation and civic engagement: Towards a typology. *Human Affairs 22*, 283–300.

Ekström, M., & Östman, J. (2013a). Information, interaction, and creative production: The effects of three forms of internet use on youth democratic engagement. *Communication Research*. Online first: http://crx.sagepub.com/content/early/2013/02/21/0093650213476295.

Ekström, M., & Östman, J. (2013b). Family talk, peer talk, and young people's civic orientation. *European Journal of Communication 28*, 294–308. doi: 10.1177/0267323113475410.

Finkel, S. (2008). Linear panel analysis. In S. Menard (Ed.), *Handbook of longitudinal research: Design measurement and analysis* (pp. 475–504). Burlington, MA: Academic Press.

Flanagan, C. (2013). *Teenage citizens: The political theories of the youth*. Cambridge, MA: Harvard University Press.

Gil De Zúñiga, H., Puig-I-Abril, E., & Rojas, H. (2009). Weblogs, traditional sources online and political participation: An assessment of how the Internet is changing the political environment. *New Media and Society 11*, 553–574. doi: 10.1177/1461444809102960.

Harris, A., Wyn, J., & Younes, S. (2010). Beyond apathetic or activist youth: 'Ordinary' young people and contemporary forms of participation. *Young 18*, 9–32. doi: 10.1177/110330880901800103.

Jenkins, H. (2006). *Convergence culture: Where old and new media collide*. New York: New York University Press.

Jennings, M. K., & Stoker, L. (2004). Social trust and civic engagement across time and generations. *Acta Politica 39*, 342–379. doi: 10.1057/palgrave.ap.5500077.

Kahne, J., Middaugh, E., & Evans, C. (2009). *The civic potential of video games*. Cambridge, MA: MIT Press.

Kennedy, P. (2008). *A guide to econometrics*. Oxford: Blackwell.

Knafo, A., & Schwartz, S. H. (2004). Identity formation and parent–child value congruence in adolescence. *British Journal of Developmental Psychology 22*, 439–458. doi: 10.1348/0261510041552765.

Lee, N.-J., Shah, D., & McLeod, J. M. (2013). Processes of political socialization: A communication mediation approach to youth civic engagement. *Communication Research 40*, 669–697. doi: 0093650212436712.

Lefebvre, H. (1991/1974). *The production of space*. Oxford: Blackwell Publishing.

Lenhart, A., Kahne, J., Middaugh, E., Evans, C., & Vitak, J. (2008). *Teens, video games, and civics*. Retrieved from Pew Internet and American Life Project: www.pewinternet.org/~/media//Files/Reports/2008/PIP_Teens_Games_and_Civics_Report_FINAL.pdf.pdf.

Livingstone, S., Bober, M., & Helsper, E. (2005) Active participation or just more information? *Information, Communication & Society 8*, 287–314. doi: 10.1080/13691180500259103.

Loader, B. (Ed.) (2007). *Young citizens in the digital age: Political engagement, young people and new media.* London: Routledge.

Mazur, E., & Kozarian, L. (2010). Self-presentation and interaction in blogs of adolescents and young emerging adults. *Journal of Adolescent Research 25*, 124–144. doi: 10.1177/0743558409350498.

McDevitt, M. (2005). The partisan child: Developmental provocation as a model of political socialization. *International Journal of Public Opinion Research 18*, 67–88. doi: 10.1093/ijpor/edh079.

McLeod, J. M. (2000). Media and civic socialization of youth. *Journal of Adolescent Health 27*, 45–51.

Mesch, G. (2012). Technology and youth. *New Directions for Youth Development 135*, 97–105.

Olsson, T. (2014). 'The architecture of participation': For citizens or consumers? In C. Fuchs and M. Sandoval (Eds), *Critique, social media & the information society* (pp. 203–215). London: Routledge.

Papacharissi, Z. (2009). The virtual geographies of social networks: A comparative analysis of Facebook, LinkedIn and ASmallWorld. *New Media and Society 11*, 199–220. doi: 10.1177/1461444808099577.

Pasek, J., Kenski, K., Romer, D., & Jamieson, K. H. (2006). America's youth and community engagement: How use of mass media is related to civic activity and political awareness in 14- to 22-year-olds. *Communication Research 33*, 115–135. doi: 10.1177/0093650206287073.

Pasek, J., More, E., & Romer, D. (2009). Realizing the social internet? Online social networking meets offline civic engagement. *Journal of Information Technology & Politics 6*, 197–215. doi: 10.1080/19331680902996403.

Prior, M. (2010). You've either got it or you don't? The stability of political interest over the life cycle. *The Journal of Politics 72*, 747–766. doi: http://dx.doi.org/10.1017/S0022381610000149.

Romer, D., Jamieson, K. M., & Pasek, J. (2009). Building social capital in young people: The role of mass media and life outlook. *Political Communication 26*, 65–83. doi: 10.1080/10584600802622878.

Shah, D. V., McLeod, J. M., & Lee, N. (2009). Communication competence as a foundation for civic competence: Processes of socialization into citizenship. *Political Communication 26*, 102–117. doi: 10.1080/10584600802710384.

Shirky, C. (2008). *Here comes everybody: The power of organizing without organization.* London: Penguin Books.

Statistics Sweden. (2010). *Utrikes födda efter län, ålder i tioårsklasser och kön. År 2001–2010.* Retrieved from www.ssd.scb.se/databaser/makro/MainTable.asp?yp=qmnggr&xu=91506001&omradekod=BE&omradetext=Befolkning&lang=1.

Stattin, H., & Kerr, M. (2002). Adolescents' values matter. In J.-E. Nurmi (Ed.), *Navigating through adolescence: European perspectives* (pp. 21–58). New York: Routledge Farmer.

Valenzuela, V., Arriagada, A., & Scherman, A. (2012). The social media basis for youth protest behavior: The case of Chile. *Journal of Communication 62*, 299–314. doi: 10.1111/j.1460-2466.2012.01635.x.

van Deth, J. W. (2000). Interesting but irrelevant: Social capital and the saliency of politics in Western Europe. *European Journal of Political Research 37*, 115–147. doi: 10.1111/1475-6765.00507.

Vromen, A. (2007). Australian young people's participatory practices and internet use. *Information, Communication & Society 10*, 48–68. doi: 10.1080/13691180701193044.

Vromen, A. (2011). Constructing Australian youth online. *Information, Communication & Society, 14*, 959–980. doi: 10.1080/1369118X.2010.549236.

Wells, C. (2013). Two eras of civic information and the evolving relationships between civil society organizations and young citizens. *New Media & Society*. Online first. doi: 10.1177/1461444813487962.

Zhang, W., Johnson, T. J., Seltzer, T., & Bichard, S. (2010). The revolution will be networked: The influence of social networking on political attitudes and behavior. *Social Science Computer Review 28*, 7592. doi: 10.1177/0894439309335162.

# 4 Political Influence across Generations

## Partisanship and Candidate Evaluations in the 2008 US Presidential Election

*Emily K. Vraga, Leticia Bode, Jung Hwan Yang, Stephanie Edgerly, Kjerstin Thorson, Chris Wells and Dhavan V. Shah*[1]

For many years, scholarship on political socialization endorsed the assumption that adolescents' political preferences were "inherited" from parents (Jennings, Stoker, & Bowers, 2009; Niemi & Jennings, 1991; Plutzer, 2002). Early perspectives on youth civic education were dominated by studies establishing parents as the principal source of political socialization, in terms of both partisanship and political attitudes (Langton & Jennings, 1968).

Yet recent work has raised questions about to what extent this unidirectional account of political socialization holds true. Pre-adult socialization into politics is context specific, impacted both by "the pressures of the times in which they first enter the electorate" (Beck & Jennings, 1991, p. 742) and by "intensive exposure to political events" (Sears & Valentino, 1997, p. 58) surrounding the process. Therefore, changes in the social, media, and political environment surrounding young adults have likely influenced the socialization process and provided new ways in which parents and children come to understand their political orientations.

In particular, recent work has led scholars to reconsider the contexts in which civic learning takes place, concluding that youth can learn about politics in diverse arenas, including media and schools (Lee, Shah, & McLeod, 2013). For example, changes in the media environment have created a shift from a mass media culture in which youth received the same messages from the same sources alongside their parents to a personalized communication culture in which youth have greater control over their media experiences. This change has produced a profound impact on how young people think about their own citizenship (Bennett, Freelon, Hussain, & Wells, 2012). Some schools are taking advantage of this environment, providing integrated and interactive lessons to encourage youth to explore news content and to form their own political beliefs and perspectives (McDevitt & Ostrowski, 2009). Moreover, digital media not only allow youth greater choice over their media consumption, but also reinforce the role of peers in developing norms of citizenship and partisanship (Glynn, Huge, & Lunney, 2009; McDevitt & Kiousis, 2007).

Altogether, these external influences may embolden young people to be active participants in their own political socialization and lead them to exert "trickle-up" influence by transforming family communication patterns (Saphir & Chaffee, 2002) and affecting parents' political orientation (Linimon & Joslyn, 2002; McDevitt & Chaffee, 2002).

Further, the political environment itself may be contributing to new pathways of socialization. The availability of political information via a wide range of news outlets and social media networks, coupled with the increased clarity of the parties' ideological positions, allows youth to more readily select a party that matches their personal priorities (Abramowitz & Saunders, 1998; Bafami & Shapiro, 2009; Wolak, 2009).

These changes call for a reexamination of some longstanding questions in political psychology: how young adults develop partisan identities and attitudes, and the relationship of these dynamics to the choices of their parents. To clarify these relationships, we use national panel data of parent–child dyads collected during the 2008 US presidential election cycle to explore different ways in which parents and children influenced each other in their partisanship and their electoral preferences for Democratic or Republican candidates. We go beyond both traditional transmission and "trickle-up" models of socialization (Linimon & Joslyn, 2002; McDevitt & Chaffee, 2000) to examine a diverse range of ways in which the partisanship and candidate evaluations of parents and children may influence one another over the course of the campaign. Equally important, we examine how change within families occurs, why some dyads remain in partisan harmony whereas others change, and why some families move toward agreement, while discord reigns in others. We pay special attention to the role of family communication patterns, civic education, peer norms, and mediated communications in predicting these relationships.

## LITERATURE REVIEW

### Partisan Socialization and the Family

Given the significance of partisanship to so many political choices, particular attention has been paid to understanding how this identification develops throughout life. The bulk of scholarly attention has focused on the role that parents play in encouraging their children to adopt a political identity in line with their own (Carmines, McIver, & Stimson, 1987; Jennings & Markus, 1984; Niemi & Jennings, 1991; Jennings *et al.*, 2009). Partisanship has generally been viewed as a "hand-me-down" orientation, with parental orientations predicting the partisan identities that children adopt (Campbell, Converse, Miller, & Stokes 1960; Lane, 1962). This research has been verified with multiple generations over decades (Jennings & Markus, 1984; Niemi & Jennings, 1991; Jennings *et al.*, 2009), with many scholars suggesting socialization occurs early and is reinforced over childhood and young adulthood (van Deth, Abendschon, & Vollmar, 2011).

While less research has considered the role of parental influence in the development of short-term political attitudes such as candidate evaluations, themselves shaped by partisan identification, parental perspectives provide important feedback for transitory political evaluations, including candidate assessments (Jennings *et al.*, 2009). Further, the same processes that influence the development of partisanship within families—direct learning of political cues and underlying characteristics like class (Beck & Jennings, 1991; Verba, Schlozman, & Brady, 1995)—should also play a role in shaping candidate evaluations.

## Challenging the Transmission Model

Efforts to expand the direct transmission model have focused on the "trickle-up" socialization model, which suggests that children, motivated by external influences discussed above, may influence their parents by initiating political discussions (McDevitt & Chaffee, 2000; 2002). Extensions of this model have focused on circumstances under which children gain their political identities, including both internal (adolescent personality) and external (campaign context) influences (Wolak, 2009).

However, existing research does not go far enough in exploring the variety of pathways by which parents and children may shift their political orientations over the course of the election. To remedy this, we build on the insight of Carmines and colleagues (1987), which recognized a variety of possible routes of parent–child agreement and disagreement. Specifically, we examine what factors increase the likelihood that a given parent–child dyad will follow any one of eight routes of socialization over the course of the election:

1   *Harmony,* in which parent–child dyads agree at early and late stages of the election.
2   *Independent child,* in which the child moves from initial agreement with the parent toward independence.
3   *Independent parent,* in which the parent moves from initial agreement with the child toward independence.
4   *Co-divergence,* in which parent–child dyads both change their views from initial agreement to disagreement.
5   *Discord,* in which parent–child dyads disagree at early and late stages of the election cycle.
6   *Indoctrination,* in which the child abandons initial independence in favor of agreement.
7   *Trickle-up,* in which the parent abandons initial independence in favor of agreement.
8   *Co-adoption,* in which parent–child dyads both change their views from initial disagreement to agreement.

We explore the distribution of parent–child dyads into these categories for several socialization outcomes and then test demographic, structural, and communicative antecedents to these parent–child relationships.

## Agents of Socialization

Socialization research has long emphasized the role that parents play in predicting children's political orientations. Research has consistently shown that the clarity and strength of parental attitudes towards politics contribute to socialization (Beck & Jennings, 1991; Carmines *et al.*, 1987; Jennings *et al.*, 2009), making it more likely that children will adopt parental attitudes.

> *H1*: Parents with stronger partisanship will encourage greater agreement with their children (e.g., more harmony, more indoctrination, less independent child, less discord) and will be less susceptible to children's influence (e.g., trickle-up).

However, recent work in socialization has established a number of challenges to the transmission model and to the assumption that family is the dominant socialization agent, emphasizing the importance of multiple socialization influences, including family communication, schools, and media habits (Lee *et al.*, 2013).

Communication is central to theoretical models linking together various agents of political socialization. The value of schools, peers, and families has been conceptualized as their being primarily sites for political discussion, which in turn both motivates and is further motivated by news media use. Early research on family interactions suggested the importance of conversation for socialization, but primarily viewed it as parent driven (Saphir & Chaffee, 2002). However, it has been argued that when children have been socialized by external influences, they have the potential to shape parents' perspectives if family communication patterns (FCP) reflect a concept orientation in which disagreement between parents and children is allowed as part of an open exchange of ideas, rather than a socio-orientation, which values conformity and adherence to parental authority (Chaffee, Ward, & Tipton, 1970; McDevitt & Chaffee, 2002; McLeod & Chaffee, 1972; McLeod & Shah, 2009).

> *H2*: Families who discuss politics more frequently will be more likely to maintain or come into agreement about politics (e.g., more harmony, less discord, less independent child).

The role of family communication may be reinforced by other opportunities for political learning. In a study comparing the effects of school-based civics curricula on political discussion and socialization outcomes, McDevitt and Kiousis (2007) argue that systematically different socialization outcomes emerge, depending on whether the influence of school-based civics interventions is channeled through the home or by peer groups. Because adolescents' motivation to differentiate the self is more salient with peers, peer-based interactions about politics are more likely to produce interest in non-conventional activism, while interaction with the family tends to reproduce existing values. Conversation, then, has the possibility of reinforcing parental norms or introducing children's political sentiments to parents.

RQ1: Will families who communicate more frequently about politics be more likely to experience trickle-up or indoctrination routes of socialization?

Schools and civic classrooms are another centrally important source of socializi Ekström and Östman ng influence. Work by McDevitt and colleagues suggests that schools can be "staging grounds" for influence when applying a civics-based curriculum, as students integrate lessons learned from the interconnected relationships between peers, mass media, and parents (McDevitt & Kiousis, 2007; McDevitt & Chaffee, 2000; Kiousis, McDevitt, & Wu, 2005; Hess 2009). Children who partake in these types of classroom activities hone their civic skills and gain confidence in their abilities (McDevitt & Kiousis, 2007; Kiousis *et al.*, 2005), giving them the agency to develop their own attitudes about the political world. Schools may offer young adults opportunities to explore new identities, whereas parents and families tend to validate and reinforce existing identities (McDevitt & Ostrowski, 2009). Moreover, as McDevitt and Chaffee (2000) suggest, children can play an active role by influencing their parents' attitudes about politics. Therefore, we expect that exposure to civics curricula will encourage children to demonstrate more freedom and power in the political socialization process.

H3: Civics education will contribute to children having more independence from parents (e.g., less harmony, less indoctrination, more discord, more independent child) and being more likely to impact parents' attitudes (e.g., more trickle-up).

Outside of traditional agents of socialization in the home and schools, research has emphasized the role of the media in helping to solidify political orientations. The news media can provide young adults with an opportunity to hear a broader range of perspectives to validate or challenge their political values and opinions (Kiousis, *et al.*, 2005; Mutz, 2002). Social media is an important new source of mediated socialization, and we expect social media to act as the more traditional media which predated it—providing information and encouraging the acceptance of shared norms of political awareness and participation (Chaffee *et al.*,

1970; Plutzer, 2002; Lee *et al.*, 2013). This is especially true in 2008, when campaign strategists extensively used social media to promote youth engagement, offering an additional means through which peer socialization might take place (Campbell, 1980; Glynn *et al.*, 2009). Evidence suggests that political uses of social media plays a role in the political lives of young people, leading us to view it as a potential factor in youth socialization (Bode, Vraga, Borah, & Shah, 2013a; Pew, 2012).

But beyond presenting young people with additional opportunities to learn about and experience political information, social media spaces are first and foremost *social*—they are places in which peers interact with, and share information with, friends. Although many people are exposed to political content on social media, only a small minority post themselves, often due to concerns about the reaction of peers within one's network (Pew, 2012; Thorson, Vraga, & Kligler-Vilenchik, in press). The role of peer relationships as a setting for everyday encounters with political content cannot be understated, as many of the settings where youth peers interact may serve as platforms for the emergence of political talk. McDevitt and Kiousis (2007) showed that civics interventions in schools can prompt youth to increase the amount of political talk both within their families and within their peer social networks. In a survey of Swedish youth, Ekström and Östman (2013) found that civic talk among peers is a particularly important predictor of a number of democratic outcomes, including participation, knowledge, and attention to political information. These findings hold in studies exploring the impact of political uses of social media on participatory outcomes (Bode *et al.*, 2013a; Vitak *et al.*, 2011). Therefore, political social media use should exert part of its power to encourage children to deviate from parents' political attitudes by heightening the salience of peer relationships.

All of these forces should offer children additional information and exposure to norms outside of their family, leading to greater independence and agency among children.

> *H4*: Children's political Facebook use will contribute to children having more independence from parental influence (e.g., less harmony, less indoctrination, more discord, more independent child), and produce greater influence on parents' attitudes (e.g., more trickle-up).

## METHODS AND MEASURES

### Data and Design

We test the different proposed routes of socialization by analyzing data from a two-wave national panel survey of adolescent–parent pairs collected by Synovate, a commercial survey firm. Four-page mailed surveys were collected from a single panel of respondents in two waves

(1st wave: May 20–June 25; 2nd wave: November 5–December 10) during 2008. Small incentives were offered for participation.

To achieve a representative pool of respondents, stratified quota-sampling procedures were employed.[2] The sample was drawn to reflect the properties of the population within each of the nine census divisions in terms of household income, population density, age, and household size; then adjusted within a range of subcategories including race, gender, and marital status to compensate for differences in return rates (see Shah et al., 2005).

This technique generated a sample of 4,000 households with children of ages 12–17. A parent in each household was contacted via mail, asked to complete an introductory portion of the survey and then to pass it to the 12- to 17-year-old child in the household who most recently celebrated a birthday. This child completed survey content and then returned the survey to the parent to complete a closing portion and return the survey. Of the 4,000 mail surveys distributed, 1,325 responses were received in Wave 1, a response rate of 33.1 percent.[3] A handful of responses were omitted, due to incomplete or inconsistent information, resulting in 1,255 questionnaires being mailed on November 4. Of these, 738 were returned, for a panel retention rate of 55.7 percent and a second-wave response rate of 60.4 percent.[4] After dropping mismatches in the age of the child and the gender of a parent who completed the first and second surveys,[5] we had a final sample of $N = 531$.

## Dependent Variables

*Political orientations.* We test three related political outcomes: party affiliation, evaluations of John McCain, and evaluations of Barack Obama. All three variables are measured for both parents and children in both waves. Partisan identifications of parents and children were measured using a 5-point scale that ranges from "Strong Democrat" (1) to "Strong Republican" (5), converted to a 3-point scale by collapsing the strong Democrat/Democrat and strong Republican/Republican categories together.[6] Candidate favorability was measured by asking "How favorable is your impression of John McCain/Barack Obama" with 5-point scales ranging from "Very Favorable" (1) to "Very Unfavorable" (5), converted to a 3-point scale by collapsing the very favorable/favorable and very unfavorable/unfavorable responses together.[7]

Next, we compared the parent/child agreement on each measure in each wave of the data collection and determined which route described the socialization process. Each route is calculated as a dichotomous measure—either the parent–child dyad took that route (coded 1) or it did not (e.g., took any other route, 0)—reflecting whether the parent and child began in agreement or disagreement and whether one or both moved over the course of the election (as described earlier). Descriptive statistics of these routes are presented in Table 4.1.

Table 4.1 Descriptive statistics for socialization routes

| Process Description | Wave 1 | Wave 2 | Political party affiliation | | | McCain favorability | | | Obama favorability | | |
|---|---|---|---|---|---|---|---|---|---|---|---|
| | | | N | % of subset | % of total | N | % of subset | % of total | N | % of subset | % of total |
| Harmony | Matched | Continue to match | 270 | 81.3 | 50.8 | 234 | 77.0 | 44.1 | 278 | 78.3 | 52.3 |
| Independent child | | Parent remains same, child changed | 44 | 13.3 | 8.3 | 30 | 9.9 | 5.6 | 35 | 9.9 | 6.6 |
| Independent parent | | Child remains same, parent changed | 14 | 4.2 | 2.6 | 26 | 8.6 | 4.9 | 28 | 7.6 | 5.3 |
| Co-diverge | | Both change to be different | 4 | 1.2 | 0.8 | 14 | 4.6 | 2.6 | 15 | 4.2 | 2.8 |
| | | Total beginning matched | 332 | | 62.5 | 304 | | 57.3 | 356 | | 67.0 |
| Discord | Not Matched | Continue to not match | 72 | 58.1 | 13.6 | 84 | 42.6 | 15.8 | 55 | 37.2 | 10.4 |
| Indoctrination | | Parent remains same, child moves to parent | 32 | 25.8 | 6.0 | 63 | 32.0 | 11.9 | 45 | 30.4 | 8.5 |
| Trickle-Up | | Child remains same, parent moves to child | 15 | 12.1 | 2.8 | 27 | 13.7 | 5.1 | 28 | 18.9 | 5.3 |
| Co-adopt | | Both change to match | 5 | 4.0 | 0.9 | 23 | 11.7 | 4.3 | 20 | 13.5 | 3.8 |
| | | Total beginning not matched | 124 | | 23.4 | 197 | | 37.1 | 148 | | 27.9 |
| No answer | | | 75 | | 14.1 | 30 | | 5.6 | 27 | | 5.2 |

## Independent Variables

*Demographics.* In our analyses, we controlled for parental education and child gender, measured in Wave 1, as well as child's age in Wave 2. See Table 4.2 for descriptive statistics. All variables were measured in Wave 2 of the survey, unless otherwise noted.

*Party identification.* To measure party identification, parent and child were each asked in Wave 1, on the 5-point scale ranging from "Strongly Democrat" (1) to "Strongly Republican" (5), which option best described their party affiliation. Partisan strength variables were constructed by folding the same item on a scale of 1 to 3, such that a higher number indicates greater partisan strength.

*Table 4.2* Descriptive statistics for key predictor

| Variables | N | Min | Max | Mean | SD |
|---|---|---|---|---|---|
| Parent | | | | | |
| Education[a] | 527 | 1 | 5 | 3.31 | 1.11 |
| Traditional news use | 530 | 0 | 7 | 2.84 | 1.42 |
| Online news use | 530 | 0 | 7 | 0.57 | 0.89 |
| Party ID[a] (1: Strong Democrat, 5: Strong Republican) | 507 | 1 | 5 | 3.00 | 1.07 |
| Strength of party ID[a] | 507 | 1 | 3 | 1.88 | 0.61 |
| Family | | | | | |
| Concept-orientation | 531 | 1 | 5 | 3.82 | 0.85 |
| Socio-orientation | 531 | 1 | 5 | 2.86 | 1.04 |
| Family political talk | 531 | 1 | 6.50 | 4.15 | 1.37 |
| Child | | | | | |
| Age | 531 | 12 | 18 | 14.90 | 1.64 |
| Gender (1: Male)[a] | 531 | 0 | 1 | 0.48 | 0.50 |
| Traditional news use | 529 | 0 | 7 | 1.34 | 1.22 |
| Online news use | 528 | 0 | 7 | 0.34 | 0.73 |
| Political social media use | 528 | 1 | 4 | 1.27 | 0.53 |
| Social media posting | 527 | 1 | 4 | 1.80 | 1.02 |
| Party ID[a] (1: Strong Democrat, 5: Strong Republican) | 471 | 1 | 5 | 2.89 | 0.92 |
| Strength of party ID[a] | 471 | 1 | 3 | 1.71 | 0.59 |
| School/friend | | | | | |
| Civic education | 528 | 1 | 8 | 3.56 | 1.99 |
| Enjoy civic education | 529 | 1 | 5 | 2.99 | 1.06 |

*Note:* [a] Variables measured in Wave 1 of the panel. All other variables were measured at Wave 2.

*News media use.* To measure news consumption, we asked how many days in a typical week both parent and child respondents used particular media. Traditional news use included broadcast news use, comprised of national, local, and cable TV news, and print news media use, reading a print copy of national or local newspapers ($\alpha = .58$ for parent; $\alpha = .70$ for child). Online news use measures news consumption via Web sites of mainstream news organizations and via liberal and conservative political blogs ($\alpha = .63$ for parent; $\alpha = .78$ for child).

*Family communication patterns.* Two dimensions of family communication patterns were constructed, combining responses from parents and children within the same family. Concept-oriented family communication measured the acceptance of disagreement between kids and adults, asking both parents and children on a 5-point scale from strongly disagree to strongly agree "In our family, kids learn it's OK to disagree with adults' ideas about the world." These measures were averaged to create an index ($r = .43$, $p < .001$). Socio-oriented family communication examined parents' dominance in decision-making, using agreement with the statement: "In our family, kids are taught not to upset adults," averaged across parents and children ($r = .47$, $p < .001$).

*Family political talk.* Family political talk averaged two items from parent and child: "I often encourage my child to talk about politics" (parent) and "Talked about news and current events with family members" (child) ($r = .34$, $p < .001$).

*Civic education.* Children were asked on an 8-point scale from "not at all" to "frequently" how often during the past three months they had: "followed the news as part of a class assignment," "learned about how government works in class," "discussed/debated political or social issues in class," "participated in political role playing in class (mock trials, elections)," and been "encouraged to make up your own mind about issues in class," combined into an index ($\alpha = .90$).

*Enjoyment of civic education.* Children were also asked how much they enjoyed and how much they participated in classroom activities about politics and current events, on a 5-point scale ($r = .67$, $p < .001$).

*Political social media use.* We measured adolescents' social media use by asking how frequently respondents had participated in a variety of activities on "Facebook, MySpace, or other social networking sites" on a 4-point scale, from never to regularly. An exploratory factor analysis using Promax rotation produced two factors. The first factor, explaining 47 percent of the variance, was labeled *political Facebook use,* including "displayed your political preferences on your profile," "became a 'fan' or 'friend' of a politician," "joined a 'cause' or political 'group'," "used a news or politics application/widget," "exchanged political views on a discussion board or group wall," and "been invited to a political event by a friend," which were combined into an index ($\alpha = .86$). A second factor, accounting for an additional 15 percent of variance, was labeled *social media posting* and combined "sharing your photos or videos online" and "updated a blog or journal" into an index ($r = .68$, $p < .001$). These two factors were moderately correlated ($r = .40$, $p < .001$).[8]

## RESULTS

### Predicting Socialization Routes

In examining the processes of parent–child socialization of political orientations, we begin by noting that for all three orientations the majority of parent–child dyads report agreement in their party affiliation, evaluations of McCain, and evaluations of Obama. Thus, those routes that begin with agreement are necessarily more likely to occur.

Looking specifically at party affiliation, we see that *harmony,* or when a parent and child remain in agreement, dominates the pathways across political orientations. Meanwhile, *discord,* or remaining in disagreement throughout the campaign, is the second most common pathway. Across the models, those routes in which a parent adjusts their political orientations—either away from agreement with the child in the *independent parent* route or to match the child in the *trickle-up* route—are less common than a child changing their position, either to come into agreement with the parent via *indoctrination* or to move away from initial agreement via the *independent child* route. Further, it is worth noting that the independent child route, which increases disagreement with parental attitudes, is roughly as common as the indoctrination route, where children adopt parental attitudes to create agreement. Finally, routes in which both parents and children change their attitudes during the campaign, either through *co-adoption* or *co-divergence,* prove very uncommon.

### Understanding Different Routes

Next we turn to our primary interest: *why* these different processes occur and the factors that predict socialization patterns. We examine the most common routes for political orientations, excluding the rare cases of independent parent, co-divergence, and co-adoption. For each dependent variable reflecting a specific path that a parent–child dyad may take, we estimate a separate logistic regression.

To test our first set of hypotheses, we examine the role that parental partisanship played in encouraging routes that produce greater agreement with their children in political orientations. This hypothesis is largely supported for party affiliation (Table 4.3). Parents with stronger partisanship inhibit the independent child ($\beta = -.80$, $p < .05$) and trickle-up ($\beta = -2.29$, $p < .01$) routes of socialization, while marginally increasing the likelihood that indoctrination ($\beta = .70$, $p < .10$) will occur for party

Table 4.3 Logistic regression analyses predicting dyadic influence routes for party identification

| | Harmony | | Independent Child | | Discord | | Indoctrination | | Trickle-Up | |
|---|---|---|---|---|---|---|---|---|---|---|
| | B (SE) | OR | B (SE) | OR | B (SE) | OR | B (SE) | OR | B (SE) | OR |
| Parental controls | | | | | | | | | | |
| Education | -.13 (.11) | .88 | .01 (.16) | 1.01 | .17 (.14) | 1.18 | .16 (.21) | 1.18 | .39 (.31) | 1.47 |
| Party ID | -.47** (.15) | .63 | .15 (.27) | 1.17 | .55** (.18) | 1.73 | .19 (.24) | 1.21 | .85 (.53) | 2.33 |
| Strength of party ID | -.02 (.21) | .98 | -.80* (.34) | .45 | .85** (.27) | 2.34 | .70† (.37) | 2.02 | -2.29** (.69) | .10 |
| Traditional news use | -.10 (.09) | .90 | -.03 (.14) | .97 | .15 (.12) | 1.16 | -.01 (.17) | .99 | -.26 (.28) | .78 |
| Online news use | .32* (.15) | 1.38 | -.18 (.25) | .83 | -.26 (.21) | .77 | -.02 (.27) | .98 | -.24 (.48) | .79 |
| Child controls | | | | | | | | | | |
| Age | .04 (.07) | 1.04 | -.13 (.11) | .88 | .06 (.09) | 1.06 | .01 (.13) | 1.01 | -.08 (.22) | .92 |
| Gender (1: Male) | -.13 (.22) | .87 | .40 (.35) | 1.49 | .02 (.30) | 1.02 | -.33 (.44) | .72 | 1.09 (.70) | 2.97 |
| Party ID | .47* (.19) | 1.59 | .53† (.29) | 1.71 | -.90** (.29) | .41 | -1.11† (.61) | .33 | -.65 (.42) | .53 |
| Strength of party ID | 1.64*** (.24) | 5.16 | -.20 (.35) | .82 | -2.01*** (.34) | .13 | -2.66*** (.65) | .07 | 1.63* (.66) | 5.10 |
| Traditional news use | .01 (.12) | 1.00 | .10 (.19) | 1.11 | -.05 (.15) | .95 | .11 (.21) | 1.12 | -.08 (.42) | .92 |
| Online news use | .06 (.18) | 1.07 | -.20 (.30) | .82 | .06 (.24) | 1.06 | -1.39* (.72) | .25 | -.82 (.91) | .55 |

(Continued)

*Table 4.3* (Continued)

| | Harmony | | Independent Child | | Discord | | Indoctrination | | Trickle-Up | |
|---|---|---|---|---|---|---|---|---|---|---|
| | B (SE) | OR | B (SE) | OR | B (SE) | OR | B (SE) | OR | B (SE) | OR |
| Family communication | | | | | | | | | | |
| Concept-orientation | -.17 (.34) | .85 | .28 (.57) | 1.33 | -.31 (.44) | .74 | -1.19† (.69) | .30 | 1.67 (1.07) | 5.28 |
| Socio-orientation | -.07 (.46) | .98 | .09 (.80) | 1.09 | -1.03 (.66) | .36 | -.80 (.79) | .45 | 3.31** (1.21) | 27.47 |
| Socio X concept | .05 (.11) | 1.05 | -.04 (.19) | .96 | .16 (.16) | 1.17 | .32 (.20) | 1.37 | -.76** (.29) | .47 |
| Family political talk | 0.05 (.10) | .95 | .01 (.16) | 1.01 | -.09 (.14) | .91 | .01 (.21) | 1.01 | .61* (.31) | 1.83 |
| Child social media | | | | | | | | | | |
| Political Facebook use | -.49* (.24) | .62 | .35 (.35) | 1.43 | .59† (.31) | 1.80 | .39 (.44) | 1.47 | -.61 (.91) | .54 |
| Facebook updates | -.18 (.12) | .84 | .28 (.18) | 1.33 | -.14 (.17) | .86 | .03 (.23) | 1.03 | -.27 (.45) | .77 |
| Child school | | | | | | | | | | |
| Civic education | .00 (.07) | 1.00 | -.06 (.10) | .94 | .02 (.09) | 1.02 | .06 (.13) | .64 | -.11 (.19) | .90 |
| Enjoy civic education | .02 (.12) | 1.02 | -.05 (.19) | .95 | -.09 (.16) | .91 | .35 (.23) | 1.42 | -.26 (.36) | .78 |
| Constant | -.87 (1.86) | | -2.34 (3.09) | | 1.60 (2.53) | | 3.51 (3.89) | | -11.32† (5.96) | |

*Notes:* N = 448

†$p < .10$, *$p < .05$, **$p < .01$, ***$p < .001$

affiliation. However, in contrast to our expectations, stronger parental partisanship also predicted discord ($\beta = .85$, $p < .01$) in party affiliation. The role of parental partisanship is much less clear for predicting which routes explain candidate evaluations, emerging to significantly predict an increased likelihood of indoctrination ($\beta = .69$, $p < .05$) only in evaluations of McCain (Table 4.4).

Next, we examine the role that family discussion of news and politics plays in encouraging agreement between parents and children, as well as its contributions to trickle-up vs. indoctrination processes to limit disagreement. *H2* receives limited support: while more family communication marginally increases the odds of harmony ($\beta = .18$, $p < .10$) and decreases the odds of discord ($\beta = -.27$, $p < .05$) in evaluations of McCain, it has little impact on other pathways. One other significant relationship emerges: families who talk about politics more frequently ($\beta = .61$, $p < .05$)—and who also engage in more pluralistic styles of communication ($\beta = -.76$, $p < .01$)—have greater odds of seeing trickle-up socialization for party affiliation. However, the role of family communication in determining how socialization occurs is limited overall, except for evaluations of McCain.

Our third hypothesis predicted that civic education would increase child independence in socialization patterns. While we find consistent support that civic education increases the odds that children will move away from their parents in their evaluations of both McCain ($\beta = .24$, $p < .05$) and Obama ($\beta = .25$, $p < .05$; Table 4.5), as well as decreases the odds of a harmonious relationship in evaluating McCain ($\beta = -.13$, $p < .05$), it does not significantly predict one route over another for those dyads that start with disagreement, nor does it explain which routes occur for socialization of party affiliation. Therefore, civic education contributes to a child's independence from their parents for candidate evaluations, as suggested in *H3*, but does not appear to explain socialization more broadly.

Turning to the role that political social media use plays in socialization, we find stronger support for our hypotheses. Children who engage in more political Facebook use are less likely to maintain harmony with parents in party affiliation ($\beta = -.49$, $p < .05$), and are instead more likely to experience discord ($\beta = .59$, $p < .10$). This heightened potential for discord among youth using more political social media is also evident for evaluations of John McCain ($\beta = .76$, $p < .01$), where it also lessens the potential for indoctrination to occur ($\beta = -.82$, $p < .10$). However, political social media use does not help to explain socialization pathways in evaluations of Obama. Therefore, we find mixed support for *H4*. Further, posting non-political updates on social media never significantly predicts which pathways occur in the socialization of these political orientations.

Table 4.4 Logistic regression analyses predicting dyadic influence routes for McCain evaluations

| | Harmony | | Independent Child | | Discord | | Indoctrination | | Trickle-Up | |
|---|---|---|---|---|---|---|---|---|---|---|
| | B (SE) | OR | B (SE) | OR | B (SE) | OR | B (SE) | OR | B (SE) | OR |
| Parental controls | | | | | | | | | | |
| Education | −.14 (.10) | .88 | −.31 (.20) | .73 | −.02 (.13) | .98 | .30† (.16) | 1.35 | .32 (.22) | 2.02 |
| Party ID | −.05 (.14) | .95 | .04 (.29) | 1.04 | .20 (.18) | 1.22 | .13 (.22) | 1.14 | .09 (.31) | 1.10 |
| Strength of party ID | .03 (.19) | 1.03 | −.01 (.39) | .99 | −.05 (.25) | .95 | .69* (.30) | 1.80 | −.20 (.41) | .82 |
| Traditional news use | .13 (.08) | 1.14 | −.00 (.17) | 1.00 | −.01 (.11) | 1.00 | −.08 (.13) | .93 | −.23 (.19) | .80 |
| Online news use | .12 (.13) | 1.13 | −.70† (.38) | .50 | −.05 (.20) | .95 | .21 (.20) | 1.24 | −.07 (.29) | .94 |
| Child controls | | | | | | | | | | |
| Age | −.03 (.06) | .97 | −.08 (.13) | .93 | .02 (.08) | .78 | .08 (.10) | 1.08 | −.33* (.16) | .72 |
| Gender (1: Male) | .06 (.21) | 1.06 | −.38 (.44) | .69 | −.06 (.28) | .83 | −.35 (.34) | .71 | −.14 (.47) | .87 |
| Party ID | .08 (.17) | 1.09 | −.14 (.38) | .96 | −.30 (.23) | .74 | −.17 (.29) | .85 | .11 (.33) | 1.11 |
| Strength of party ID | .35† (.20) | 1.43 | −.72† (.43) | .49 | −.29 (.27) | .29 | −.36 (.32) | .70 | .30 (.42) | 1.35 |
| Traditional news use | −.01 (.11) | .99 | −.07 (.21) | .94 | −.09 (.15) | .91 | −.24 (.19) | .79 | .46* (.22) | 1.59 |
| Online news use | .24 (.18) | 1.27 | .03 (.28) | .49 | −.83* (.39) | .44 | .12 (.32) | 1.12 | .14 (.31) | 1.16 |

| | | | | | | | | | |
|---|---|---|---|---|---|---|---|---|---|
| **Family communication** | | | | | | | | | |
| Concept-orientation | .01 (.33) | 1.01 | .07 (.67) | 1.08 | .09 (.45) | 1.10 | -.43 (.52) | .65 | -.69 (.71) |
| | .50 | | | | | | | | |
| Socio-orientation | -.13 (.42) | .88 | .28 (.82) | 1.33 | .12 (.58) | 1.13 | -.27 (.64) | .76 | -.38 (.78) |
| | .68 | | | | | | | | |
| Socio X concept | .02 (.10) | 1.02 | -.08 (.20) | .92 | -.04 (.14) | .96 | .12 (.16) | 1.12 | .10 (.20) |
| | 1.10 | | | | | | | | |
| Family political talk | .18† (.10) | 1.20 | .06 (.19) | 1.07 | -.27* (.13) | .76 | .03 (.16) | 1.03 | .04 (.23) |
| | 1.04 | | | | | | | | |
| **Child social media** | | | | | | | | | |
| Political Facebook use | -.14 (.22) | .87 | .45 (.41) | 1.56 | .76** (.29) | 2.13 | -.82† (.49) | .44 | -.65 (.58) |
| | .52 | | | | | | | | |
| Facebook updates | .12 (.11) | 1.13 | -.16 (.24) | .86 | -.17 (.16) | .85 | .10 (.18) | 1.11 | -.28 (.30) |
| | .75 | | | | | | | | |
| **Child school** | | | | | | | | | |
| Civic education | -.13* (.06) | .88 | .24* (.12) | 1.26 | .08 (.08) | 1.08 | -.09 (.10) | .91 | .12 (.13) |
| | 1.13 | | | | | | | | |
| Enjoy civic education | .08 (.11) | 1.09 | -.29 (.22) | .75 | 1.9 (.15) | 1.21 | -.09 (.18) | .91 | .31 (.27) |
| | 1.36 | | | | | | | | |
| Constant | -.97 (1.72) | | .46 (3.49) | | -1.36 (2.35) | | | | 2.26 (3.72) |

*Notes:* $N = 435$

†$p < .10$, *$p < .05$, **$p < .01$, ***$p < .001$

Table 4.5 Logistic regression analyses predicting dyadic influence routes for Obama evaluations

| | Harmony | | Independent Child | | Discord | | Indoctrination | | Trickle-Up | |
|---|---|---|---|---|---|---|---|---|---|---|
| | B (SE) | OR | B (SE) | OR | B (SE) | OR | B (SE) | OR | B (SE) | OR |
| Parental controls | | | | | | | | | | |
| Education | -.11 (.10) | .90 | .23 (.19) | 1.26 | -.03 (.15) | .97 | .10 (.18) | 1.10 | .18 (.21) | 1.20 |
| Party ID | -.33* (.14) | .72 | .23 (.26) | 1.26 | .16 (.23) | 1.17 | .57* (.26) | 1.77 | .12 (.31) | 1.13 |
| Strength of party ID | .28 (.19) | 1.32 | -.15 (.37) | .86 | -.32 (.31) | .73 | -.03 (.36) | .97 | -.41 (.41) | .67 |
| Traditional news use | .04 (.08) | 1.04 | -.17 (.16) | .85 | .01 (.13) | 1.01 | -.18 (.15) | .84 | -.21 (.17) | .81 |
| Online news use | -.06 (.14) | .95 | .17 (.27) | 1.18 | -.20 (.25) | .82 | .05 (.30) | 1.05 | .44† (.24) | 1.56 |
| Child controls | | | | | | | | | | |
| Age | -.02 (.06) | .98 | .26* (.13) | 1.30 | .08 (.10) | 1.09 | -.09 (.12) | .91 | .20 (.14) | 1.22 |
| Gender (1: Male) | .11 (.21) | 1.11 | .10 (.40) | 1.10 | -.49 (.34) | .61 | .27 (.39) | 1.31 | -.54 (.45) | .58 |
| Party ID | .44* (.18) | 1.54 | -.64† (.38) | .53 | -.10 (.28) | .91 | -.74* (.32) | .48 | -.51 (.39) | .60 |
| Strength of party ID | .62*** (.21) | 1.86 | -.83* (.43) | .44 | -.34 (.32) | .72 | -.08 (.38) | .92 | -.23 (.45) | .79 |
| Traditional news use | .18 (.11) | 1.19 | -.12 (.22) | .89 | -.16 (.18) | .85 | .10 (.21) | 1.11 | .06 (.23) | 1.06 |
| Online news use | .03 (.18) | 1.03 | -.07 (.36) | .93 | .06 (.28) | 1.06 | -.98 (.69) | .37 | -.18 (.38) | .83 |

| | | | | | | | | | | |
|---|---|---|---|---|---|---|---|---|---|---|
| **Family communication** | | | | | | | | | | |
| Concept-orientation | −.05 (.33) | .95 | .30 (.64) | 1.34 | .02 (.52) | 1.02 | .08 (.63) | 1.08 | −.15 (.75) | .86 |
| Socio-orientation | −.06 (.43) | .94 | .46 (.75) | 1.58 | .04 (.69) | 1.05 | −.03 (.82) | .98 | −.38 (1.06) | .69 |
| Socio X concept | .00 (.10) | 1.00 | −.10 (.18) | .91 | −.01 (.17) | .99 | .02 (.20) | 1.02 | .11 (.25) | 1.12 |
| Family political talk | .15 (.10) | 1.16 | −.23 (.19) | .78 | .10 (.15) | 1.10 | −.25 (.18) | .78 | −.02 (.20) | .98 |
| **Child social media** | | | | | | | | | | |
| Political Facebook use | −.25 (.22) | .78 | −.04 (.42) | .96 | .40 (.34) | 1.49 | −.53 (.55) | .38 | −.10 (.47) | .90 |
| Facebook updates | .05 (.12) | 1.05 | −.09 (.22) | .91 | −.22 (.19) | .81 | .22 (.20) | 1.25 | −.14 (.25) | .87 |
| **Child school** | | | | | | | | | | |
| Civic education | −.07 (.06) | .94 | .25* (.12) | 1.30 | .03 (.10) | 1.03 | −.01 (.12) | .99 | −.07 (.13) | .93 |
| Enjoy civic education | −.05 (.11) | .95 | .18 (.22) | 1.20 | −.19 (.17) | .83 | .01 (.20) | 1.01 | .13 (.23) | 1.14 |
| Constant | −.84 (1.73) | | −5.89 (3.56)† | | −2.05 (2.72) | | .27 (3.39) | | −2.94 (3.92) | |

*Notes:* $N = 437$

†$p < .10$, *$p < .05$, **$p < .01$, ***$p < .001$

## DISCUSSION

This project sought to deepen our understanding of the ways in which parents and children orient themselves towards politics. Building on traditional models of socialization (see Carmines *et al.*, 1987; Jennings *et al.*, 2009; McDevitt & Chaffee, 2002), we began by exploring a wide range of diverse pathways that parents and children can travel during the election as they navigate their attitudes towards political candidates and their party affiliation.

Our results indicate that for most dyads, orientations towards politics were established before the 2008 general election. For party affiliation, 64 percent of dyads maintain their co-orientation during the campaign—a percentage largely replicated for candidate evaluations. With roughly half of dyads entering the campaign in agreement in their political attitudes, the most common outcome is to preserve a harmonious relationship, which may explain the long-time dominance of the transmission model of socialization (Jennings *et al.*, 2009; van Deth *et al.*, 2011).

But our results also show that political orientations are not immutable. Contrary to the transmission model, the *independent child* route (in which children move away from initial agreement with their parent) is just as prominent as *indoctrination* (in which children move to align with parents). Similarly, many teens are willing to remain in discord with their parents throughout the election, rather than bow to pressures to adopt a parent's attitudes. Thus, transmission of political orientations often does not overwhelm disagreement between a parent and a child—and teens as often move away from or maintain disagreement with their parents' beliefs over the course of the election as they move into alignment.

In our investigation of the factors that predict one socialization route over another, we found parental partisanship to play an important, but not defining, role in socialization—in line with previous literature (Jennings *et al.*, 2009). More partisan parents tended to be more successful in transmitting their party affiliation to their child during the election, and limited the potential for a child to move away from their parent or influence their parents' political identity. But parental partisanship also increased the odds that discord remained in party affiliation throughout the campaign, a finding that ran counter to initial predictions. It may be that strong parental partisanship is especially likely to encourage children to adopt a parent's party affiliation before the general campaign, but those partisan parents who have *not* successfully transmitted this strong party affiliation to children by the end of a contentious primary remain unable to do so during the general election.

This study primarily focused on the role of influences outside the home, and our results largely support the contention that civic education in the classroom and political social media use promote greater independence of the child in their political orientations. Children who used social media for political purposes demonstrated greater autonomy in their political orientations: social media use increased the likelihood that children would maintain existing disagreements with their parents, reduced the likelihood of being recruited to a parent's position (at least when considering evaluations of McCain), and lessened the odds that the family would maintain a harmonious relationship with regards to party affiliation. Altogether, these results point strongly to the conclusion that engagement in political discussion and activity through social media offers children an alternative way to understand their political identity to what is available at home.

Civic education showed similar patterns, particularly for evaluations of presidential candidates. Civic education increased the odds that children moved away from initial agreement with parents in evaluating both McCain and Obama. It is intuitive that civic education should be more potent in influencing candidate evaluations than in influencing party affiliation. Civic education is designed to facilitate an understanding of the political process and current events information, including that related to presidential candidates, and provide independent information to children for them to consider in developing political preferences (Lee *et al.*, 2013; McDevitt & Ostrowski, 2009), yet not necessarily making the link to longstanding party affiliations.

In contrast to social media use and civic education, our work provides little evidence that family communication about politics and news explains socialization pathways, with a notable exception. Frequent, pluralistic family discussions of news and politics were more likely to produce trickle-up socialization for party affiliation, wherein a child's political orientation influenced their parents'. But, given how few families in our sample experienced this route (less than 3 percent of dyads), this finding must be considered exploratory.

There is an alternative reading of these findings. From one perspective, the observed relationships support the view that the rapidly changing communications landscape, particularly the rise of digital media sources and an increased emphasis on civic education, may enhance youth agency in parent–child dyads, as compared to previous generations. However, this begs the question of whether earlier researchers examined the possibility of mutual influence. It may be that young people in previous generations who actively consumed information sources (reading newspapers, listening to radio, going to movies, watching television) who talked about this information with peers, or who participated in more civic activities in school, exercised more agency in their parent–child relationships. It may be possible to reexamine these relationships in existing datasets, depending on whether relevant questions are asked of parents and children at multiple points in time. It is also possible that this burst of youth agency was a feature of this particular election context, which was historic in many respects, reinforcing the need for future research on parent–child dyads, inside and outside of presidential election contexts.

While our work provides several new insights into the political social-ization process, it also illuminates gaps in our knowledge. We employed a unique methodology to gather responses from a nationally representative panel survey of parent–child dyads, but the complexity of the processes that we examined limited our ability to discern effects. Especially in study-ing party affiliation, for several of the theoretically proposed pathways, the small number of dyads that reported a given pattern precluded us from performing statistical analyses to explore predictors of these path-ways. Furthermore, unequal sample size among the remaining pathways may have heightened our statistical power in some cases but not others, limiting comparability. Although those pathways that include the few-est dyads—in particular, those which had parents shifting in their party affiliation or candidate preferences—are theoretically expected (Campbell *et al.*, 1960; Green *et al.*, 2002), future research should investigate in more detail what contributes to those cases in which this pathway does occur.

Further, we chose to explore these questions of political socialization during a salient event—the 2008 presidential election—when dyads were likely to be most focused on the political process (Sears & Valentino, 1997; Valentino & Sears, 1998). Given this limited window, it is notable that the effects we uncovered were detectable; but our results also sug-gest that many young adults—over two-thirds in our sample—entered the general election campaign with their political orientations vis-à-vis their parents established. This may have been exacerbated by the fact that our initial wave of data collection occurred after an already vocal political discussion surrounding the 2008 primary campaigns. The clear need here is for research designs that can consider potential interactions and pathways for co-orientation over wider time periods that include times of heightened political awareness and discussion, as well as more quiet periods.

The particular context of the 2008 campaign also bears mentioning. In describing the socialization pathways that occurred across three types of political orientations, our models and key predictors functioned less well in explaining which pathways dominated for evaluations of Obama. Barack Obama was not a typical candidate and did not run a typical campaign (Dalton, 2009; Walker, 2008). Further, the long-fought Demo-cratic primary, which kept Obama in the media spotlight longer than his political adversary, may have meant that attitudes towards Obama's candidacy were solidified before the period of our study, as evidenced by greater agreement among dyads in Wave 1 in evaluations of Obama.

Political socialization can also be studied from multiple vantage points. Two research agendas seem particularly important: expanding the types of democratic orientations studied and broadening the lens of inquiry outside the family. Individuals, young and old, have a wide array of tools at their disposal to facilitate individual and collective forms of participa-tion (Ekman & Amnå, 2012). As such, the different socialization routes can be expanded to consider various acts of participation, like political consumerism or civic participation (Bode *et al.*, 2013b). It's likely that, when looking at different outcomes, new relationships between parent and child will emerge and the importance of diverse socialization agents will shift (Thorson, 2012). Similarly, this study remained focused on examining the routes of socialization within the family unit. However, the pathways and dynamics uncovered here may function similarly—or very differently—within peer relationships. Future research should continue to expand the lens in which pathways to socialization are studied to gain more insight into this complex yet important process.

Ultimately, this research provides an important step in theoretically establishing and testing the diverse ways in which parents and children establish political orientations during elections. Transmission and trickle-up socialization are only two of many potential pathways through which parents and children develop and adjust their political attitudes and identities. As we have seen, which pathway is followed is largely dependent on the characteristics of both parents and children, the ways in which they engage each other, and a range of other potential socialization agents. This study thus supports and challenges classic political socialization research, encouraging political communication scholars to consider a wider range of processes that shape socialization norms. In particular, information and communication technologies play an important role in socializing political attitudes, challenging parental dominance and rivaling classroom influences.

## NOTES

1  The research team acknowledges support from the following sources: the Diane D. Blair Center of Southern Politics at the University of Arkansas; the William Allen White School of Journalism and Mass Communications and the Robert J. Dole Institute of Politics at the University of Kansas; the Robert Wood Johnson Foundation Scholars in Health Policy Research Program at the University of Michigan; the Reynolds Journalism Institute at the University of Missouri; the University of Texas Office of the Vice President for Research; and the Hamel Faculty Fellowship, the Graduate School, and the Department of Political Science at the University of Wisconsin. Dhavan Shah of Wisconsin is principal investigator for this survey panel. The authors of this paper received additional support from the Spencer Foundation to conduct further analyses of these data. Any conclusions or recommendations expressed are those of the authors and do not necessarily reflect the views of the supporting sources or participating faculty.
2  Rates of agreement vary across demographic categories. For example, 5 to 10 percent of middle-class recruits typically consent, compared to less than 1 percent of urban minorities. It is from this pre-recruited group of roughly 500,000 people that demographically balanced samples are constructed for collection.
3  We acknowledge that this is not an ideal means by which to sample both children and parents. Ideally, we would conduct separate interviews or send separate surveys to parents and children. However, this would dramatically lower

our response rate of complete parent–child dyads (as it would be more likely that either parent or child would complete their survey but not both), which would therefore increase non-response bias, already a growing concern in survey research (Groves, 2006). We acknowledge that privacy concerns are valid in this context, and that parents and children completing a joint survey may lead to more biased answers from both, as they try to please or meet expectations of their family members. Despite of these concerns, the fairly high concept-oriented family communication patterns ($M = 3.82$, $SD = .85$ in a 5-point scale) among our sample indicates that the parents are very open to their childrens' disagreement, which alleviates potential bias in children's responses. This survey met ethical guidelines, including approval from the Institutional Review Board at University of Wisconsin-Madison.

4   To see if our final panel might be subject to selection bias, we compared those respondents in our final panel ($N = 531$) with those who completed only our first-wave survey ($N = 517$). The final panel and the first-wave-only participants were not different in terms of age, gender, or other demographic and political orientations. The only difference discovered was in household income, with panel participants slightly lower than non-participants.

5   About a third of the mismatches are due to adolescent respondents failing to provide information on their age in either wave. We also compared our panel respondents with the second-wave respondents whose responses were discarded in the panel data analysis, due to mismatches of their personal information between the two waves of data collection ($N = 207$). Panel respondents were not different in terms of other demographic and social-structural variables from those second-wave respondents whose responses were dropped from the analysis. With proper controls, we have little reason to believe that the nature of the relationships among our key variables is different in the general population than it is in our matched panel respondents.

6   Democrat: 36%, Independent: 23.9%, Republican: 35.6% (Wave 1), Democrat: 37.5%, Independent: 23.7%, Republican: 36.3% (Wave 2) for parent; Democrat: 32.6%, Independent: 32.4%, Republican: 23.7% (Wave 1), Democrat: 39.2%, Independent: 27.7%, Republican: 30.1% (Wave 2) for child.

7   McCain favorability: Favorable: 34.7%, Neutral: 26.9%, Unfavorable: 35.4% (Wave 1), Favorable: 33.5%, Neutral: 18.6%, Unfavorable: 46.5% (Wave 2) for parent; Favorable: 34.8%, Neutral: 35.2%, Unfavorable: 27.3% (Wave 1), Favorable: 40.8%, Neutral: 22%, Unfavorable: 36.3% (Wave 2) for child. Obama favorability: Favorable: 42.4%, Neutral: 21.3%, Unfavorable: 33.7% (Wave 1), Favorable: 38.6%, Neutral: 15.6%, Unfavorable: 44.6% (Wave 2) for parent; Favorable: 38.1%, Neutral: 25.4%, Unfavorable: 34.3% (Wave 1), Favorable: 31.6%, Neutral: 18.5%, Unfavorable: 48.9% (Wave 2) for child.

8   One item—organized as a group activity—was dropped from these indices, as it cross-loaded with both factors.

## REFERENCES

Abramowitz, A. I., & Saunders, K. L. (1998). Ideological realignment in the US electorate. *The Journal of Politics, 60,* 634–652. doi: 10.2307/2647642.

Bafami, J., & Shapiro, R. J. (2009). A new partisan voter. *The Journal of Politics, 71,* 1–24. doi: 10.1017/S0022381608090014.

Beck, P. A., & Jennings, M. K. (1991). Family traditions, political periods, and the development of partisan orientations. *The Journal of Politics, 53,* 742–763. doi: 10.2307/2131578.

Bennett, W. L., Freelon, D. G., Hussain, M. M., & Wells, C. (2012). Digital media and youth engagement. In H. A. Semetko & M. Scammell (Eds.) *The SAGE Handbook of Political Communication* (pp. 127–140). Los Angeles, CA: SAGE.

Bode, L., Vraga, E. K., Borah, P., & Shah, D. V. (2013a). A new space for political behavior: Political social networking and its democratic consequences. *Journal of Computer-Mediated Communication,* online first. doi: 10.1111/jcc4.12048.

Bode, L., Edgerly, S., Thorson, K., Vraga, E. K., Wells, C., Yang, J., & Shah, D. V. (2013b). Participatory influence within parent–child dyads: Rethinking the transmission model of socialization. Paper presented to the International Communication Association (Political Communication), London, UK.

Campbell, B. (1980). A theoretical approach to peer influence in adolescence socialization. *American Journal of Political Science, 24,* 324–344.

Campbell, A., Converse, P. E., Miller, W. E., & Stokes, D. E. (1960). *The American Voter.* New York: Wiley.

Carmines, E. G., McIver, J. P., & Stimson, J. A. (1987). Unrealized partisanship: A theory of dealignment. *The Journal of Politics 49,* 376–400.

Chaffee, S. H., Ward, L. S., & Tipton, L. P. (1970). Mass communication and political socialization. *Journalism Quarterly, 47*(4), 647–666.

Dalton, R. J. (2009). *The Good Citizen: How a Younger Generation Is Reshaping American Politics.* Washington, DC: CQ Press.

Ekman, J., & Amnå, E. (2012). Political participation and civic engagement: Toward a new typology. *Human Affairs, 22,* 283–300. doi: 10.2478/s13374-012-0024-1.

Ekström, M., & Östman, J. (2013). Family talk, peer talk and young people's civic orientation. *European Journal of Communication, 28*(3), 294–308. doi: 10.1177/0267323113475410.

Glynn, C. J., Huge, M. E., & Lunney, C. A. (2009). The influence of perceived social norms on college students' intention to vote. *Political Communication, 26,* 48–64. doi: 10.1080/10584600802622860.

Green, D. P., Palmquist, B., & Schickler, E. (2002). *Partisan Hearts and Minds.* New Haven, CT: Yale University Press.

Groves, R. M. (2006). Nonresponse rates and nonresponse bias in household surveys. *Public Opinion Quarterly 70*(5), 646–675. doi: 10.1093/poq/nfl033.

Hess, D. (2009). *Controversy in the Classroom.* New York: Routledge.

Jennings, M. K., & Markus, G. B. (1984). Partisan orientations over the long haul: Results from a three-wave political socialization panel study. *American Political Science Review, 78,* 1000–1018.

Jennings, M. K., Stoker, L., & Bowers, J. (2009). Politics across generations: Family transmission reexamined. *The Journal of Politics, 71,* 782–799. doi: 10.1017/S0022381609090719.

Kiousis, S., McDevitt, M., & Wu, X. (2005). The genesis of civic awareness: Agenda setting in political socialization. *Journal of Communication, 55,* 756. doi: 10.1111/j.1460-2466.2005.tb03021.x.

Lane, R. E. (1962). *Political Ideology.* New York: The Free Press.

Langton, K. P., & Jennings, M. K. (1968). Political socialization and the high school civics curriculum in the United States. *The American Political Science Review 62,* 852–867.

Lee, N., Shah, D. V., & McLeod, J. M. (2013). Processes of political socialization: A communication mediation approach to youth civic engagement. *Communication Research, 40,* 669–697. doi: 10.1177/0093650212436712.

Linimon, A., & Joslyn, M. R. (2002). Trickle up political socialization: The impact of Kids Voting USA on voter turnout in Kansas. *State Politics & Policy Quarterly, 2,* 24–36. doi: 10.1177/153244000200200102.

McDevitt, M., & Chaffee, S. H. (2000). Closing gaps in political communication and knowledge: Effects of a school intervention. *Communication Research, 27,* 259–292. doi: 10.1177/009365000027003001.

McDevitt, M., & Chaffee, S. H. (2002). From top-down to trickle-up influence: Revisiting assumptions about the family in political socialization. *Political Communication, 19,* 281–301. doi: 10.1080/01957470290055501.

McDevitt, M., & Kiousis, S. (2007). The red and blue of adolescence: Origins of the compliant voter and the defiant activist. *American Behavioral Scientist, 50,* 1214–1230. doi: 10.1177/0002764207300048.

McDevitt, M., & Ostrowski, A. (2009). The adolescent unbound: Unintentional influence of curricula on ideological conflict seeking. *Political Communication, 26,* 1–19. doi: 10.1080/10584600802622811.

McLeod, J. M., & Chaffee, S. H. (1972). The construction of social reality. In J. T. Tedeschi (Ed.) *The Social Influence Processes.* Chicago: Aldine Atherton.

McLeod, J. M., & Shah, D. V. (2009). Communication and political socialization: Challenges and opportunities for research. *Political Communication, 26,* 1–10. doi: 10.1080/10584600802686105.

Mutz, D.C. (2002). Cross-cutting social networks: Testing democratic theory in practice. *American Political Science Review, 96,* 1, 111–126. doi: 10.1017/S0003055402004264.

Niemi, R. G., & Jennings, M. K. (1991). Issues and inheritance in the formation of party identification. *American Journal of Political Science, 35,* 970–988.

Pew (2012, September). Politics on Social Networking Sites. Pew Internet and American Life Project. Retrieved from http://pewinternet.org/~/media//Files/Reports/2012/PIP_PoliticalLifeonSocialNetworkingSites.pdf.

Plutzer, E. (2002). Becoming a habitual voter: Inertia, resources, and growth in young adulthood. *The American Political Science Review, 96,* 41–56. doi: 10.1017/S0003055402004227.

Saphir, M. N., & Chaffee, S. H. (2002). Adolescents' contributions to family communication patterns. *Human Communication Research, 28,* 86–108. doi: 10.1111/j.1468-2958.2002.tb00799.x.

Sears, D. O., & Valentino, N. A. (1997). Politics matter: Political events as catalysts for preadult socialization. *The American Political Science Review, 91,* 45–65.

Shah, D. V., Cho, J., Eveland, W. P. Jr., & Kwak, N. (2005). Information and expression in a digital age: Modeling Internet effects on civic participation. *Communication Research, 32,* 531–565. doi: 10.1177/0093650205279209.

Thorson, K. (2012). What does it mean to be a good citizen? Citizenship vocabularies as resources for actions. *The Annals of the American Academy of Political and Social Science, 644,* 70–85. doi: 10.1177/0002716212453264.

Thorson, K., Vraga, E. K., & Kligler-Vilenchik, N. (in press). Don't push your opinions on me: Young citizens and political etiquette on Facebook. In J. A. Hendricks & D. Schill (Eds.) *Presidential Campaigning and Social Media: An Analysis of the 2012 Campaign.* New York: Oxford University Press.

Valentino, N. A., & Sears, D. O. (1998). Event-driven political communication and the preadult socialization of partisanship. *Political Behavior, 20,* 127–154. doi: 10.1023/A:1024880713245.

van Deth, J. W., Abendschon, S., & Vollmar, M. (2011). Children and politics: An empirical reassessment in early political socialization. *Political Psychology,* *32,* 147–173. doi: 10.1111/j.1467-9221.2010.00798.x.

Verba, S., Schlozman, K. L., & Brady, H. E. (1995). *Voice and Equality: Civic Voluntarism in American Politics.* New York: Harper and Row.

Vitak, J., Zube, P., Smock, A., Carr, C. T., Ellison, N., & Lampe, C. (2011). It's Complicated: Facebook Users' Political Participation in the 2008 Election. *Cyberpsychology, Behavior, and Social Networking, 14,* 107–114. doi: 10.1089/cyber. 2009.0226

Walker, M. (2008). The year of the insurgents: The 2008 US presidential campaign. *International Affairs, 84,* 1095–1107. doi: 10.1111/j.1468-2346.2008.00759.x.

Wolak, J. (2009). Explaining change in party identification in adolescence. *Electoral Studies, 28,* 573–583. doi: 10.1016/j.electstud.2009.05.020.

# 5 Facing an Uncertain Reception

## Young Citizens and Political Interaction on Facebook

*Kjerstin Thorson*

The popularity of social network sites as a venue for sociability among young people has brought about renewed optimism for the role of online media in political engagement. Studies show that use of *Facebook* and other social network sites (SNS) can contribute to higher levels of social capital and rates of civic engagement (Ellison, Steinfield, & Lampe, 2007; Gil de Zúñiga, Jung, & Valenzuela, 2012), and can enable incidental exposure to diverse news and political content (Baumgartner & Morris, 2010; Brundidge, 2010; Gil de Zúñiga & Valenzuela, 2012).

However, studies show that these desirable outcomes of SNS use depend on *how* the sites are used. In particular, informational uses of SNS as well as forms of online political interaction predict both online and offline forms of political participation (Ekström & Östman, 2013). Also, interest-driven and information-seeking (as opposed to sociability oriented) uses of SNS have been linked to increased exposure to divergent political views (Ellison, Steinfield, & Lampe, 2010; Kahne, Middaugh, Lee, & Feezell, 2012). Political uses of SNS are less widespread than the general popularity of social media among youth might suggest. A third of 18- to 24-year-olds interviewed in 2012 reported seeing news on a social network site "yesterday" (Rainie *et al.*, 2012). But many fewer reported posting news links, and even fewer still reported posting content about politics. In the run-up to the 2012 US elections, 85 percent of young SNS users posted little or no political content (Rainie *et al.*, 2012). In sum, there is much hope invested in Facebook as a place where youth encounter politics, but we know little about how political Facebook interactions emerge out of everyday usages of the site.

This stands in contrast to what we know about the role of social settings in shaping political interactions in both face-to-face groups and interest-driven online communities (Eliasoph, 1998; Walsh, 2004; Wojcieszak & Mutz, 2009). Eliasoph's rich ethnographic study of political talk within social and volunteer groups showed that political talk in many contexts is itself quite a social accomplishment. Political conversation can be difficult (and unattractive) for many people, in part because talking about politics is less well governed by the routine rules of interaction than are other forms of talk (Warren, 1996). Engaging with politics opens up the risk of encountering disagreement, of offending or disrupting an otherwise amiable social relationship, and of experiencing discomfort (Mutz, 2006). These and other studies have demonstrated that social settings vary in their capacity to facilitate or hinder political talk, primarily based on the unwritten rules of interaction that guide appropriate social behavior in a particular context.

A crucial task for the study of politics and social media is therefore to explore the sociological possibilities for political interaction within the new online social settings where youth interact. As the primary spaces for youth interaction shift from those based in group-membership settings of the types Eliasoph (1998) studied to self-created "lifestyle networks" supported by the affordances and social practices of diverse social media sites (Bennett, 1998), how will the changing context for interaction shape the forms of political talk that emerge?

I explore this question first with a brief review of cultural approaches to understanding political talk in groups. I next outline factors about Facebook in particular that are expected to shape political talk on the site. These include the ambiguity of the imagined audience, the unknown "publicness" of any given post, due to the replicability and spreadability of online content; the capacity for individuals (and organizations) to analyze responses to their posts; and the constantly changing affordances of the platform itself.

Based on this review, I propose that one important effect of the increased role of SNS in the lives of young citizens is to amplify what Warren (1996) has called the "social groundlessness" of political interaction. That is, SNS increase the uncertainties and risk associated with political talk by increasing the ambiguity of the social setting, in terms of both the potential audience and the context within which a political message will be received. In posing this argument, I do not claim that SNS are "bad" for political interaction. On the contrary, conditions of groundlessness, where norms, identities, and modes of speech are more open and contestable, do not only produce discomfort and self-censorship (Warren, 1996). They can also produce an opportunity structure within which new forms of interaction and engagement can be invented and explored.

Two sets of interviews with young citizens are presented by way of illustration. In these data we will see both outcomes of social groundlessness on SNS. Those who are motivated and willing to "do politics" in these spaces appear as entrepreneurs of political talk. They are playfully (and sometimes painfully) testing genres of political expression and their suitability across multiple social media platforms. On the other hand, a second set of interviews, focused specifically on Facebook as a platform for political interaction, show the power of social uncertainty to hinder political self-expression.

## WHAT DOES IT TAKE TO ACCOMPLISH POLITICAL TALK?

One of the major themes in recent political communication research is the increased interpenetration between politics and everyday life (Bakardjieva, 2009; Dahlgren, 2009). Nowhere has the crossover between politics and everyday life received more attention than in the study of political talk. Casual political conversation is increasingly seen as a form of political participation in and of itself, as well as being a central mechanism through which citizens work through their own opinions, process what they read in the media, and gain exposure to alternative facts and frames through which to understand issues (Kim & Kim, 2008). However, cultural approaches to the role of political talk in democratic life have demonstrated the need to explore *how* the political emerges within different conversational contexts. These scholars urge us to go beyond quantitative counts of interaction partners, memberships, and ties to consider how political talk is structured within the social settings of everyday life (Eliasoph, 1998; Mansbridge, 1983; Warren, 1996).

Social settings matter for political talk because contexts provide cues to people as to how to behave and, as such, offer a shared ground, a shared schema that serves as a basis for action (Goffman, 1959). Studies of political talk in social groups show that, over the course of repeated interactions, a rule set emerges that determines "what constitutes good or adequate participation in the group setting" (Eliasoph & Lichterman, 2003, p. 737). This "group style" works to define the way group members think about group boundaries, group bonds, and the speech norms within the group. For example, in some social groups political talk is "forbidden," while in others the forms of such talk are constrained: polite, "civic" talk may be allowed but partisan politics is not (Eliasoph & Lichterman, 2003). Mutz (2006) and others have suggested that more heterogeneous social settings make the emergence of political talk more difficult. Hayes, Scheufele, and Huge (2006) tie willingness to self-censor in political conversation both to personality characteristics and to the perceived "publicness" of a given setting for political interaction.

Although unwritten rules of interaction shape the permissible forms of political talk within a given setting, it is important to note that these shared rules also *enable* citizens to overcome the groundlessness that accompanies certain forms of political conversation (Warren, 1996). It is confidence in a social situation that makes higher-risk forms of interaction possible. In the absence of such rules, when a social situation appears ambiguous and poorly defined, it may be more difficult to know how to behave, and a greater degree of variation in perceived norms and behaviors is likely to be present (Goffman, 1959; Lapinski & Rimal, 2005). Scholars of impression management have shown that such circumstances can produce "protective" behaviors, such as avoidance and self-censorship (e.g., Rui & Stefanone, 2013).

## GROUNDING POLITICAL DISCUSSION ON FACEBOOK

Most of what we know about the cultural practices of political talk comes from ethnographic studies within face-to-face membership-style groups. In the brief review below, I highlight four clusters of Facebook affordances and usage practices that serve up contrasts to the social settings that have been examined in previous work on political talk.

First is the particular strangeness of the imagined audience on Facebook. Posting to SNS requires speaking to a "context collapsed" networked audience (Marwick & boyd, 2011). The networked audience combines social contacts from across a variety of contexts from one's own life. A post to Facebook might reach high school friends, work colleagues, family members, and neighbors. This is a peculiar context for political interaction, more like the challenges faced by a candidate giving a speech to a diverse audience than like talking about news or the latest scandal in a coffee shop with friends (Meyrowitz, 1985). The mixing of audiences on SNS requires posters to negotiate a self-presentation that will be acceptable across a complex imagined audience that itself may vary depending on the perceptions of the network owner (Litt, 2012; Rui & Stefanone, 2013). Notably, one's own networked audience on Facebook may not only be more politically diverse in actuality than many offline settings, but the extent of that diversity is also much more difficult to ascertain.

Second, the affordances of SNS combine to make for a rather extreme degree of unpredictability concerning the reception of any post. Content posted to social media can be copied, it can be spread widely—including beyond the privacy settings of the original poster—it lasts over time and remains searchable (boyd, 2010). What will happen to your content once it has been posted and who will see it, in what context, and how they react cannot be known with any certainty in advance (Litt, 2012). In addition, your friends can create content that becomes attached to your Facebook profile by commenting on your posts or re-sharing them to a wider audience, loosening even further the reins of personal control over representations of self-image (Rui & Stefanone, 2013).

Third, SNS enable users to track direct responses to their posts. On Facebook, a user can see the number of likes or comments a particular post receives. Although the topic is as yet little studied, these analytics may provide cues to users as to the composition of the imagined audience, or, more importantly, serve as the salient representations of an otherwise ambiguous "real" audience on Facebook (Litt, 2012). Tracking feedback over time may also encourage individuals to make "data-driven" decisions about personal expression in a way analogous to the strategic maneuvering of professional content-creation organizations (Lohr, 2012).

Finally, the affordances of SNS are constantly in flux. The corporate owners of these platforms have an incentive to make frequent adjustments to their services as part of the effort to attract and retain users, as well as to better connect advertisers with consumers (Nocera, 2013). These goals have inspired companies like Facebook to change privacy settings, alter the visibility of certain kinds of content through changes to the news feed algorithm, insert promoted or sponsored content into individual feeds, and make it easier to search for topic-related content across the full corpus of the platform. Because these changes are usually outside of individual control and are often poorly explained to users, they add to the uncertainty concerning audience, visibility, and publicness of any given post. Any certainty achieved as to "how Facebook works" or "who sees my posts" is likely to be undercut in short order.

There is little question that this collection of factors influences the way individuals communicate on Facebook, even if much less is known about the ramifications of this social ambiguity for political talk. Personal broadcasts on SNS offer challenges to common strategies of self-presentation (Marwick & boyd, 2011; Rui & Stefanone, 2013). Binder, Howes, and Sutcliffe (2009) showed that more diverse Facebook networks were predictive of experiencing tension online. A recent paper using a large set of Facebook data—3.9 million users—found that 71 percent of posters engaged in self-censorship while posting a status update to the site, either deleting their first draft altogether or making minor edits (Das & Kramer, 2013). Notably, the rate of self-censorship is higher for those who had more distinct friendship groups within their network, although identified diversity of political opinion (that is, diversity *visible* to the user) within the network had no effect.

I propose that the net result of these uncertainties of content reception is to create not a widely shared "group style" for political talk on Facebook but, rather, to promote a constantly renewing sense of social groundlessness among young citizens when it comes to political talk on the site. These uncertainties should, in turn, shape the form and content of Facebook political interaction as youth react in different ways to the potential consequences of opinion expression to an unknown audience. Exploring these propositions is the central purpose of the interviews reported below.

## EXPLORING THE AMBIGUITY OF FACEBOOK POLITICS: THE INTERVIEW DATA

Investigating questions about the social grounding of politics on social media presents a series of methodological challenges. Unlike online communities that are built around repeated interactions and some degree of consistency among participants—that is, something akin to a membership structure—SNS are based on egocentric publics (Wojcieszak & Rojas, 2011): even if two people are friends on Facebook, the content they are exposed to in their news feeds and the particularities of their (imagined) audiences will differ because not all of their friends will overlap. For example, my largest

Facebook friend overlap is with my husband of more than a decade and we have slightly less than 50 percent of our friends in common.

This set of circumstances makes it difficult to engage in something resembling a virtual ethnography, akin to the procedures followed in previous studies of the cultural contexts for political talk (e.g., Eliasoph, 1998). Instead, I draw on two distinct interview methodologies. The first is comprised of fifteen in-depth interviews with young adults (ages 18–29) who were identified by participants in a much larger sample of interviews as individuals who "post a lot of news or political content on *Facebook* or *Twitter*" (Thorson, 2012). Therefore these interviews focus on investigating a *practice,* not a platform. (In fact, as we will see, this practice is in most cases carried out across multiple social media sites.) I refer to this practice as social politics curation. Eight men and seven women were interviewed in 2011 and 2012. All either were in college or had attained a college degree.[1] Interviews lasted approximately one hour and consisted of a short life history followed by a detailed discussion of news media consumption, political behavior, and SNS use.

The second set of interviews was designed to capture perceptions of politics on Facebook in particular, and to come closer to the social contexts where potential political interactions occur. These interviews focused not on a practice, but on a topic (political interaction) and a platform (Facebook). Interviewers sat down with participants and conducted an in-depth interview while looking together through several days of the participant's Facebook news feed. Twenty interviews were conducted (eleven females, nine males, in college or with college degrees). None of these participants was an active social politics curator, although a third reported occasionally posting about news or politics on Facebook.[2] These interviews were conducted between September and November 2012, covering the period of the three US presidential debates, the vice-presidential debate, as well as the election itself.[3]

## INVENTING POLITICS ON SOCIAL MEDIA: THE SOCIAL POLITICS CURATORS

"Oh yeah, I know I'm an outlier in my Facebook crowd," one young woman told me, laughing:

> I know a lot of things I know are obscure and I don't talk about it because I don't like being that person like, well did *you* know that? That's why I don't get comments on my things . . . I joke about it with my friends, oh yeah, I'm posting that stuff again.

The social politics curators are very aware that their posts about politics are unlikely to be popular across their array of Facebook friends.

Many (but not all) feel that their passions set them apart from many friends, family, and acquaintances they are connected to through the site, and a majority of respondents think that Facebook is a harder place to talk about politics than Twitter, a more interest-driven network. These are youth who, over the course of a day, engage in media and politics content consumption repertoires that span multiple platforms and outlets, often starting with news and politics aggregators and their own finely honed Twitter news feeds and moving through readings of the *New York Times* and *Wall Street Journal* and across email listservs from issue organizations. Given what we know about news consumption among this age cohort, their sense that they are in the minority is correct (Rainie *et al.*, 2012).

When our conversation turns from media consumption to curation and content sharing on SNS, it is clear that motivations to post about politics are complex. A few respondents—primarily those who are frequent posters on Twitter—are seeking to make a name for themselves in campaign politics, or are motivated more generally by the desire to be influential within professional networks (Marwick & boyd, 2011). On the other hand, nearly all of the interview respondents emphasized their desire to let people know about content they find interesting or important: they see themselves as helping to inform or mobilize their friends. This was the primary motivation for posting to Facebook specifically. Said one young woman,

> It's more like even if somebody is like oh my god I learned something today and now I care, they're going to tell somebody else, and maybe one person tells one person and at the end of the day maybe only twenty people will know about it and nothing is going to happen or change . . . I'm not trying to be some beacon, but like, I like to share information. And even if one person is shared with, that's cool. For me, you know.

When asked why he shares political content on Facebook, another respondent said,

> Partially it's the, you know, savior or hero mentality that I have [laughs], but I think mostly it's because I want them [his friends on Facebook] to think in a different way as well. Don't just take what people are telling you, read stuff, read opposing views and then decide what you think. When you decide for yourself, you do end up with a sensible opinion.

The interviews reveal that what we might call "social news judgment"— story selection and framing choices made around posting political content to SNS—is profoundly entangled with concerns about self-presentation and strategic desires to be read. Social politics curators worry about posting something that isn't credible or that could expose a lack of knowledge, they worry that the flow of their posts corresponds to their sense of self, and, most importantly, they experience a high level of uncertainty about how their posts will be received by their mix of friends who are more and less interested in viewing posts about news and politics. This uncertainty is heightened on Facebook as compared to Twitter.

For example, one respondent contrasted Twitter to Facebook, explaining that Facebook has too many "wild card" commenters, too many people who will not engage in what she views as reasonable political discourse.

> People on Facebook are quick to an opinion without really knowing an issue. And I don't really want to have that interaction . . . They're like, Obama sucks, he's so stupid, and they don't even know why they're saying it. Or people will be like, people will say something completely off base and it's only to say it, because it seems like the right thing to say. Those kinds of things are just like, ugh. Thanks for uninforming me.

Another respondent reports similar feelings, but she doesn't laugh it off. After a family member and an acquaintance (two people who don't know each other, either in offline life or on Facebook) got into a shouting match beneath a news story she posted about the Israeli–Palestinian conflict, she swore off news sharing or discussions of politics on Facebook altogether. Her posts were either ignored or, she felt, misunderstood.

> On Facebook [my political posts] are mixed in with, you know, where I went on vacation and the bridesmaid dress that my sister wore. It's mixed in with all this stuff so it's not—people could be getting these really strong political statements, or actually not strong political statements, just a political statement, that because of the context that it's in seems like this really strong political statement. Whereas if it were in a different context, for example the context of my blog, where that is one article among many that they can see, they would have a better understanding of my perspective, of where I'm coming from and what I stand for.

For her, Facebook presented an unmanageable level of uncertainty not only in terms of *who* might see and comment on a particular post, but the way that post might be interpreted. She recognizes that each person's news feed is unique. Her posts on the tensions between Israel and Palestine will appear in different contexts—next to different content—for various of her Facebook friends, and the display algorithms of the platform make it possible that two people who have never met and will never meet, that are not even friends on Facebook, could come together in an unpleasant clash visible to hundreds.

> It was just lame. My feeling about it was, I don't want this [fight] to be on my Facebook page. If you guys want to go do this, fine, but you are now affecting what people see on my Facebook page. I don't want that. Especially because I think that diplomatic and honest and respectful conversations about politics are really important. That's something that I really value and I want to encourage, but I think that the character of that conversation was not representing what I wanted my page to represent.

Scholars of impression management identify this motivation for self-censorship as related to perceived discrepancies between actual and ideal self-image (Rui & Stefanone, 2013). However, this young woman can be seen as engaging in self-censorship only if we consider her behavior on Facebook in isolation. Even as she withdrew her political content from that site, she was building up an audience for her opinions on her blog, and sees herself as building a different, less uncertain audience for her posts on Twitter. This removal of politics from one site and shifting to others is one possible strategy for dealing with the "groundlessness" of Facebook.

Another approach to managing the challenges of Facebook uncertainties is to experiment with different ways to present news or political content within the platform to make it more palatable to a wider array of readers. The social politics curators pay attention to how their posts are received. That is how the young woman above knows that she is "an outlier on her Facebook." A majority of respondents reported attending to reactions to their posts (although they were often embarrassed to admit it) with an eye to maximizing attention for their opinions and content, or to mobilizing their friends and promoting conversations on topics they care passionately about.

In some cases, use of these analytics resulted in "data-driven" political posting, one outcome of which is a focus on delivering novelty, or what more than one respondent referred to as "the oh my god factor."

> It really, honestly just depends if I find something personally worth sharing. I don't know if there's a litmus test other than just an 'oh my god' factor. Either in a good way or a bad way.

This young woman believes, based on her own Facebook analytics, that the "oh my god" factor determines the popularity of her political posts.

Another respondent reported adopting a politics-humor hybrid persona in order to appeal to a wider audience on Facebook—an approach he adopted after his many more sincere, serious statements of political opinion were ignored. "I definitely post politics and real news stories, but I also have a Colbert sense of politics and the approach to the way I talk about it," he explained. He posts hard news stories but undercuts their seriousness with his own jokey commentary or shares political cartoons and images he thinks will resonate with his imagined audience:

> Most of the stuff that I post is more like graphics or cartoons because those are obviously going to be clicked on or looked at more because we're such a graphic oriented society, especially the younger folks. And I seriously doubt that many people actually click on long news stories too often unless it's got a really catchy headline or a really provocative headline.

He also makes sure to balance any political posts with status updates that are funny but not on political topics, based on the theory that too much politics will lead people to "unfriend" him.

Other respondents reported withdrawing their political posts from the uncertainties of the networked audience by making use of the filtering features on Facebook. One started a private group with ten likeminded libertarian friends where they can "post articles with snide comments about the opposing viewpoint." Another divided his 600 friends into three lists, one of which specifically filters out his religious friends so he can post news stories or opinions that support his stance against organized religion.

Finally, a smaller number of respondents reported *enjoying* the potential for conflict on Facebook, and took pleasure in the social surprises that occur when people from different parts of their lives collide and argue. One young woman explained,

> My friends always call me out, you post the most inflammatory stories, and it's not even that inflammatory, it's just people are so passionate about their views one way or another. I told you I have several friends who are extremely left, extremely right, very smart people, very dumb people. I know a lot of people and it's funny to see them [argue]. They don't even know each other but they get so passionate . . . It amuses me to watch my friends who don't even know each other duke it out with each other.

Analysis of the life-history portion of the interviews revealed that these "provocateur" respondents were those socialized into a love of political debate by their families, and who commonly engage in political debate with their friends in a variety of offline and online settings. As has been seen in many cases, offline practices strongly shape online practices, particularly when the appropriateness of certain behaviors online remains ambiguous (e.g., McLaughlin & Vitak, 2012).

## ENCOUNTERING POLITICS ON FACEBOOK:
## THE FACEBOOK PLATFORM INTERVIEWS

"On Facebook everyone sees everything. Everyone knows your Facebook. Even someone you just met can see everything you post on your profile," explained one young woman as she and the interviewer looked at her Facebook news feed. The funny thing is, for most topics of interaction, respondents in the second round of interviews reported having little problem managing the networked audience. Notions of public and private are complex in the context of SNS (boyd, 2010; West, Lewis, & Currie, 2009). What studies of such complexities often show is that SNS can seem like a much smaller world than the average number of friends or followers would imply. Individuals may have a certain person in mind when they add a post, or post based on the hunch that the Facebook algorithm really displays their posts to only a few of their closest friends (Marwick & boyd, 2011; Litt, 2012). This ability to bracket uncertainty appears in these interviews as well. One young woman described how she handles incidental encounters with content not "meant" for her:

> I'll see stuff that someone posted to another friend's wall. I'm like, "Oh my god, yes." I'll like that and maybe comment on it. But if other people want to like and comment, then that's cool. It's only if they get the inside jokes. Some people just comment, and they're like, "What are you talking about?" I have no need to include them in the conversation. I just don't respond.

But interview transcripts reveal that this comfort stops where politics begins. The pattern appears again and again in the interviews: Facebook is really a smaller world than you think, the interviewer is told, I don't worry about it too much. Oh, politics? No, Facebook is too public for politics. One female respondent said,

> I'm aware that other people can see it, so I try to avoid political things, or abortion things. Even though it's important to me, I think Facebook is very public. While it's your personal page, I think you really have to be careful. You still don't want to portray yourself as one-sided or something.

Another respondent explained,

> Yeah, I think generally with the things that I say and stuff, like I don't really like saying things that I know will make waves. So that's why I don't post anything about politics or post any rivalry things. I feel like if I have really strong opinions about something, Facebook's not necessarily the place that I'd want to put it on.

The "publicness" of Facebook is contextual, and politics is a topic that makes the public character of the site salient. This finding reinforces the work of scholars who have argued that talk about politics is in a special category, one that challenges our day-to-day habits of social interaction (Mutz, 2006; Warren, 1996; Eliasoph, 1998).

The interviews revealed a series of strategies used by non-social politics curators to manage the complexities of politics on Facebook, strategies that converge in important ways with the behaviors of the social politics curators we met above. Foremost among these is self-censorship—in a particular form. Respondents focused on the importance of neutrality and not being "one-sided." One male respondent, who does occasionally post about politics, said he is careful not to do so in an opinionated fashion. He explains, "I think the reason why I'm more neutral is just because when you pick a side, you alienate the other group of people." When asked if she ever posts about politics, another respondent said,

> I don't think so. I usually don't [post about politics]. I want to remain neutral and stuff unless somebody is going out of line . . . I don't want people to get the wrong perception of me.

Neutrality is a "protective" strategy well known to scholars of self-presentation (Rui & Stefanone, 2013). In fact, Hogan (2010) argues that the possibility of constricting social media posts to the "lowest common denominator" is what makes is possible for people to use SNS at all. The inability to conceive of a "neutralized" option would make for paralysis when confronted with the status update box.

Respondents don't want to "push" their ideas on others and they don't want others' ideas pushed on them.

> I really, really, really don't like when people push things on other people, which is why I take a step back from that if I can . . . I just don't like to shove anything on anyone else. I guess part of that goes to Facebook because that's such a public thing and everybody sees that. I don't want that to be the only little blurb because my political views and my religious views are a lot more than that little blurb.

In the interviews, a recitation of this preference for neutrality is often accompanied by a contrasting narrative about a Facebook friend who does post political opinions. The salient stories—the ones recited in the interviews—describe the kind of provocateurs introduced above, people who post to get others riled up and to cause a reaction.

> I think people are more trying to be politically neutral on Facebook, because unless they're [neutral] they want controversy. I see people like my friends fighting over things. I remember one of my friends

posted up a very controversial status. It just blew up. And then the mob. It just became nasty. Just like people unfriending each other. And just like, "I unfriended you now."

That the political provocateurs offer the most easily accessible examples of politics on Facebook is not without consequence. In a sea of uncertain audiences and unknown contexts for reception, these relatively rare actors have an outsized influence on perceptions of Facebook as a setting for political interaction. Political neutrality appears as an effective self-presentation strategy not because our interview respondents have no opinions or are not capable of debate (on the contrary, many reported talking politics with friends in offline settings), but because it seems like the safest form of interaction under conditions of social ambiguity. It is a strategy to avoid the very kinds of argumentative responses that the political provocateurs desire.

On the other hand, humor is appreciated as a strategy to express political opinions without violating the safety of neutrality. Nearly every respondent in the second round of interviews took the time to tell the interviewer that humorous content is what they find most valuable on Facebook, and if political content is couched in humor that makes it okay. One respondent who reported occasionally posting about politics explained,

I thought [Romney] won the debate, objectively, but I thought the funniest thing was the "Big Bird comment." I posted about that. I think both sides would just think that that was randomly funny, not making fun of Mitt Romney, not saying Obama won, but something in the middle and funny about it.

The appreciation of humor extended to the reading of political posts by friends as well. Humorous posters were contrasted positively with the widely loathed political "ranters." One woman said,

I like reading political posts that are funny and that are rhetorical and ironic like that. I don't like rants and raves. I don't like paragraphs that are telling people how they should vote. I get it, and I think, you know, dissemination of information is important. But I don't like it in that form.

Finally, when it comes to managing incursions of politics into one's personal news feed, respondents have carefully cultivated the ability to strategically ignore. When an interviewer and respondent were looking over a pro-Mitt Romney post on the respondent's news feed, she expressed surprise that it was there. Her explanation took the form of noting that she never reads posts from this person:

I scroll right past it, specifically because that's a person that is constantly posting her opinion and I've read threads where people ask her why she feels this way and there's never any substance. It's not offensive to me. It's her opinion. She's not hurting anyone by it. I would just scroll past it and roll my eyes.

## DISCUSSION

Social settings shape the extent and form of political interactions that emerge within them. The dinner table at your house may be forbidding to political debate; dinner at our house is ripe for argument. Whether a setting encourages or constrains political talk or the ways in which sociability shapes acceptable forms of talk depends on an etiquette that is learned over time, across repeated interactions. The existence of a shared schema offers a secure ground from which to decide how to behave, whether to speak out or remain silent, whether to argue or avoid.

On Facebook, no such shared schema has emerged. Rather, a fuzzy sort of social politics logic is emerging out of the convergence of varied posts by social politics curators and the social concerns of everyone else. The status quo for everyday political interaction on the site is defined by uncertainty, ambiguity, and a high level of variation in both behavior and perceptions of what is appropriate. This ambiguity is tied to the affordances of the platform itself. Facebook enhances the flattening of distinct social spheres not only by its very nature (an ego-based social network) but by making it relatively effortful to post selectively to a subset of your friends. In addition, a second kind of context collapse appears in the presentation of posts. Not only do Facebook users often have no firm grasp of *who* will see their posts, they have no control over the context within which that post will be presented. Your call to political action may appear in my feed awkwardly sandwiched between a cat video and a picture of my friend's new baby; one friend's post of a *New York Times* editorial may sit uncomfortably next to another's personal expression of his conservative views.

That the algorithms, privacy settings, and other rules of the road of Facebook usage are constantly changing only enhances the challenges for young citizens to define imagined audiences and likely reception contexts for risky political posts. Taken together, these circumstances produce a constant renewal of social groundlessness, an always-new set of unknowns. For many forms of interaction this uncertainty can be bracketed. The interview data show youth managing this brave new world and something like norms emerging around the appropriate amount to post, whether to tag a friend in a racy photo, and so on (McLaughlin & Vitak, 2012). But for the topic of politics—at least for the interview respondents in this study—the uncertainty persists. One collection of motivated, passionate youth experiment with ways to "do politics" on everyday

Facebook and others engage in protective strategies to avoid the possibility of offense or misinterpretation or an inaccurate presentation of self.

The social politics curators are entrepreneurs of political interaction. While the current study cannot tell us a great deal about why these inventors of politics on social media behave differently from their politics-avoiding counterparts (Vraga, Thorson, Kligler-Vilenchik, & Gee, 2013), we can see them navigating the ambiguities of Facebook in creative ways, reaching out to their friends using humor, a careful mix of fun and serious content, and sometimes simply by bringing in novel content or embracing the role of provocateur. Some of these strategies tend toward "evaporating" political content on Facebook (Eliasoph, 1998). For example, take the young woman who became fed up with the unpleasant social surprises that occurred in response to her political posts and moved all her political expressions to Twitter and a personal blog. Social pressures against Facebook as a space for news or politics may work against the possibility that political content will reach the gaze of those young people we would most like to reach, particularly if changes to the Facebook content display algorithm push in the direction of showing each of us only content we like, as evidenced by our history of interactions.

The Facebook-aided interviews showed clearly how social groundlessness on Facebook works against the emergence of political interaction on the site in some cases, and how those ambiguities shape the *kind* of politics that is accepted and shared within the space. Here we see the dominance of what Kahne and Westheimer (2006) have called "civics without politics." The most common strategy to manage social ambiguity and preserve self-presentation is to endorse only "neutral" versions of politics. Neutrality is defined against the expression of political opinion. Humor is seen as a mechanism to neutralize political opinion, to make it safe to share.

These findings help us to consider the macro-level implications of Facebook as a social setting for the kinds of information we can expect to flow through the site. By macro-level, I mean not only considering what individual youth will post or share or read, but exploring how these behaviors in turn shape the curation practices of news outlets, campaigns, interest groups, and other strategic organizations as they attempt to promote their content through the social flows of youth networks. In the wake of the 2012 debates, one study of public posts about the debate on Facebook showed that 60 percent of content shared by individuals originated with a strategic organization of some kind (Edgerly, Thorson, Bighash, Gee, & Hannah, 2013). Looking at the list of top ten most shared posts about the debate showed that campaigns and interest groups had widely adopted the humorous "image meme" style that has earned a reputation for spreadability on social media. Another example is Upworthy.com, a (very successful) site dedicated to curating "social good" content and repackaging it to make it more spreadable on platforms like

Facebook. In a recent interview, one of Upworthy's curators reported that "despite the fact that Upworthy skews liberal," they avoid partisanship in their posts. He recommends, "don't take a strong stance in a headline that will make people uncomfortable when they pass it—you don't want people afraid to tell their conservative uncle" (Kaufman, 2013).

Our understanding of "what spreads"—and the experimentation enabled by analytics built into social media platforms—thus shapes flows not only of peer-created content but of content inputs from professional media actors as well. This is political interaction performed strategically, by both individuals and organizations, governed by an evolving set of social perceptions that are themselves subject to change as quickly as Facebook launches a new algorithm. A great deal more research is needed to investigate how the social pressures (and beliefs about how those pressures work) are acting to shape and possibly narrow the range of political discourse that flows through Facebook and other SNS. Understanding the culture of political talk on Facebook can provide important insights to help us make sense of the flows of political content through social media and open a new window into the impact of the changing media environment on democratic processes.

## NOTES

1 Notably, this was not true of the original sample, which was designed to vary across levels of educational achievement.
2 For more information on the sampling strategy, interviews, and data analysis, see Thorson (2012) and Thorson, Vraga, & Kligler-Vilenchik (forthcoming).
3 This window for the interviews was chosen as a time when political content would be relatively common on participants' Facebook news feeds. However, for the majority of participants (80 percent), no news- or politics-related content was found in the last ten posts of their news feed.

## REFERENCES

Bakardjieva, M. (2009). Subactivism: Lifeworld and politics in the age of the internet. *The Information Society, 25*(2), 91–104.

Baumgartner, J. C., & Morris, J. S. (2010). MyFaceTube politics: Social networking web sites and political engagement among young adults. *Social Science Computer Review, 28*, 24–44.

Bennett, W. L. (1998). The uncivic culture: Communication, identity, and the rise of lifestyle politics. *PS: Political Science & Politics, 31*(4), 741–761.

Binder, J., Howes, A., & Sutcliffe, A. (2009, April). The problem of conflicting social spheres: Effects of network structure on experienced tension in social network sites. In *Proceedings of the SIGCHI Conference on Human Factors in Computing Systems* (pp. 965–974). ACM.

boyd, d. (2010). Social network sites as networked publics: Affordances, dynamics, and implications. In Z. Papacharissi, ed., *A networked self: Identity, community, and culture on social network sites*, pp. 39–58. New York: Routledge.

Brundidge, J. (2010). Encountering "difference" in the contemporary public sphere: The contribution of the Internet to the heterogeneity of political discussion networks. *Journal of Communication, 60*(4), 680–700.

Dahlgren, P. (2009). *Media and political engagement.* Cambridge: Cambridge University Press.

Das, S., & Kramer, A. (2013). Self-censorship on Facebook. Association for the Advancement of Artificial Intelligence, Seventh International AAAI Conference on Weblogs and Social Media.

Edgerly, S., Thorson, K., Bighash, L., Gee, E., & Hannah, M. (2013). Posting about politics: Media as resources for debating the debates on Facebook. Paper presented to the Association for Education in Journalism and Mass Communication (Communication Technology), Washington, DC.

Ekström, M., & Östman, J. (2013). Information, interaction, and creative production: The effects of three forms of internet use on youth democratic engagement. *Communication Research.* Online first, doi: 10.1177/0093650213476295.

Eliasoph, N. (1998). *Avoiding politics: How Americans produce apathy in everyday life.* Cambridge, UK: Cambridge University Press.

Eliasoph, N., & Lichterman, P. (2003). Culture in interaction. *American Journal of Sociology, 108*(4), 735–794.

Ellison, N. B., Steinfield, C., & Lampe, C. (2007). The benefits of Facebook "friends": exploring the relationship between college students' use of online social networks and social capital. *Journal of Computer-Mediated Communication, 12*(4): 1143–1168.

Ellison, N. B., Steinfield, C., & Lampe, C. (2010). Connection strategies: Social capital implications of Facebook-enabled communication practices. *New Media & Society, 13*(6): 873–892.

Gil de Zúñiga, H., Jung, N., & Valenzuela, S. (2012). Social media user for news and individuals' social capital, civic engagement, and political participation. *Journal of Computer-Mediated Communication, 17,* 319–336.

Goffman, E. (1959). *The presentation of self in everyday life.* Garden City, NY: Doubleday.

Hayes, A. F., Scheufele, D. A., & Huge, M. E. (2006). Nonparticipation as Self-Censorship: Publicly Observable Political Activity in a Polarized Opinion Climate. *Political Behavior, 28*(3), 259–283.

Hogan, B. (2010). The presentation of self in the age of social media: Distinguishing performances and exhibitions online. *Bulletin of Science, Technology & Society, 30*(6), 377–386.

Kahne, J., Middaugh, E., Lee, N. J., & Feezell, J. T. (2012). Youth online activity and exposure to diverse perspectives. *New Media & Society, 14*(3), 492–512.

Kahne, J., & Westheimer, J. (2006). The limits of political efficacy: Educating citizens for a democratic society. *PS: Political Science & Politics, 39*(2), 289–296.

Kaufman, L. (2013, October 13). Viral content with a liberal bent. *New York Times,* p. B1. Retrieved October 15, 2013 from www.nytimes.com/2013/10/14/business/media/upworthys-viral-content-with-a-liberal-bent-is-taking-off.html?src=rechp&_r=0.

Kim, J., & Kim, E. J. (2008). Theorizing dialogic deliberation: Everyday political talk as communicative action and dialogue. *Communication Theory, 18*(1), 51–70.

Lapinski, M. K., & Rimal, R. N. (2005). An explication of social norms. *Communication Theory, 15*(2), 127–147.

Litt, E. (2012). Knock, knock. Who's there? The imagined audience. *Journal of Broadcasting & Electronic Media, 56*(3), 330–345.

Lohr, S. (2012, February 11). The age of big data. *New York Times,* p. SR1. Retrieved September 15, 2013 from www.nytimes.com/2012/02/12/sunday-review/big-datas-impact-in-the-world.html?pagewanted=all&_r=0.

Mansbridge, J. J. (1983). *Beyond adversary democracy.* Chicago: University of Chicago Press.

Marwick, A. E., & boyd, d. (2011). I tweet honestly, I tweet passionately: Twitter users, context collapse, and the imagined audience. *New Media & Society, 13*(1), 114–133.

McLaughlin, C., & Vitak, J. (2012). Norm evolution and violation on Facebook. *New Media & Society, 14*(2), 299–315.

Meyrowitz, J. (1985). *No sense of place: The impact of electronic media on social behavior.* New York: Oxford University Press.

Mutz, D.C. (2006). *Hearing the other side: Deliberative versus participatory democracy.* Cambridge: Cambridge University Press.

Nocera, J. (2013, October 18). Facebook's new rules. Retrieved October 18, 2013 from www.nytimes.com/2013/10/19/opinion/nocera-facebooks-new-rules.html.

Rainie, L., Smith, A., Schlozman, K. L., Brady, H., & Verba, S. (2012). Social media and political engagement, *Pew Research Center's Internet & American Life Project.* Retrieved February 15, 2013 from pewinternet.org/Reports/2012/Political-engagement.aspx.

Rui, J. R., & Stefanone, M. A. (2013). Strategic image management online: Self-presentation, self-esteem and social network perspectives. *Information, Communication & Society, 16*(8), 1286–1305.

Thorson, K. (2012). What does it mean to be a good citizen? Citizenship vocabularies as resources for action. *The Annals of the American Academy of Political and Social Science, 644*(1), 70–85.

Thorson, K., Vraga, E., & Kligler-Vilenchik, N. (forthcoming, 2014). Don't push your opinions on me: Young citizens and political etiquette on Facebook. In *Presidential Campaigning and Social Media.* Oxford: Oxford University Press.

Vraga, E. K., Thorson, K., Kligler-Vilenchik, & Gee, E. (2013) Personalities, perceptions and "drama": How individual sensitivities to disagreement shape youth political expression on Facebook. Unpublished manuscript.

Walsh, K. C. (2004). *Talking about politics: Informal groups and social identity in American life.* Chicago: University of Chicago Press.

Warren, M. E. (1996). What should we expect from more democracy? Radically democratic responses to politics. *Political Theory, 24*(2), 241–270.

West, A., Lewis, J., & Currie, P. (2009). Students' Facebook "friends": public and private spheres. *Journal of Youth Studies, 12*(6), 615–627.

Wojcieszak, M. E., & Mutz, D.C. (2009). Online groups and political discourse: Do online discussion spaces facilitate exposure to political disagreement? *Journal of Communication, 59*(1), 40–56.

Wojcieszak, M., & Rojas, H. (2011). Correlates of party, ideology and issue based extremity in an era of egocentric publics. *The International Journal of Press/Politics, 16*(4), 488–507.

# Part II

# Civics and Citizenship Education

# 6 Australian Reflections on Learning to Be Citizens in and with the Social Web

*Suzanne Mellor*

Claims are commonly made, both in the popular press and in the professional education literature, about the significance of the social web in facilitating civic learning and participation. However, empirical evidence supporting these claims is sparse, not strongly indicative and contested. This chapter draws upon data from a research project undertaken in late 2011 in Melbourne, Australia and contributes to the discussion about the ways in which the social web might support the civic participation, especially, of young people. It did this by examining the ways in which social media was integrated into teaching and learning in three schools and by identifying any other processes of civic socialisation that were consciously adopted in three schools.

This research examined general school administrative practices that could be construed as being supportive of the development of a school community and citizenship behaviours, the roles allocated to social media in teaching, and also teachers' engagement with their students in terms of explicit civics and citizenship curricula and activities. The research was predicated on the view that each of these strands of educational work has potential for inducting students into participatory citizenship dispositions and civic behaviours, and the norms and practices, rights and responsibilities of democratic citizenship. The research also examined the young people's experience of social media platforms such as Google, Facebook, Twitter, YouTube and also shared content sites such as Flickr, blogs and discussion forums in their school-based learning and in their lives and sought their views and understandings on the potential of these processes for broader civic engagement.

Specifically, the use of the social web in schools and its implications for enhancing young people's civic learning and citizenship engagement were investigated. The research methodology, in which senior teachers and Year 9 (age 14) students in three schools were interviewed, was designed to develop evidence-based hypotheses and arguments about ways in which young people's civic socialisation might be mediated by social media.

The key research questions were:

1   In what ways are social media technologies effectively used in teaching and learning and in administration in schools, and specifically in civics and citizenship education programmes?
2   How do schools' policy and practice reflect their view of a school's role in supporting active citizenship?
3   In what ways do school students use social media technologies in their social/informal community-based networks?
4   What are the similarities and significant differences in young people's use of social networking technologies in their schooling, as compared with in their personal settings?
5   How do young people perceive their personal use of social media in relation to supporting enhanced citizenship participation and engagement?
6   What are the implications of these different applications of social media technologies for civics and citizenship learning and for political socialisation generally?

Underpinning these research questions is a view about the importance of civic engagement as being critically important to the 'health' of a democracy, and the perception that social networking has a potentially (and increasingly demonstrated) significant role in that civic and democratic engagement. If the projected potential role of social media in civic engagement occurs, it may well impact on the more conventional established traditional practices of political and civic engagement, which, for most citizens in Australia, is confined to voting in state and federal elections. The citizens who are most likely to use social media in their participation with democratic processes are those who are already the most active users of social media—that is, those under 30 years of age. This project is a manifestation of the belief that it is important to better understand the changing context of civic engagement by young citizens and to identify ways of supporting their civic learning. It also conveys the hypothesis that social media may play a significant role in this learning, and possibly, by implication, in young people's future engagement with active civic participation, through social networking. We need to know more of how young people might learn to engage with these civic and citizenship participation options.

Three factors were identified as possible key drivers in supporting student learning about engagement: the role of a school's culture in student learning and engagement; the contribution of social media in student learning and engagement; and the role that an explicit civics and citizenship course plays in student learning and engagement. Each of these three factors impact on the students' sense of identity; their feeling of belonging to the wider school community; the students' efficacy in decision making and governance; and their learning and knowledge generally, including skills development. The hypothesis was that these three drivers, with their subsets, can contribute to students learning how to act as engaged citizens in their present circumstances and, as such, may contribute to the likelihood of their acting similarly in their adult lives.

## RESEARCH METHODOLOGY: SAMPLING OF SCHOOLS AND STUDENTS

The three case-study schools, A, B and C, located in Melbourne, Victoria, Australia, were selected as suitable for the study, as they asserted on their websites that they had an interest in ICT (information and communication technology) teaching and learning, and also as having a programme at Year 9 which encompassed some explicit Civics and Citizenship Education (CCE) objectives. Taken together, these three schools encompass a range of types: state/government and private schools, relatively recently and long-established schools, single sex and co-educational, student cohorts from different socio-economic backgrounds and in different types of locations within Melbourne.

The selected grade sample was Year 9, where the majority of students in Australia are aged 14 years. In part, this year level was selected as the state curriculum requires a minimum of half a term's work to be allocated to CCE. It also was chosen as other assessment research work had been conducted in Australia with this age group, enabling the project to be conducted within this context and allowing for possible comparative additional research to be subsequently conducted. The International Association for the Evaluation of Educational Achievement civics studies (Mellor *et al.*, 2002; Schulz *et al.*, 2010) used this year level.

In the three cycles of the Australian *National Assessment Program— Civics and Citizenship (NAP-CC)*, (MCEETYA, 2006; MCEETYA, 2009; ACARA, 2012), the students assessed were in Years 6 and 10, these being the concluding years for Australian students in primary and compulsory secondary schooling. Although not identical in age to the Networking Young Citizens pilot project sample, the student civic and citizenship knowledge and understandings demonstrated in these NAP-CC assessment reports and the associated commentary on that student knowledge were taken as indicative of the CCE learning—knowledge and dispositions—expected for the sampled cohort.

The school visits were conducted over a two-month period late 2011. Two of the sampled schools provided access to Year 9 students. The third school made only a class of Year 8 students available to be interviewed, and the data indicates that their life and school experiences are, unsurprisingly, less complex than those of students a year older.

## RESEARCH METHODOLOGY: INTERVIEWS

Interviews were scheduled with one teacher for each school, selected by each of the three schools as the person most appropriate to represent the school's position, vis-à-vis the project outline and objectives. Two were classroom teachers of the students who were subsequently interviewed and the third teacher had a pastoral role with the interviewed students. In each school, the teacher was first interviewed and then, independently, the students. The same two interview schedules were used in each of the three schools, with different questions for the staff and students. All interviews lasted at least an hour. The project interviewees' responses were noted, and full audio tapes of all interviews were taken and reviewed and analysed in terms of the three interpretative framework elements.

## FINDINGS

### Learning and Teaching

This project was predicated on the view that participatory learning, or gaining of the disposition and competency to engage, is no different from other learning domains. Participation skills, like any other skills, need to learnt and honed, and that requires practice by learners, ideally in a variety of fields of action. Moreover, the provision of many appropriate learning opportunities, affirmation of achievement and reinforcement, through modelling and other pedagogic and cultural processes, are important because they actively support the learning previously achieved. It pays to recall that learning is cumulative; that deeper understandings are built upon what has already been learnt.

> Other research is providing insights into the nature of *learning progress* within particular learning domains. This research is answering such questions as: What is it that develops as individuals become more expert in a domain? What new knowledge, skills and understandings do they typically develop? What are common sequences and pathways of development? What are prerequisites for further learning? How does new learning build on and extend existing learning within the domain?
>
> (Masters, 2013: 18–19)

The School C teacher affirmed that reflective learning was integral to the school ethos:

> 'the focus is on being articulate about what they have learnt and how their ideas have altered/progressed, over time, over the years . . . Students keep a digital portfolio of their work over the year, are encouraged to reflect on themselves in an audience-appropriate manner.'

> 'The mainstream attitude is the very high value placed on learning—for all students and all learnings . . . Staff have the responsibility to make it [the curriculum] a real fit for kids.'

'Teachers need to innovate if first attempts at engagement don't work.'

The school adopted 'an inclusive pedagogy', commonly requiring that 'students work together', in and outside school. Emphasis in teaching and learning was placed on the importance of having *quality* specific knowledge, and the need for it to be verified, before advancing an argument or position on anything. The students knew that 'opinion is not enough'. They knew that 'a case had to be made' in their submissions—private and public, paper and electronic. That is what they were taught, what they practised.

## TEACHING AND LEARNING WITH SOCIAL MEDIA AND WEB 2.0

Web 2.0 was first so termed in 1999, and its non-static nature is critical to its character. The associated technologies, the social media, are not static technologies; communication traffic is multi-dimensional, not under the control of any single person or institution. Teaching and learning with new technologies utilises recent understandings about how the brain works (Masters, 2013). It incorporates the social learning that students acquire outside classrooms and school and has radical effects on what can be a legitimate 'learning space'. Additionally, and crucially, its usage is interactive—the 'conversation' now can go in many directions at once. So the skill sets, attitudes, knowledge and creativity required for effective teaching and learning have grown exponentially. These new technologies have changed all teaching and learning.

The interviewed teacher from School C reported the school's attitudes to and commitment to the resourcing of Web 2.0 in teaching and learning:

'School C is a Google Apps school and has an IT department of eight or nine technical support staff who will support anybody with anything they want to learn or do or make.'

'Teachers understand that you can't just chalk and talk anymore, there's an expectation of teaching staff, of everyone, that they will use the technologies in teaching and learning.'

'IT staff are always trialling new things—iPads, whiteboards with laptops/USBs, social media to some extent, channels where we put teacher stuff for students, or where their stuff goes up for watching [by others]—creating sites and portals for many subjects and groups . . . and wireless is coming.'

Web-based tools are used to facilitate students' interests and to present their work.

'There are clubs and societies in the school which have Facebook pages/groups . . . School C Radio, internet, has been set up and students talk about what is coming up.'

'various audio-visual technologies . . . a video resource is being created to add value'.

The students affirmed that accessing ICT-based tools provided important learning skills and increased satisfaction and efficacy in learning.

'It introduces interest into your work. If you interpret in your own way and make a video, it suddenly becomes more interesting, you put your own twist on it [the topic]—[also] it's more interesting [for you and others] to watch.'

The teacher confirmed that cyber safety remains a significant issue, with the school providing instruction to parents and students.

'Constant alertness that Web 2.0 can open the school up too much to outsiders [. . .] [so] no photos are put up.'

No one should underestimate the challenge these technologies represent for educational practitioners, especially those for whom this technology occurred part way through their professional life. Little wonder, then, that some practitioners show a reluctance to become fully engaged with the technologies in the classroom.

The teacher at School A said of incorporating Web 2.0 technologies into pedagogy:

'That takes time and teachers don't have time . . . That'd be so time consuming to set up and manage and oversee . . . you don't get that sort of time.'

The students in School C were sympathetic to late-learning adults.

'If you weren't brought up with modern technology your lives would not revolve around Facebook and social networking technology as much. You'd just have to learn how to use it—for us it's just part of the range of [communication] tools.'

For students and staff at School C, Web 2.0 and associated technologies were

'recognised as a powerful interchange. Most teachers use Web 2.0 to tailor almost-individualised instruction . . . Web 2.0 portal tools are commonly used to facilitate individual learning and whole-class learning.'

School C's expectation is that students will also be using these Web 2.0 portal tools in their work, 'and they do'. Parents, students and staff all believe it is the students' role to seek to catch up if a class is missed, but equally, teachers are expected to have resources and planned instruction available to them. 'There's a YouTube channel for keeping up.'

Katherine Moyle has argued that

> Including [new] technologies in teaching and learning requires a re-conceptualisation of the curriculum and how it can be taught. Using technologies to simply replace blackboards with whiteboards and pens with computers and word processors does not constitute a re-conceptualisation of teaching and learning, nor the nature of school education. Such an approach will not support students to 'learn, unlearn, and relearn'.

> Building innovation with technologies and placing the learner at the centre of education offers many creative opportunities for students and educators. . . . In the 21st century the school education sector, as a whole, faces the challenge of determining what constitutes teaching and learning, of deciding what does and will truly build students' innovation and creativity capabilities. Technologies are seen as a way to radically alter traditional learning and teaching patterns. Such approaches to learning place students, not as passive recipients of information, but as an active author, co-creator, evaluator and critical commentator. (Redecker, 2008).
>
> (Moyle, 2010: 60)

Given that this level of innovation is rarely approximated in schools, she points to another issue, which students in the three schools experienced differentially:

> But currently young people's uses of technologies differ between home and school, with children and young people often 'powering down' for school and 'powering up' at home (Project Tomorrow, 2009). It is time that educators construct learning with technologies in sufficiently complex ways for students to feel they are not only 'powering up' in their personal activities with technologies, but for them to also have a similar sense about learning at school.

> A challenge for all Australian schools then, is how to make real the promise of blended learning opportunities, where classrooms make optimal use of both the face-to-face and the virtual environments available to them, so that viable and meaningful learning with technologies is achieved for students and teachers.
>
> (Moyle, 2010: 60)

Only one of the case-study schools in this project demonstrated that it had achieved this level of blended learning opportunities, and both students and teachers at School C could explain how it was achieved. The School C students were totally at ease with Web 2.0 and social media technologies, both for learning and for personal use. They observed, in relation to Moyle's concerns about blended learning and powering down at school, that:

> 'Technologies have personal, social and academic uses—and they overlap.'

> 'Computer use is just part of everyday life. [We] use them for reading the news, and not just sport or personal interests, watching TV, social networking, gaming, entertainment, talking with others, homework, especially planning.'

Students had a clear view about the difference between participating in conversation face-to-face and online.

> 'You behave differently online than otherwise—You feel like you're speaking in a different voice'.

> 'Compared to the phone you can't hear intonation.'

> 'Things seem more literal.'

Students reiterated the importance of trust in the use of social networking, both when using it in a personal space, for example with peers, and also when using it as a learning and exposition tool, for example in making of their videos.

> 'Online you have to imagine the emotion, you can misinterpret—sometimes the conversation has to go for a bit more/longer before you can be sure . . . because you can't be sure of boundaries [that is, of the other's opinion/positioning on an issue,] 'vis-à-vis you'.

School B had explicit goals and strategies for achieving these blended learning opportunities, but lack of resources, internal and external, human and technological, was said to be working against the achievement. School B's region was reported as having the worst broadband and wireless access in Melbourne, inhibiting Web 2.0 and social media use in teaching and learning. The interviewed teacher had set up outward-facing blogs:

> 'for example I have set up a blog for the humanities domain and we use it as our front door for the school in terms of the domain. Parents can go there, there's no passwords required, so there is access to see what the curriculum is, broadly what they are going to look at each term plus lots of links to resources, interactive games and other

kinds of alternative learning tools. It is open to all humanities teachers to be contributors, but not students. [The reasoning behind this was] because we are a new school, and we started with such young children, one of the risks of putting them out into cyberspace, that putting out unedited work, very very embryonic work . . . public criticism . . . can actually inhibit whether they continue to do that. We also have a duty of care with young people and the internet.'

The teacher reported that she and others

'used wikis which were private/closed—You can only be a member if you belong to our school group. We put assignments up there, and resources, and we allow discussion forums to happen. Although students haven't taken to it initially well.'

Two additional online tools provided some opportunities for peer-to-peer interaction:

*Collaborize Classroom*: 'You can post work, questions, opinion polls. Students can engage then with the work. . . . they did for a while but then the interest dropped off.'

*Edmodo*: 'This is what we call "Facebook teaching" . . . it looks and acts a little like Facebook. You get a wall. As a teacher you can go in and create groups for each of your classes. You can post anything you want, questions, comment, a bit of advice, resource links, assignments, due dates, polls, all sorts. Students can get it from anywhere because it is web technology. They don't have to be logged into the school network. They can actually respond and reply to each other and I have found that they [students and staff] have really taken to it. I have only come back from PD [professional development] on it three weeks ago and it is already gone like wildfire through the school. Last week I ran a remote lesson . . . It's like instant messaging, posting on a Facebook page . . . I would post up a question and wait for someone to respond to it because I know they have it up while they're doing their other work.

'I try to book laptops for my kids as often as possible. We've got kids out on other activities and they really get concerned about missing out so if you post the assignment or the lesson activity up there on Edmodo, then they can come into it at any time of the day, go in and see what they were supposed to do then go off and do it. So that seems to be working quite well.'

As previously indicated, School A did not have blended learning goals for its students.

## Teaching and Learning within a Supportive School Culture

Underpinning the concept of blended learning (technological and face to face) and all the pedagogical relearning that it entails for staff, is the view that a school culture which advocates placing a high value on explicitly developing and supporting students' sense of their identity and belonging plays a key role in the work of teaching and learning to be. Johanna Wyn argues that

> Changing expectations of youth will increase the expectation that education plays a greater role in creating actively engaged, critical citizens who are well informed about civic life.
>
> (Wyn, 2009: 42)

> Identity work is increasingly acknowledged as central to education. It is often hidden work done by students, but not acknowledged by their teachers . . . The role of identity work in learning for life is an important consideration because it addresses the way in which all the other partners in education see young people and *their* role. If young people are to be seen as partners in learning, it is important to provide them with opportunities to be active partners and so to shape identities that are premised on belonging, making decisions and having the capacity to influence their own learning.
>
> [ . . . ] One of the ways in which individuals manage this is through an intense focus on 'becoming': watching, practising and learning the mix of social skills, knowledge and practical skills that are required to achieve success. They can be supported in this endeavour in school. Indeed, identity work should be actively supported in schools, with acknowledgement given to the way in which learning and identity are intertwined.
>
> (Wyn, 2009: 48–49)

Again, case-study School C demonstrated that it had a full set of explicit strategies for achieving all these goals, for all students (although it did not suggest that it had been successful for all). Asked about the reference in the school charter to identity and belonging, the teacher said:

> 'The whole school's teaching and learning environment and culture and the Civics and Citizenship course have an explicit identity focus.'

The teacher further commented on the concept of multiple identities:

> 'our students belong to many communities—it's part of who they are. They are not racially homogenous but harmonious.'

School C students said

> 'When you ask yourself who you are, you feel like you want to know yourself better. It's about finding the relationship between what you do, why you do it and who you do it with.'

Teachers and leaders in School C clearly articulated how they intended to reach these goals, and how they supported each other in achieving them. The school and its staff were said to have an awareness of the importance of lifelong learning.

> 'The curriculum and its delivery are structured to facilitate links to futures and future learning students might want to have. [. . .] assessment and programme evaluations [are] routinely undertaken, with all stakeholders actively involved.'

The school's emphasis was said to be on students being responsible for their

> 'learning and in participating in the life of the school in a positive, broadly defined way . . . every opportunity [is] given for students to try something [in or outside of school]; [. . .] staff and kids talk up *trying*.'
>
> '. . . students should take all [the opportunities] and sort out which ways are best for them.'

School C students reckoned that they had been allowed and supported to learn and practise all these skills, and regarded themselves as lucky indeed.

> 'At this school you can decide to belong, and most do feel that, especially to some part of it.'
>
> 'To explore, and to find out where and with whom you fit, is a responsibility and an obligation.'

The students' view on the teaching and learning philosophy of the school was succinct:

> 'They want you to do well, but they want you to find yourself and your interests too.'

They knew they would be affirmed at the school assemblies and on the school website:

> '. . . which the students support and can upload to too'.
>
> 'If you want to contribute you can, but no one forces you to take on a public role.'

'When reading in a newspaper article about the school you feel connected to it and positive, you feel proud about it.'

School B had some of those independent learning objectives but failed to actively implement all the elements. An example of ethos/action dissonance was evident in the setting up of students' gravatars [globally recognised avatar], for using Edmodo.

'The most important thing for students, is to get their gravatar set up, they need their image . . . It is about their online identity I think, who they are. Because we make them use a username—a name which identifies you as a classroom. So there is a transition period of them getting used to doing that. We have to allow that to happen. Edmodo does allow you to lock students out if they're mucking around or give them read-only access if they are posting inappropriately.'

Some confusion shows here regarding learning goals (student identity versus adult control).

The characteristic that separated these three schools with regard to school culture was the degree to which all elements illustrated in Figure 6.1 were developed, and equally addressed, in the implementation. The underlying requirement for a school to create the kind of learning environment capable of achieving the interrelated goals previously mentioned in this chapter is that *all* elements be implemented in a congruent manner. Dissonance between expressed intentions and implementation can ruin student belief.

The *Networking Young Citizens* report argues that:

Creating and managing an environment or climate in a school which will actively support the students' sense of self and of belonging, requires a school prioritising knowledge, attitudes and skills that enable students to learn the importance of having evidence to make a case, not just assert a view, to explore and form views on dilemmas associated with their interests and their futures actions, and that will support productive relationships between students and between staff and students. It includes prioritising ways in which school structures can provide encouragement for all students to deal with identity issues (theirs and those of others), to experiment and practice their skills in decision-making, especially with a view to considering the context of the views of others. Civics and citizenship curricula explicitly deal with these matters, thus developing a disposition for engagement and participation in individuals and in the institution. Active engagement of all participants becomes the underlying modus operandi of the whole school community. The figure below [Figure 6.1] is a diagrammatic representation of the conceptualisation of the inter-related elements of such a school culture.

(Mellor & Seddon 2013: 12)

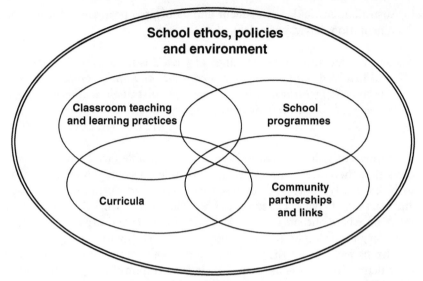

*Figure 6.1* A conceptualisation of a school learning culture supportive of student engagement and active participation

Figure 6.1, in various forms, has frequently been used in Australia for over a decade, particularly in CCE professional learning (Holdsworth & Mellor 2004; Mellor 2008). Its validity lies in the need for all four sub-elements to be implemented in a way that is consistent with the school's expressed goals: its ethos, policies and environment. But if a CCE programme is not complemented by the whole-school approach, if, for example, it is the only learning space where equity is provided for student voice, then the students will recognise it as a fraud and may not engage with it, and will certainly not adopt the hoped-for attitudes, behaviours and learnings. Modelling these outcomes is effective for student learning only if students can then practise them in their own worlds. This is most evidently the case if the goal is to have students actively engage and participate in their communities in their current and later lives. Why promise them something and then restrict their capacity to practise it? Students' engagement will, at least initially, be based on their perception of what interests them. This mantra is manifestly the case for all learning. Effective schools and teachers have to link the students' interests to a broader base—they have to stretch their students' interests and learnings.

## Civics and Citizenship Learning

Civic learning and citizenship participation are political socialisation processes which depend upon formalised teaching and informal induction into the social and cultural practices of responsible and active citizenship.

In Australian curricula, assessment and associated professional learning documentation, 'civics' was defined as:

> Knowledge and Understandings of Civic Institutions and Processes and involved *'knowledge of key concepts and understandings relating to civic institutions and processes in Australian democracy, government, law national identity, diversity, cohesion and social justice.'*
>
> (MCEETYA, 2006: 98–102)

This apparently simple definition refers to knowable facts, but also indicates that there are contestable, interpretable concepts which will need to be explicitly addressed, analysed and unpacked during the teaching and learning of civics. The notion of how democracy works depends very much on where one sits in society, as one's interests and capacity to influence vary accordingly. Knowing how the 'system' works is a precursor to citizens feeling that they might take the opportunity to exercise both their democratic rights as well as their civic responsibilities. More than this civic knowledge is needed, however.

The concept of 'citizenship' was defined in the NAP-CC Assessment Domain as:

> 'Dispositions and Skills for Participation' and involved the development of *'the skills, attitudes, beliefs and actions that underpin active democratic citizenship.'*
>
> (MCEETYA 2006: 98–102)

> The Assessment Domain indicates that without civic knowledge, plus a disposition to engagement, a person cannot demonstrate the required citizenship skills or effectively practice citizenship.
>
> (Mellor *et al.*, 2010: 5)

The six identified dimensions of civics and citizenship learning identified by Prior are:

> *Dimension 1*: Civic knowledge:
> (ie. understandings about political organizations, decision making processes, institutions, legal requirements)
> *Dimension 2*: A sense of personal identity:
> (ie. a feeling of self-worth, belonging efficacy, resilience)
> *Dimension 3*: A sense of community:
> (ie. locating oneself within a community(s), some perhaps imagined communities)
> *Dimension 4*: Adoption of a code of civil behaviours:
> (ie. civil and ethical behaviour, concern for the welfare of others)

*Dimension 5*: An informed and empathetic response to social issues:
(ie. environmental issues, social justice, equality and equity)
*Dimension 6*: A skilled disposition to take social action:
(ie. community service, active participation in community affairs)
(Prior, 1999; 2006: 6–10)

In the context of the above published research and the project's goals, Prior's initial conceptualisation of the CCE dimensions links civic knowledge to citizenship action and links identity to belonging. Prior was affirming the need for a school to operate within a learning culture as shown in Figure 6.1. Experience in decision making is fundamental to students achieving and demonstrating the skills and disposition defined in Dimension 6.

## Teaching and Learning Decision Making: Participation in School Governance

The explicit civics and citizenship curriculum at School C is a manifestation of the school's charter expectations regarding joint student and school responsibilities and accountability. The interviewed teacher, the course's developer, charged with its delivery, affirmed that:

'the course and school environment have an explicit identity focus, and it operates within a culture where voting on a range of matters within the school is common'.

As required by state curricula standards, the civics and citizenship curriculum is compulsory for half a term for all Year 9 students. It is conducted in half-class groups. It is a multimedia course and links citizen engagement and civic process.

'"Auzzie Democrazy" is a taster course in civics/citizenship, and will provide students with context for their politics study in Year 12. It demonstrates that policy is formed by people who care. It has explicit socialisation objectives. It requires rapport development, extends sense of self. It teaches kids to become wary of spin.'

Students select an issue which was a live political one at the time of Federation and is still a politically current issue; for example, immigration (boat arrivals) and defence (support for a war, financing etc.). The explicit CCE course

'requires a developing and testing of students' own ideas. It gets students to discover and clarify their interests and think in terms of their futures. Many of them start thinking/deciding what careers/futures they want to follow in their lives. . . It helps them work out more about their identity, about who they are . . . [The course] models negotiation, and allows students to experience and question governance, decision and policy making, exterior to the school.'

Asked if some students didn't closely engage with this course the teacher was emphatic.

'*No,* kids don't switch onto the course and its requirements. We help them find an issue they care about [and it works because] it shows them how the outside world is relevant to them.'

Using a full range of web-based and other research tools, students identified and researched the historical and current context. Despite the teacher's urging, they remained contemptuous of engaging with Twitter.

'Twitter is for celebrities.'

'No one wants to show or listen to your everyday thoughts.'

'[You] can stalk with it' and

'[Those who use it] are old people who think they are hip.'

They interviewed their local federal member and an education journalist on their topic, and formed a policy view on their issue. Finally, with the additional learning goal of practising audience awareness,

'each [student] wrote and created and videoed a maiden speech, trying to adopt a politician persona'.

The student videos were watched and critiqued by the class group. The teacher intended that

'[the videos, with texts ] will be sent to ABC Open for uploading there [and also] put them onto a school website—perhaps a blog—for internal audience [and personal affirmation].'

School C students had a precise view of the governance and decision-making options available to them, and they exercised them frequently. Their Student Representative Council (SRC) experience had been that when only students were in charge, the process was chaotic. The students expressed frustration that they could not resolve the conflicting stances on issues brought to the SRC by students. 'There are too many opinions, they can conflict.' Without adult mediation they could not effectively negotiate or implement decisions. Decision-making processes were clearly understood, but they did not yet have the skills to effectively exercise them alone.

Students knew that school was not a fully functioning democracy and why it could not be.

'There are constraints on what you can do—school is not like Australia, it's not so much a democracy.'

But participating had felt good, and they all knew the choice was there, and that another time they could actively engage on an issue that concerned them.

'Plus school's pretty good, we have good teachers, programmes, curriculums and we don't need much to change to make it perfect!!'

At School B, students are allocated to houses,

'we are sort of like a family within a family, I guess'.

Students can apply for the positions of house captain, but they are appointed by teachers. The students elect house representatives to the SRC, which can take issues raised by students directly to the principal. One student reported having achieved success on a recent occasion.

'I was elected to the SRC not long ago and we discussed an issue [the most frequently suggested issue from the anomymous suggestion box—how to avoid sports students having to stay in their sports uniforms all day] and we found a solution and we had to talk with the Principal and we tested our idea for a couple of weeks and it went well so we decided to keep it . . . It felt good because now we don't have to worry about the problem.'

The limitations on student governance and decision making evidenced in this quote, especially the student's comment on the outcome, indicate the dilemma that schools face when letting students try to learn governance. If the process is restricted, learning is reduced. The School B student did not learn much about governance, but had the satisfaction of contributing to fixing something that was a problem for students at the school. Additionally, there was no CCE course for students at either Schools A or B.

The long-term learning outcomes sought for those educated in a rounded CCE programme are that they will be able to confidently act as individuals in decision making within their communities. For this, both civics education and the disposition to engage are required. A comprehensive CCE programme contributes to the learning of models of civic action and other citizenship behaviours. The disposition to participate can best be taught in an environment where the processes and the outcomes of engagement are valued by the active participants, the recipients or peers and those in authority.

In a learning situation or space, engagement and self-management can be displayed in relation to all learning. School C sought to encourage students to actively engage across a huge range of activities, both within the school community and beyond. This school consciously created and operated within a culture which actively supported the development of decision making and management learning in all students. Because it comprehensively implemented all elements of its ethos (as in Figure 6.1) the school also had developed students who could demonstrate Prior's sixth dimension. Students routinely reported on their group's activity at weekly school assemblies, which were always attended by the principal, and they addressed house and club meetings:

> 'you don't have to win or anything [and the] school photographer is always present, snapping away [and these pics are] uploaded onto newsletters and a video resource'.

For this school, any active participation in learning was worthwhile, as it all contributed to the development in students of the skills and dispositions to actively engage in, and reflect on, their learning. The students agreed, saying they were confident about how they gained their learning: 'you can learn from doing anything'. The students are correct of course, though it will happen only if you have been offered the full range of learning opportunities at school, have been encouraged to participate to the full and have been taught how to reflect on your learning. Co-incidentally, this state school is one of Victoria's most sought-after secondary schools, having high achievement across the broadest of curriculum goals for a non-streamed student cohort. This project's analysis of School C's learning culture and programme delivery provides insights into how this can be achieved.

## CONCLUSIONS

This pilot case-study project examined how student participatory learning could be supported and managed by schools operating within a pro-active participation culture, using pedagogic approaches associated with CCE and ICT (including Web 2.0 and social media). The approaches to participation/engagement in learning and the curricula (witnessed especially in School C and to a lesser extent in School B) can be described as being a citizenship model of learning. Although they were still students (and therefore not generally regarded as 'full citizens' of society), the students' descriptions of their learning processes at school indicated how their behaviours and those of those around them, in those communities of which they are full members, enabled them to experience rich teaching and demonstrate many diverse learnings.

Students from School C had experienced all three elements (articulated explicit connections between the civic characteristics of the value of participation, social media and Web 2.0-based learning). The responses from these students demonstrated how such participating experiences can enrich and enhance learning processes, strengthen their sense of identity and intrinsic value (and that of others) and increase their skills in living and learning. These learnings proved to be a parallel path to growing up (becoming adults), being responsible for the outcomes of their actions and actively participating in the world they currently inhabited. They clearly articulated how their learning models enabled them to view with some comfort how they might engage in the future, in their ever-widening world. The CCE and ICT/Web 2.0 curricula acted both as tools in and as a model for achieving effective learning outcomes, both currently and for the future. They felt good about themselves, their school and their future learning.

## 1 Measuring Learning

These areas of learning are amongst the most difficult to measure. Measuring personal growth (including variables that reference the development of a sense of self and autonomy for participation) and the use of ICT, both as a tool and also as a way of seeing and acting within the world, (and the integration of Web 2.0 and social media in learning) are fiendishly complex matters. Three cycles of the NAP-CC and NAP-ICT programmes have been conducted and reported on in Australia, so it is not reasonable to argue the case that assessment of such knowledge, skills and attitudes cannot be done. Students' sense of well-being can also be tested. And general achievement levels can be taken as indicators of all the relevant variables.

## Resourcing Teaching and Learning in School Ethos, Web 2.0 and CCE

Significant factors in a school providing a rich experience of learning to be a citizen in the Web 2.0 world are the cultural, economic and symbolic resources available to a school. A full complement of these factors is required to ensure the full implementation of all elements of the School Learning Culture of Figure 6.1. A school which lacks an explicit ethos or culture or policy emphasising engagement/participation in the school community cannot prioritise and model those values in all the elements contained within the figure. Resourcing of professional learning and supporting staff to adopt the school ethos is critical to achieving this combination. Thin resources in any of the the domains negatively impact on the experiences offered in the school—limiting the sense of belonging and the participatory options that can be learnt, and taken up by, students.

## Benefits of Incorporating Web 2.0 and Social Media in Pedagogies

Schools which become much more actively engaged in using Web 2.0 and social networking in their teaching and in their administration will benefit. Web 2.0 should not be restricted to teacher-directed learning activities. When creatively and extensively utilised by all stakeholders, Web 2.0 and social networking can be powerful factors in developing student independence, in students having a positive view of the world, their place in it and their capacity to engage with it. Where Web 2.0 approaches were employed in a school—for teaching, learning and presentation of student work, for students and other stakeholders to connect to the whole school community, through the community partnership links—the benefits of such engagement were very clear. The benefits were increased participation by all in that community, and a positive sense of belonging. That students already have such a positive and personal connection with social media makes for relative ease in its wider utilisation in teaching and learning practices. This fact adds yet another practical motivation for having these pedagogies more widely adopted in schools.

## Additional Benefits from Positive Whole School Cultures

Where there is a high level of integration in school policy between the three policy areas that were the focus of this study (that is, school culture, ICT—Web 2.0 and social media—and explicit CCR) there was little dissonance between the interview responses from students and staff, and the students were more engaged on all fronts. Such synergy indicates an alignment of views about desirable learning goals held by staff and students, and suggests an explicit and meaningful dialogue about the achievement of learning outcomes is underway. This is evidence of a productive and efficacious learning culture.

## Smart Phone Use and Identity Construction in the Wider World

A common thread in the responses from students in all three schools was the ubiquitous nature of social media in their out-of-school life, of their smart phones, which were used mostly for social purposes. For those who attended a school where Web 2.0 was commonly utilised as a means of identity construction and communication, using their smart phones to participate in the wider world is not so big a step. Students in School C affirmed that they would have to first become specifically interested in a particular aspect of an issue in the outside world, and, if that happened, then having previously practised engagement within a social culture and having had some civic and citizenship education, they would readily and confidently participate. (Social action sites have gained much greater prominence worldwide and in Australia since 2011.)

## Encouraging Collaborative Student Use of Web 2.0 Platforms

Researchers noted that Schools A and B rarely seemed to suggest that students work together, especially at after-school work, via Skype for instance. There may be non-ICT reasons for this, including assessment-based concerns about distinguishing individual contribution in the work. Despite agreeing on the benefits of jointly preparing homework tasks, students rarely appeared routinely to work jointly after hours, though peer referencing, for queries and seeking opinions, was common in School C and less so in School B. However, in-class work was more frequently jointly produced, for example with YouTube being a favourite medium at School C (and mentioned in School B) for demonstrating students' ideas about issues, along with uploading text and ideas onto the school intranet. There was little evidence of schools encouraging between-school exploration of inter-student views on issues.

## Supporting Student Voice in School Governance Processes

Where a school provided opportunities for students to make explicit connections between civic knowledge and in-school governance, there were fewer complaints from students about school governance processes. This was because students gained a greater understanding of what it meant to actively engage and 'make a difference' in the school community, and on their own terms. If teaching and learning 'improves' when there is less disruption and distraction within a school's classrooms, then this is a benefit for all stakeholders. Students and teachers in each school mentioned the importance of reducing student disruption to learning and, especially in School B, the teachers and students commented on the positive role that Web 2.0 and other media played in achieving this.

## Participation in CCE Learning Governance Improves Achievement Levels for All

One major finding demonstrated by the case studies (in School C, and to a lesser extent in School B) is the way a school with a pro-active participation culture is readily able to integrate ICT (including the use of Web 2.0 and social media) and CCE into its teaching and learning programmes. Researchers hypothesise that this relative ease of implementation (assuming the necessary work on ethos and resourcing of staff in the relevant contexts and skills is done) is due to the congruence between self-expression and belonging that is inherent in social networking, the participatory objectives of CCE and modelling of the substantive concepts and concerns of civic and citizenship learning. These elements are complementary to such a school culture, having in common their engagement base and a view of all participants as having rights and responsibilities in engaging in their learning and participatory activities. The project found that being involved in decision making makes for more reflective learners and higher levels of achievement. This notable finding complements and supports the NAP-CC07 findings regarding the effect on student achievement of students participating in school governance, having other civics and citizenship-related experiences in school, and also citizenship activities outside school. (Mellor & Seddon, 2013:16–18). This study found that Web 2.0 and social media, when combined with CCE curricula, opens up significant education options by supporting participatory self-motivated and self-monitoring learners across the full breadth of the school population.

## Concluding Remarks

In conclusion, schools would do well to consider the benefits to all stakeholders of more intensively implementing ICT (including Web 2.0 and social media) and CCE approaches, both in whole-school cultures (as in Figure 6.1and in classroom pedagogies, across the full curriculum. This pilot project indicates that implementing educational policy in schools that emphasises the connectedness between pre-existing and new applications in students' learning of explicit and deep knowledge of engagement and action will result in the increased engagement of young people in a range of participations during their school lives. Consequently, as previously quoted research has indicated, the range and levels of student achievement, of learning, increase. Implementing such policies confers personal, pedagogic and social identity benefits to many parties, both during their school years and also subsequently, in adulthood.

## Further Work

This pilot study raised as many questions as it explicitly addressed. Areas for further research, using a broader cohort, are the following:

- More research is urgently required into the potential of Web 2.0, social media and CCE models of effective pedagogy and learning, across all curricula.
- Schools should develop taxonomies, across these modes, with explicit descriptors of the types of behaviours and attitudes associated with active in-school student engagement.

- Gender difference in learning associated with social media and CCE has been tangentially researched to date (in this study there appeared to be no gender-based difference), but more closely focused work may be revealing.
- A deep consideration of the long-term effects on post-school community engagement and participation of having experienced teaching and learning that incorporates various models of social media and CCE could lead to rich findings. There is a lot we don't know about the long-term impact of such learning at school.

## REFERENCES

ACARA (Australian Curriculum, Assessment and Reporting Authority), 2012, *NAP-Civics and Citizenship Years 6 and 10 Report*. Retrieved 13 April 2013 from www.nap.edu.au/verve/_resources/NAP-CC_Report_2010_251011.pdf.

Holdsworth, R. & Mellor, S., 2004, *Discovering Democracy in Action: Implementing the Program*. Melbourne: Department of Education and Training, Office of Learning and Teaching, Student Learning Division. Retrieved 23 July 2010 from www.eduweb.vic.gov.au/edulibrary/public/teachlearn/student/discoveringdemocracy.pdf.

Masters, G.N., 2013, *Reforming Educational Assessment: Imperatives, Principles and Challenges* (Australian Education Review, 57), Melbourne: ACER Press. Retrieved 12 April 2013 from www.acer.edu.au/aer.

MCEETYA (Ministerial Council on Education, Employment, Training and Youth Affairs), 2006, *National Assessment Program—Civics and Citizenship Years 6 and 10 Report, 2004*. Melbourne: MCEETYA. Retrieved 12 April 2013 from www.mceecdya.edu.au/mceecdya/nap_cc_2004_years_6_and_10_report,17149.html.

MCEETYA, 2009, *National Assessment Program—Civics and Citizenship Years 6 and 10 Report, 2007*. Melbourne: MCEETYA. Retrieved 23 July 2010 from www.mceecdya.edu.au/mceecdya/nap_civics_and_citizenship_2007_yrs6_and_10_report,26602.html.

Mellor, S., 2008, 'The National Assessment Program—Civics and Citizenship: Reflections on Practices in Primary and Secondary Schools,' *Proceedings, ACER Research Conference 2008*, pp. 26–28. Retrieved 12 April 2013 from http://research.acer.edu.au/research_conference_2008/12/.

Mellor, S., Kennedy, K. & Greenwood, L., 2002, *Citizenship and Democracy: Australian Students' Knowledge and Beliefs—The IEA Civic Education Study of Australian Fourteen Year Olds*. Melbourne: Australian Council for Educational Research.

Mellor, S., Meiers, M. & Knight, P., 2010, *The Digest, Civics and Citizenship*, No. 3, 2010, New South Wales Institute of Teachers. Retrieved 5 April 2013 from www.nswteachers.nsw.edu.au/publications.

Mellor, S. & Seddon, T., 2013, *Networking Young Citizens: Learning to Be Citizens in and with the Social Web*. http://works.bepress.com/suzanne_mellor/64/.

Moyle, K., 2010, *Building Innovation: Learning with Technologies* (Australian Education Review 56). Melbourne: ACER Press. Retrieved 12 April 2013 from www.acer.edu.au/aer.

Prior, W., 1999, 'What It Means to Be a "Good Citizen" in Australia: Perceptions of Teachers, Students and Parents', *Theory and Research in Social Education*, Vol. 27, no. 2, 215–247.

Prior, W., 2006,. 'Civics and Citizenship Education' in *Ethos*, Victorian Association of Social Studies Teachers, Vol. 14, no. 4, 6–10.

Project Tomorrow, 2009, *Media Release*, 24 March, Project Tomorrow, The Future Educators Association of California. www.tomorrow.org/speakup/pdfs/PT%20releaseFINAL.pdf.

Redecker, C., 2008, *Review of Learning 2.0 Practices*. European Union JRC European Union, European Communities. Retrieved 10 April 2013, from http://is.jrc.ec.europa.eu/pages/documents/Learning2-0Review.pdf.

Schulz, W., Ainley, J., Fraillon, J., Kerr, D. & Losito, B., 2010, *ICCS 2009 International Report: Civic Knowledge, Attitudes, and Engagement among Lower-Secondary Students in 38 Countries*. Netherlands: International Association for the Evaluation of Educational Achievement.

Wyn, J., 2009, *Touching the Future: Building Skills for Life and Work* (Australian Education Review 55). Melbourne: ACER Press. Retrieved 23 July 2010 from www.acer.edu.au/aer.

# 7  Perceptions of Students and Teachers in England about How Social Media Are Used (and How They Could Be Used) in Schools and Elsewhere

*Ian Davies and Edda Sant*

This chapter draws upon the work undertaken in Australia by Suzanne Mellor and Terri Seddon, and discussed in the previous chapter, by examining the findings that emerged from a small-scale research project conducted in England during the autumn and winter of 2012–13. In particular we seek to address four key research questions:

1  In what ways do school pupils use social media technologies in their social/informal community-based networks?
2  What are the similarities and significant differences in young people's use of social media in their schooling and personal settings?
3  How do young people perceive their personal use of social media supporting enhanced citizenship participation and engagement?
4  In what ways are social media effectively used in school-based citizenship education programmes to support active citizenship?

On the basis of questionnaire and interview data gathered from pupils and teachers in three schools, we suggest that pupils frequently use social media for personal and social reasons and that some of them consider that this technology may also be of some help educationally. More precisely, pupils and teachers feel that social media can enhance citizenship engagement, knowledge and participation insofar as people can be informed and updated; everybody has the right to give their opinion and to be listened to on an equal basis; opinions posted on websites can be discussed; people may organise and inform others about their actions; and people can engage in global citizenship by getting to know people from other cultures.

But many pupils have reservations. They feel that the content of information presented through social media cannot be easily verified; these forms of technology may be harmfully addictive; any benefits of social media can be achieved in face-to-face situations; it may merely help those who are already engaged; and there would be specific gaps in young people's knowledge if there were to be significant reliance on social media.

We found that teachers used social media less frequently than pupils, although teachers acknowledge its general educational potential and suggest possible connections that may be established with citizenship education. While teachers suggest that social media will be used extensively in educational contexts in the future, current low usage may be explained by the need to preserve professional independence; to maintain barriers between teachers' private and professional lives; and is connected with uncertainty about their expertise with technology.

On the basis of an analysis of data from all respondents, we suggest that social media may enhance citizenship education in relation to identity (generating a sense of belonging, global citizenship and forming new groups); promoting knowledge about citizenship (searching sources, commenting, discussing); and facilitating participation (informing people, organising social movements, being democratic as opinions are developed). However, although there seems to be a general consensus in the academic community about the potential of social media platforms in citizenship education, our general argument is that there is—in light of our respondents' reservations about the nature and extent of social media and citizenship education—an urgent need for more research about the development of high-quality educational programmes using the social web.

In this chapter we attempt to do several things: we outline some of the developments about social media and citizenship education, drawing attention to the context in England where our research was undertaken; we describe and discuss our methods; we present findings; and we develop the argument referred to above.


## BACKGROUND

There is little doubt that social media and citizenship education are seen as matters of great significance.

Broadly it may be suggested that

> Civic engagement is involvement in the public sphere, incorporating participation in constitutional politics as well as less formally constituted activity. Social media are relatively new forms of technology (principally, but not exclusively, social networking sites) that allow users to interact.
>
> (Davies *et al.*, 2012: 294)

There is an almost overwhelming amount of material that refers to the seismic shifts that are occurring or will occur in society as a result of social media and associated educational potential. However, it is important in such contexts to approach such claims constructively and critically. Elsewhere (Davies *et al.*, 2012) we have asked questions that would help us to develop such an approach to this field, discussing whether or not there is sufficient access to—and relevant usage of ? social media; whether civic engagement is congruent with social media (or, to put it crudely, if there is at least as much potential for social media to be used by dictators as by democrats—Morozov, 2011); and what sort of educational processes could be experienced and what would need to be done by teachers and others in order to develop that work.

All research takes place in a context and we need to sketch the situation in England that pertained at the time of our project. That picture is generally unclear. Ofsted (2004), the UK government inspection agency, has long declared that 'new' technologies have the potential to raise educational achievement. And yet the most recent (2010) general election in the UK saw the influence of traditional media (in the form of TV debates) and very little evidence of the impact of social media. There are concerns about differential take-up of civic engagement opportunities which may or may not be ameliorated by the use of new technologies. On the one hand, it is argued that young people of lower socio-economic status are more likely to be both distrustful of government and disadvantaged in terms of access to and skills for technology and civic learning efficacy (Merien *et al.*, 2010); but there are others who suggest that 'There are hints that forms of civic engagement anchored in blogs and social networking sites could alter long-standing patterns that are based on socio-economic status' (see http://pewresearch.org/pubs/1328/onlinepolitical-civic-engagement-activity).

More specifically, in relation to education, Kerr *et al.* (2007) have reported low usage of new technologies in schools. In the National Curriculum's current citizenship programme of study in England there is only one relevant statement to technology use (number nine in a list of ten 'curriculum opportunities'). In the version of the National Curriculum for citizenship that will be in place for school year 2014–15 there is no reference to new technologies. It is possible that new technology, if used at all, might 'merely' enhance presentation skills in the teacher's recitation script, and little else (Smith *et al.*, 2006: 455). Livingstone, Bober and Helsper (2005) suggest that young people lack key skills in evaluating online content and perhaps little is being done to address that need. But Selwyn and Gorard argue that 'the evidence does not suggest the "new learning technologies" imply or precipitate "new forms of learning"' (2003: 178). However, these reservations about digital learning are not in themselves an argument for failing to explore the potential to generate new forms of learning in relation to civic engagement. Beldarrain (2006) notes the potential transition from teacher as deliverer of knowledge to facilitator of online interaction, reflecting the two tenets of constructivism: learning as an active process of constructing knowledge rather than acquiring it; and instruction as a process that involves supporting that construction rather than a process of communicating knowledge. Some (e.g. Merien *et al.*, 2010: 187) have suggested that radical change is occurring in civic engagement and that educators have a responsibility to push forward with these opportunities.

We need to know more about the extent and nature of the usage of technology generally and of social media in particular if we are to be able to make judgements about the development of civic engagement through education that uses social media. And at this point the methods of our project should be described and discussed.

## METHODS

This research was conducted using mixed methods through numeric and narrative approaches allowing for the exploration of those areas which are contested (Johnson *et al* 2007; Cohen *et al.*, 2011; Miles & Huberman 1994; Bergman, 2008). Within this general approach our principal emphasis was qualitative. Our aim was to understand and interpret the perceptions that pupils and teachers have about social media and citizenship education.

The original intention was to sample from only those schools which are already well known for their expertise in the educational use of social media. Advice was gathered from experts in the field as to which schools could be approached. However, it was not entirely straightforward to gain recommendations about schools with that expertise, and, of those that were recommended and invited, only one agreed to join the project. We feel that it would be unreasonable to draw any conclusions from these difficulties, as schools are under such a range of pressures, but we did not form the impression that schools were eager to display their expertise in this field. The two schools that agreed to join the project but that had not been recommended by experts in the field of social media and citizenship education nevertheless had notable regional expertise in citizenship education as well as interests in the possibility of developing further work generally in that area, and wished to explore specifically the potential of social media. The demographics of the schools varied greatly in terms of several factors, including religious affiliation, funding (independent and state) and size of town. As such, the sample provides a snapshot of a variety of practice from different starting points and is not intended to be representative.

The main characteristics of each of the teachers and the schools they work in are summarised in Table 7.1. The sample of pupils who completed the survey was selected in agreement with the teachers and with the permission of the pupils themselves.

In School 1, all Year 9 pupils (aged 13–14) who agreed participated in the questionnaire. In School 2, all the girls from Year 9 and Year 10 (aged 14–15) answered the questionnaire. In School 3, three of the seven Year 9 tutor groups were surveyed in accordance with practical circumstances and a desire not to disrupt the smooth running of the school. A total of

Table 7.1 Characteristics of the project teachers and their schools

| Teacher | | | School | | |
|---------|--------|---------|---------|---------|---------|
| Gender | Subjects Taught | Principal Curricular Responsibility | Location in England | Type of School | |
| Female | PSHE* and religion | PSHE | North | State school | Co-educational school |
| Female | PSHE and arts | PSHE | North | Independent school | Female school |
| Female | Citizenship and history | PSHE and citizenship | South | State school | Co-educational school |

Note: *Personal, social, health and economic education.

247 pupils comprised the sample (Table 7.2). The main characteristics of these pupils are described below.

Sixteen of the 247 pupils surveyed volunteered to join the focus group sample. Four focus group interviews were carried out (two in School 1; one in School 2; and one in School 3). Teachers selected those pupils who had some experience of voluntary activities (and so would, perhaps, be better able than others to comment on citizenship) and a range of academic ability and, in two of the schools, sought to provide a balance of male and female pupils.

The questionnaire included both open and closed questions and was divided into three sections: perceptions about citizenship; pupils' current use of social media in personal and educational contexts and in relation to identity; and perceptions about the connection between social media engagement and knowledge. The four focus group interviews of pupils were conducted in the three project schools in order to identify, in greater depth than had been provided by questionnaire data, pupils' practices and perceptions and their preferences in terms of the possible enhancement of social media use in citizenship education. Semi-structured interviews were used in order to investigate teachers' perceptions about the nature of and the extent to which social media are already in use specifically in citizenship education, and teachers' preferences for the future in terms of the possibility of enhancing social media use in citizenship education.

Mixed methods analysis was conducted by exploring qualitative meaning, in part through reflections made in relation to quantitative indicators (Biesta, 2012). Exploratory qualitative analyses of the whole data set (from the surveys, focus groups and interviews) were undertaken using the online software www.wordle.net (which counts the number of words used). Subsequently, deeper qualitative analyses (Creswell, 1998; Miles & Huberman, 1994) were completed using the online software www.dedoose.org.

Table 7.2 Characteristics of the pupils who answered the survey

| | Gender | | Age | | | | | Year | |
| | Male | Female | 12 | 13 | 14 | 15 | 16 | Year 9 | Year 10 |
| | Frequency | Frequency | Freq | Freq | Freq | Freq | Freq | Frequency | Frequency |
|---|---|---|---|---|---|---|---|---|---|
| School 1 | 61 | 71 | 1 | 98 | 31 | 0 | 0 | 133 | 0 |
| 2 | 0 | 54 | 0 | 17 | 23 | 13 | 1 | 23 | 31 |
| 3 | 35 | 25 | 0 | 47 | 13 | 0 | 0 | 60 | 0 |
| Global Frequency | 96 | 150 | 1 | 162 | 67 | 13 | 1 | 216 | 31 |
| Valid per cent | 39.0 | 61.0 | 0.4 | 66.4 | 27.5 | 5.3 | 0.4 | 87.4 | 12.6 |

The main steps followed in the process of data analysis are as follows:

1 creation and organisation of data documents (Creswell, 1998)
2 reading and first impressions about data; first codes created by means of www.wordle.net (Creswell, 1998)
3 direct interpretation, category summaries and development of first classification criteria following the steps described by Miles and Huberman (1994):
   a data codification
   b code scheme creation
   c memorandum development to describe the codes
   d data recodification according to the new codes
   e creation of matrix nets and schemes to achieve the first interpretations.

Finally, the data from the surveys were analysed using the codes previously created in the qualitative analyses and shown in the tables below. Data were quantified using descriptive statistics (frequencies and percentages) using SPSS.

## FINDINGS

We show below our four research questions and the responses to them.

### 1 In what ways do school pupils use social media in their social/informal community-based networks?

In summary, we found heavy usage, principally for the purposes of maintaining contact with friends, but very few considered that social media would help them achieve educational goals. Pupils do, however, feel that social media helps them to have a sense of belonging to groups and this, perhaps, has some civic potential.

Pupils use social media (principally Facebook, Twitter and Skype) at home and elsewhere, checking at least once each day in order to keep in contact with their friends, talk with them, arrange meetings, find people with similar interests, create new groups and develop confidence. They principally use Facebook (89.6%), Twitter (56.1%) and Skype (50.2%). Some of them also use Tumblr (14.9%), Instagram (10.9%) or other sites (33.9%) (Figure 7.1).

There is a sense of incredulity on the part of pupils if they are asked if anyone does not have access to these technologies.

*Interviewer*: Have you got some pupils here who don't have social media?

*School 3 Teacher*: Who don't have?

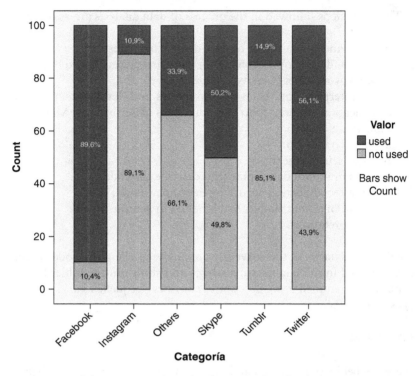

*Figure 7.1* Valid percentage of pupils who use each technology

*Interviewer*: Who don't!

*School 3 Teacher*: I'd think there is a few but not very many . . . I'd think . . . The vast majority have access by mobile phones and . . .

Most of the pupils who said that they were using social media 'all the day' explained this by referring to their use of a smartphone. It was common for pupils to reply: 'All the time. On phone walking home from school' (ID41) or 'Whenever I have it on my phone so notifications come through' (ID93). Some (4.7%) claimed that they use social media at least once per hour: 'Quite often, every 1/2 hour just to check' (ID41) (Figures 7.2, 7.3).

More than half of the pupils use social media mainly to talk (59.1%), and also to be updated on the latest news from their friends (32.7%). Some of the pupils also said that they used it to keep in contact (27.4%), to share photos (5.8%), to give their opinions (4.8%), to arrange meetings (4.8%) and to play games (4.8%). Six pupils said that they used it to spend time when they were bored, and only eight pupils (3.8%) reported that they use it in order to achieve school-related aims.

*Interviewer*: Yeah . . . Why do you think young people use social networks?

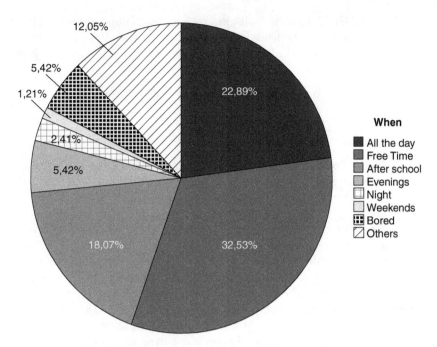

*Figure 7.2* When do they use these technologies?

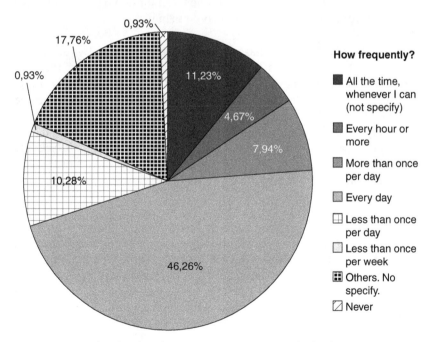

*Figure 7.3* Graph related to the question 'How frequently do they use them?'

*School 3 Girl 2*: Usually . . . It's just to . . . like . . . I don't know . . . Contact friends . . . And just you know talk to friends . . . But usually . . . It's like . . . Social networking are used for that . . . Just friends . . .

*Interviewer*: To communicate with your friends, do you mean?

School 3 Girl 2: Yeah . . .

*Interviewer*: Do you think it can be used for any other goal?

*School 3 Boy 1*: Mm . . . I suppose you can make friends . . . Probably it's not advised to . . . If you aren't in touch with them . . . Yeah . . . I think that yeah . . . it's mostly like talking to friends and . . .

However, it is possible that this personal usage also allows for the development of civic potential. A majority (71.5%) of the pupils consider that social media contributes to their sense of belonging to a group(s) of people, and Figure 7.4 shows that they feel these technologies allow them to know more about the other group members (29.4%), prepare future meetings (25%), feel connected (19.1%) and talk to them (8.8%).

A considerable number suggested that these technologies allow them to interact with new people (finding people with similar interests, 20.6%; and meeting them, 19.1%). For example, one girl explained in the focus groups that she could meet people through Tumblr (a blog site) who have the same problems as she and who would help her.

*School 2 Girl 1*: Yeah! I mean . . . I've got Facebook and Twitter . . . But the one I use the most is Tumblr, which is a blog in kind of . . . and yeah I use that all the time . . . I think . . . Mainly . . . Because it's really enjoyable for me and it's nice to . . . so if . . . You can like . . . talk to people who have similar interests than you . . . And then . . . It's just . . . That I really . . . really like it . . . It's nice . . . And you can feel connected . . . I think because not that many people have Tumblr I saw . . . It feels like it's just a small sort of thing . . . And I like that . . . And it's nice to feel connected to . . . with people . . .

(. . .)

*School 2 Girl 1*: I think it can help some people . . . Especially things like Tumblr . . . I mean people can like . . . post problems on that and then you can find people who are in like . . . the similar situation and so you don't feel so as alone . . . Like . . . And I think that condition really . . . really helps me to know this people, right across the world maybe . . . That I've never met before that kind of . . . do you feel them . . . and do you care about problems . . . And I think it's a big thing . . .

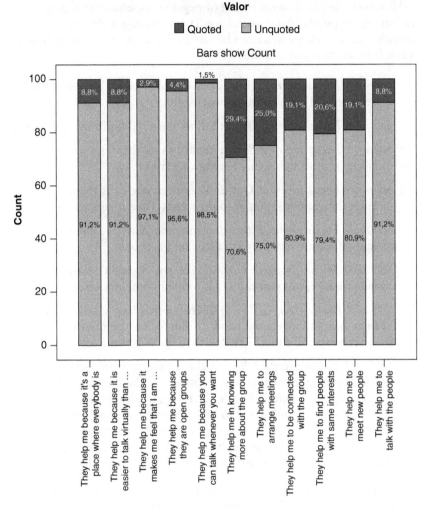

*Figure 7.4* Valid per cent of pupils who said each reason that explains why these technologies help them in be part of a group(s)

The ease of use and the possibility of instilling confidence through social media meant that there is the possibility of bringing people together:

> *School 3 Boy 1:* (. . .) A lot of groups become closer over social networking sites . . . Cause you also you can be with someone like 24/7 and you have like . . . Facebook or something you've access to people . . . to being able to match with people like . . . the most of the time . . . And so that . . . it keeps . . . it keeps people so close together . . . So people is not just a part . . .

However, the pupils were aware of negative aspects of this communication. Some pupils blame social media for causing a decrease in their confidence, or perhaps what can be interpreted as problems that arise as a result of an excess of confidence:

> *School 1 Focus group 2 Boy 1*: But I think it could be some benefits if we never did have social networks sites . . .
>
> *School 1 Focus group 2 Boy 2*: I think we would be more confident!
>
> *School 1 Focus group 2 Boy 1*: Yeah! I think there is a lot of falling-outs happen through social networking sites . . .
>
> *School 1 Focus group 2 Girl 2*: Then everyone calls them a coward because they're not saying it to their face. Then it gets worst . . .
>
> *School 1 Focus group 2 Boy 1*: Sometimes like . . . comments that shouldn't been made, they are made on Facebook . . .
>
> *School 1 Focus group 2 Girl 2*: Like you wouldn't dare say it to someone's face, but you can say it to their computer screen . . .
>
> *School 1 Focus group 2 Boy 1*: There is something you wouldn't say to their face and it gets out hand . . . But for the majority of the time, the Facebook and things like that they do help you a lot . . .
>
> *School 1 Focus group 2 Boy 2*: But I think people would be nice to each other like face-to-face, because it's like they wouldn't have Facebook, they wouldn't like say . . . things like horrible to each other, because they wouldn't say it to each other like to their face . . . They wouldn't do it . . . So, in this times, they do on real life . . . Cause they can do it in the computer first, and so I think we never go to that stage without Facebook and stuff . . .

In short, we suggest that there is frequent use of social media and that, in its connection with identity formation and facilitation of communication, it may have some civic potential. However, there is little evidence available in the data referred to above to support the idea that young people are using social media explicitly for civic purposes or to help them realise educational goals.

## 2   What are the similarities and differences in young people's use of social networking technologies in school and personal contexts?

In summary, there is a rather sceptical approach to the educational value of social media. Approximately half of the pupils feel positive to some extent about social media at school, and in particular about the help that may be generated in relation to homework. But throughout the data there is a clear sense that our pupil respondents quite simply do not connect social media is with school. Teachers are aware of these pupil perceptions.

Those pupils who considered that social media networks were not helpful in terms of the aims of schooling argued that they waste pupils' time (42.3%), that education is not the purpose of social networking sites (30.8%) and that the content of websites is not verified and so is inappropriate for learning (23.1%). There are elements of a more positive stance. Of the pupils surveyed, 7.7% reported that social media is not helpful simply because it is not used in schools (thus implying that use could occur). Those pupils who considered that social media is educationally helpful explained that it can be used in order to do homework (73.3%), assist with the learning of new knowledge (16%), improve communication skills (8%), improve their computer skills (5.3%), develop confidence (2.7%) and allow for the use of videos as educational tools (1.3%).

When interviewed, pupils were asked about the use of social media in regard to schooling goals. Most of them mentioned that social media can be helpful in order to do homework:

> *School 1 Focus group 1 Girl 1*: Yeah! My sister is at university, and I struggle with homework on English or something like that, so I may use Skype or something like that . . . She is not . . . It's not easy to see her, even in the same thing is not easy to see her explaining things and she (even just post sort of her) 6:51 it's like you do this and this so . . . I've done some times, but I wouldn't necessary do it with my friends and probably not likely to do it . . . With family . . .

> *School 1 Focus group 1 Boy 1*: Also like . . . If you forget your homework then most people just go on Facebook, and it's just like ask someone in the class . . .

> *School 2 Girl 1*: Yeah . . . I mean . . . On Facebook sometimes if I am not sure what to do on homework, then I can just say to people what do you do for question three . . . And then . . . I get people who reply to that . . . And that's really . . . really helpful . . .

> *School 2 Girl 2*: We have . . . Just for our year, we have sort of a group . . .

Pupils also reported that they can work in groups through social networking sites and that this was at times regarded more positively than working through conventional means such as through telephone calls.

But most opinions were quite sceptical. A typical response is the following:

> *School 3 Boy 1*: Mm . . . I suppose you can pick up a few bits of the . . . Meet you people, like . . . asking people for question on work or something . . . Yeah, I suppose . . . Sometimes you can but . . .

Furthermore, pupils considered that most of the school activities that can be done using social media can also be done using conventional methods:

> *School 2 Girl 2*: Yeah . . . I don't think . . . But again . . . I don't think it's the only thing you can use . . . I don't think you are limited to just using social networks. I think they are one of many tools . . .

Teachers are aware that pupils use social media, but lack detailed knowledge about what pupils do and whether or not those activities have educational potential:

> *School 2 Teacher*: I think they do, how much they use it, I don't know . . . I wouldn't like to even guess . . . But where they do use it, the levels they may use . . . I don't know . . . It's hard to say . . . I think it would be worth . . . (. . .)

As a result of analysing data in questions 1 and 2 there is an overwhelming sense that pupils regard social media primarily in terms of its social functions and most are negative or sceptical about its educational potential. Given the rather heightened rhetoric about social media and education, this reaction should be of interest to policy makers, academics and practitioners. We need now to explore whether young people regard social media to have potential in relation to civic engagement.

### 3    How do young people perceive their personal use of social media in relation to enhanced citizenship participation and engagement?

There does seem to be civic potential in relation to social media. Although there are some differences of outlook and a range of understanding about what social media can be used for, most pupils (79.3%) (Figure 7.5) consider that social media makes a difference to engagement.

For those pupils (who were in the minority) who were reluctant to see the civic worth of social media there were a variety of reasons given. Some felt that social media was for personal and not civic matters. Approximately 20% of pupils said that they did not agree with developing knowledge that would facilitate engagement in society. Of those surveyed, 62.5% argued that they could not or did not want to learn citizenship knowledge by means of social media because that was not the reason they used these technologies. For instance, one girl wrote 'No, because I mainly use these sites for communication purposes' (ID10) and one boy mentioned 'No it's not like the news you only learn what your friends are doing' (ID27).

Some argued that these technologies do not help with acquiring knowledge relevant to engagement because people would become addicted to

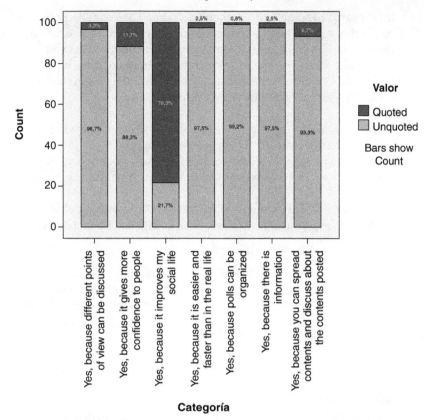

*Figure 7.5* Valid per cent of the positive reasons the pupils gave to the question 'Do you think social networks make a difference to your relationship with others or to your engagement in society?'

networking (e.g. 'You could get addicted to them so it could affect you badly', ID115) and some of them argued, again, that everything that could be learned by means of social media could be also learned outside social networks (e.g. 'I read the newspaper if I want to know about my community or listen to the radio', ID202).

Some pupils reported that information available in social media was not always credible and so it would not contribute to make them a 'good citizen':

*School 1 Focus group 2 Boy 2*: I really would say it make you a citizen . . . Because you can hear stuff, but not necessarily a good citizen . . . Cause some of the stuff that gets posted is just rumours and isn't true . . . And so if you start talking like that, you can become like a citizen . . .

*School 1 Focus group 2 Girl 2*: People find easier to spread stuff . . . They find easy to say . . . Like . . . Instead of saying it to like someone's ear they'd say it to someone's Facebook account. They would say so-and-so did this instead of saying so-and-so did this to their face. Cause then they know, like you can just hide your post and pretend that you never said it, like when you say it in words, you can't take it back if you've said it and like. If someone says you've said this, the person that said it could then just go 'no I didn't' and delete the post.

However, the majority of pupils asserted the positive potential of social media for civic engagement.

There is some suggestion that connections with friends and engagement in society might be closely linked in the minds of young people.

*Interviewer*: OK, last question guys . . . Do you think that social media can help you to participate, to be engaged in your community?

*School 1 Focus group 1 All*: Yeah . . .

*School 1 Focus group 1 Girl 2*: Yeah, definitely . . . Because if you have more chances to communicate, then you have more chances to be a part of it . . . So . . . Like . . . If you use social networking sites you may cross your community . . . So if you have chances to speak out about things, you may have chances to . . .

Pupils were asked if they thought their citizenship knowledge would increase as a result of using social media and most of the pupils (80.1%) agreed with that idea.

There were particular emphases to the sorts of connection that were made between social media and civic engagement. There was acceptance of the suggestion that knowledge of what is happening in society could improve.

Of the pupils surveyed, 63.6% reported that they could participate more in society thanks to social networks because they could be more informed. This emphasis on the role of information was interesting. Some pupils in the surveys (16.8%) and also in the focus group also characterised social media as being a source of information. For instance one girl said in a focus group interview:

*School 3 Girl 2*: Oh yeah . . . Definitely, because if you can, to find out something that is currently happening in a political party, you can search it out on Facebook or something . . . And find pages straight away and information about it . . . Cause without it, I don't think it'd be that easy or that we'd bother to do it . . .

Although just 15% of the pupils reported in their questionnaire responses that social media could help them to learn about other people and cultures, in most of the focus group interviews, pupils reported this to be relevant and possible (Figure 7.6).

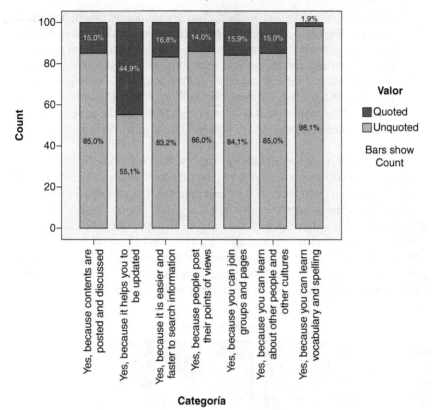

*Figure 7.6* Valid per cent of the positive reasons the pupils gave to the question
'Do you think that social networks can help you in having more
knowledge related to your community, your country and the world?'

*School 3 Boy 1*: (. . .) It would just be easy, you can pretty much
make a friend in Australia, be aware of what he thinks about the
Australian like . . . presidential or something . . . And so . . . I think
with time it will grow in and become easier . . . It still is quite easy at
the moment to manage but in time especially you can . . . It's quite of
possibilities . . . of quite big . . . for you be able to do . . .

(. . .)

*Interviewer*: And do you think you can learn something about their
culture or their country?

*School 3 Boy 1*: Oh, yeah . . . Definitely . . . definitely . . . Cause you
are . . . Like I've said on Facebook especially . . . You got . . . you got
people with walls and stuff who post different things and you may
be and you may have a friend who is going out to holiday to a different country . . . Like taking pictures and posting on there . . . And

so that . . . you like I've said . . . You are schooling through without sort of knowing . . . You're learning cause you looking at it, for different people who are posting in it . . . You're looking at pictures and you're learning about that different cultures . . . Like going on holidays to look a different country . . . You, without knowing it, you're learning and picking up things by looking at what people are doing and . . . Also from a person . . . a person from a different culture or a different country posting . . . you feel that you're learning as well . . .

But this emphasis on knowledge was not the only thing highlighted by pupils. Of those surveyed, 74.4% pupils considered that social media could help them participate more in their communities and society and they gave a variety of reasons why they thought this would occur (Figure 7.7).

It seems that school pupils were seeing the spreading of information both as an act of participation and as a creation of a space in which participation could occur. For some focus group participants, social media represent a sort of democratic process where everybody has the same right to participate and the same chances to be listened to.

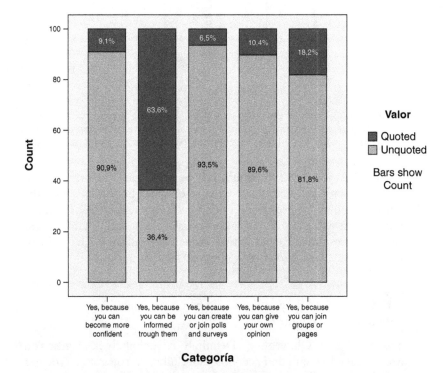

*Figure 7.7* Valid per cent of the positive reasons the pupils gave to the question 'Do you think that social networks can help you participate in your community and in society?'

*Interviewer*: (. . .) Do you think that this social media can contribute that you can participate more in your society?

*School 3 Boy 1*: Oh yeah! Definitely . . . cause you think on a . . . On . . . In Facebook, for example, everyone . . . everyone is . . . is . . . virtual profile . . . and so no one it's more important than someone else . . . And so . . . Everyone . . . Everyone gets heard not like basically . . . It's not like no one gets heard or anything . . . Everyone . . . Everyone gets their community across . . . and so everyone is learning from other people . . . And so it's like a big collaboration sort of side web . . . Where people just learn of each other . . .

Thus the data we have gathered in relation to our third research question suggests that pupils perceive the potential to enhance civic engagement by means of social media. However, it is interesting to reflect on the differences between pupils within this generally positive reaction to social media and civic engagement. Although the evidence is not entirely clear it seemed that the biggest users of social media see the greatest civic potential. Those who do not use it as frequently as others are more likely to downplay its potential. A question thus remains as to whether these differences tell us anything about the nature of the effect of using social media in relation to civic engagement or whether those who are already inclined to engage will do so with whatever means are available.

We now need to turn to the issue of how current usage and possible future usage might allow for an educational perspective to be developed through the use of social media.

## 4   In what ways are social media effectively used in school-based citizenship education programmes?

In summary, we suggest that teachers are convinced about the importance of social media, make some limited educational use of it currently and perceive significant barriers that lie in the way of further development. This is not to suggest that teachers do not wish to see increased educational use of social media or feel that it will not happen. It is nevertheless interesting to contrast these findings about limited usage with the rhetoric of those who champion the educational value of social media.

Just one of the three schools that took part in this research used social media explicitly in its school-based citizenship education programmes. The teacher explained how this project was working:

*Interviewer*: Do you use social media in your classes?

*School 3 Teacher*: I do . . . I do yeah! I do in citizenship and the Key Stage 4 classes . . . So Year 10 and 11 they use social media cause we do campaigning so we use it as part of the campaigns and they would set off Facebook and sites of them, from a view of online petitions . . . to get people be aware of the causes they've chosen . . . Not so much Twitter, to be honest . . . But definitely, Facebook we use it for online petitions . . .

*Interviewer*: And how does it work?

*School 3 Teacher*: So . . . To be honest . . . Because we don't have so much access in the school, most of them we do that at home . . . So they would choose to do that in addition to what we do in school, in lessons . . . So they will do things, for example in the school . . . We'd do, we do Amnesty International causes and the people would write letters and do posters and speeches on the samples and things like that . . . And then on their own, they'd go and set off the Facebook so the people . . . Where they would give information about Amnesty case and then they may advertise that in the school and get people to follow . . . And they sign online petitions, they set up on those as well.. So . . . It's about this kind of (. . .) And we do use it certainly in citizenship . . .

*Interviewer*: In which is the last goal of these activities? Why did you choose to work with social media instead of doing it in a more conventional way?

*School 3 Teacher*: I guess because of the impact, because the amount of people you can reach is just so much greater, so many greater . . . people you can reach them, than by using conventional, sort of posters they would just put up around the school . . . And . . . But . . . Obviously things like Facebook and Twitter they get much . . . Great coverage . . . And so . . .

(. . .)

In this case the teacher reported using social media with citizenship education aims in one part of the citizenship education course in Years 10 and 11. The activity consists of pupils using Facebook to post online polls related to Amnesty International campaigns they are working with, and it works as an additional activity to that which pupils do at home.

In the independent school, one teacher decided to work with social media in order to make connections between her pupils and those in Russian schools and to encourage discussions about local problems. The pupils were again Year 10, Year 11 and also Year 12. However, in this case the activity was not explicitly related to citizenship aims even though the relationship can be suggested. In that case the school uses IT to communicate with pupils and parents but the communication is one-directional. The same situation is described in School 3, where the school sends tweets but it is not possible for others to comment on these tweets.

*School 3 Teacher*: We use it . . . sort of . . . I think, I've said before, like Twitter feeds we do use it to promote things the school is doing, or give information to parents as well . . . So . . . For example, if we go on a school trip, we may send back photos and information about how trip is going so parents can keep update with . . . How the trip is going . . . And if we've got sort of an inset day it will go out on Twitter as well . . . It's at our school website . . . We use a lots of texts phone as well . . . So . . .

*Interviewer*: And are the pupils able to comment if you . . . for instance . . .

*School 3 Teacher*: I don't think so . . . I think it's locked . . . so . . .

*Interviewer*: One direction!

The three teachers were asked if they used social media in order to facilitate work in the school council, to elect representatives or in-other activities related to the decision making process in the school. In all three cases, the teachers responded negatively.

Teachers considered that the lack of availability of technology was a huge hindrance to the use of social media in the schools:

*School 1 Teacher*: It's not really something that we have even thought, because we don't have access to it. So in school, in this building, we don't have wireless internet, we do in that building across there, we don't have the money for laptops, and those kind of things, so at the moment it's not really an issue, the only way I can see it working it would be like a homework task, but again not all our pupils have computers at home. So this few little barriers that we have to be . . . Look to . . . But I do accept . . .

One teacher suggested that social media sites could be used in such matters as homework perhaps by using pupils' smartphones. In spite of this, the schools have different—and not always positive—approaches to the use of smartphones in class.

*School 1 Teacher*: You know a lot of our pupils have got smartphones, a lot of them, you know, could take pictures of their work on their camera phone and email them and print them off . . . or . . . You know, if you need to do some quick research they can use their iPhones . . . You know . . . To a degree, I wouldn't . . . at least sixth formers or seventeen–eighteen years old do that, but the youngest pupils we don't really want them to be on their phones in lessons . . .

According to the teachers' perception, some of their colleagues or themselves are reluctant to use social media in their classes. This concern is related to several reasons. Teachers reported that some teachers were not confident with social media technologies and that they were concerned that their pupils knew more about them than themselves. Teachers reported that their concerns related to the fact that their work could be constantly observed and assessed. For instance, Teacher 2 explained:

> *School 2 Teacher*: (. . .) I think other people do use it . . . I think that there is a sense in teachers that you do have these . . . It's supposed to be fair technology, and fair in their use and way (. . .) . . . Just the other day, for instance, I was doing a photography project, in Arts, and I was getting to use them and SLR digital camera, sorry . . . and SLR manual camera . . . So it was entirely manual, no digital aspects at all . . . And I said they all . . . You know you can use your phones just to record and then I found myself saying that, but . . . Please, make sure that it just ends up on Facebook because it was just . . . Oh! My Goodness! They are all wearing the (name of school) uniform! But some of the ideas we were looking at . . . We were looking at . . . You know . . . Making small things look big, and big things look small . . . And one of the girls, she was lying across the troll train track, tied up . . . Trying to be, rolled by the train . . . And I though . . . Oh! If that ends up on Facebook, she's got the (name of school) uniform, because of her jacket, you know . . . I could be in serious trouble! And so . . . You know . . . Please make sure that it must in your phone . . . You know . . . This is just to record that . . . I must introduce your friends to record it! So, you have a personal record of your work . . . It must not go on in any other site! And it was . . . Why? And you know . . . And it was . . . You know, they were Year 9 and so they were fourteen and they couldn't understand why, why it wasn't ok for that to be put out there . . . So . . . I think that's our biggest fear . . . That something could be misinterpreted so easily . . . And that makes you think! So perfect example . . . Some ordinary thing . . . And you know . . . You know . . . Used as a tool, but they could absolutely be putting out there on, using Web 2.0 technology . . . And it could be totally misinterpreted and misconstrued and you could . . . You know . . . You could be without a job . . .

Finally, teachers' concerns are related to the boundary between their personal and professional lives.

> *School 1 Teacher*: I think that as teachers we are very wary of it, in terms of the boundary between, you know as a teacher using social media with the pupils, the boundary between school and outside of school becomes a little bit blurred and I think that I would never ever be friends with a pupil, you know on Facebook, even you know . . . all our pupils have an email account, and if I have to contact pupils via email I always do, you know in school time, because I think social media can be great in terms of having an instant response . . . as a

teacher, I would be wary of that kind of relation, relationship with pupils, you know . . .

*Interviewer*: The professional role, you mean . . . ?

*School 1 Teacher*: Yeah, the professional role . . .

One teacher did report having a social media profile and suggested that private and professional life can be unlinked by means of using the privacy sections. She also claimed that the use of social media in her school did not cause more problems than those associated with the use of other forms of communication.

*School 3 Teacher*: Yes! Yeah . . . I do, yeah . . . So it's just privacy sections . . . So I make me sure they are all settled at the highest levels and we have very strict rules and guidelines about . . . You know . . . Not being friends with pupils or . . . As I've said, the departments ones . . . who have department Twitter feeds they definitely locked so . . . So . . . People can look at them, and followed them . . . So they can get the access and get and get the benefits of being able to access them . . . But they can't, as I've said, comment and link on those . . .

*Interviewer*: Have you got any kind of troubles using these technologies?

*School 3 Teacher*: Mmmm . . . I mean . . . We haven't had any massive one . . . But I think there've been one or two instances of Facebook being in issues out the school suddenly, and that's build into school life while somebody is using the negative way patterns to bully somebody and then that's obviously continuing in the school . . . I think we have a couple of issues there . . . Which go on obviously in the school . . . But . . . And again in terms of . . . we've got quite clear guidelines, other people should be aware of that . . . And the mobiles . . . Unless you would be nasty use as part of the . . . part of the lesson . . . by the teacher . . . Then the mobiles should be switched off and in their bags and . . . But they are allowed to use them at the two break times that they have . . . So it's something that the school council work with . . . Y.Z. he set off geography, he work with them and bringing the policy together, the mobiles device policy so . . . So it's quite clear guidelines that people have and then teachers obviously know what they are so . . . Follows a usual procedure if they haven't . . . For example, people refuse to find away . . . Then, basically they just refuse to follow the teachers' instructions then they'd get punishment as anything else they did that . . . involved on not following the instructions . . . So . . . It's done . . . In that way really . . . But, nothing specific other than I've said . . . and issues that's not in the school, but that's come back into school really . . .

All three teachers agreed that in the future social media should play a role in citizenship education. However, the ways they suggested to develop that use were quite diverse. The teacher in School 3 considered that the sort of activities she was working with should form part of this citizenship education programme in the future.

> *School 3 Teacher*: I think definitely . . . And I am going to use the example again, but it's kind of one we use it in the Amnesty, I think, we make something where they can . . . obviously something that is a global issue, cause it's a case that Amnesty is talking about before . . . Somebody will campaign for cases in Mexico and Gambia and China . . . So across the world really . . . So in that aspect, they're also play a part in a international citizens and global citizens really . . . And they . . . Definitely it also encourage them and we'd look at things like politics and we look at manifestos . . . and various as well . . . All the political parties now have, you know, just feeds and Facebook . . . We do encourage them to look at those and particularly we may look at the same manifestos . . . We look at some of the party websites and definitely Facebook and twitters we encourage them to go and look at those . . . So, I think they can play more of a part and I think that looking at the things like in the future we took a . . . about styles of voting, so that's an area that they sort of keen to perhaps introduce some social media into things like voting cause they say they would get more involved if it was done by Facebook and twitters . . . and so . . . I think definitely it can play a part in all of that . . .

According to this teacher, social media should be used in order to take advantage of the impact it has. But for this teacher and also for the teacher in School 1, social media should mainly be used in order to bring pupils closer together with people from diverse contexts who live in the same country, and also with those around the world, in order to create a sense of belonging to a common citizenship.

> *School 1 Teacher*: I suppose it would be interesting if you are getting people from different schools to communicate, because our pupils don't have a great understanding about cultural diversity, I think . . . diversity or these kind of things, we try to discover them in lessons but you need more participants from other schools maybe to engage with that kind of thing . . . So it would be thinking about, so does actually to be a good citizen and what does it mean to be a British citizen?

What seems striking about the above is the awareness of educational potential, the very limited usage and the fear of creating new learning spaces.

## DISCUSSION

In this small-scale research, our data analyses from three schools suggest that most of the pupils investigated are social media users and most of them consider that it can contribute to enhancing peoples' engagement, citizenship knowledge and participation. However there are also some user pupils who consider that social media platforms are not and should not be used in order to achieve these goals. Indeed, those who are not social media users consider that, rather than providing an improvement, it has some negative effects.

Some teachers seem enthusiastic about the use of social media as an educational tool but others show a considerable amount of concern. Some of this wariness is related to a perception of power loss and some of it is based on the current situation of IT infrastructures at their schools. In spite of this, all of them consider that social media technologies will increase in importance in education in the future.

Data analysis also suggests different applications of these social media with citizenship education aims. First, social media sites have several implications for engagement. Engagement can be related to identity, and some of the 'sense of belonging' qualities that pupils attribute to some school activities (sports, clubs, school council) can be transferred easily to the use of social media as an educational tool: e.g. sharing a purpose, considering everybody's work relevant, taking decisions. Moreover, according to the data analysis, some pupils already describe a feeling of global citizenship that is developing through social media platforms. For these respondents communications technologies allow them to have an explicit 'place in the world'. These 'talking activities' could enhance pupils' identity in relation to their nearer contexts (e.g. schools, towns), but also in relation to farther and wider contexts, such as achieving a global identity. Second, social media also could increase pupils' knowledge about citizenship by means of some of the activities mentioned previously, but also by searching, discussing and commenting on some of the content posted on these sites. Finally, pupils and teachers also reported the links between social media sites and citizenship participation. According to most of them, social media could contribute not only by informing people about events and proposals and being an organisational tool for some movements, but also by providing a democratic way for pupils to give their own opinions and to spread their views.

What needs to be done in the future is to continue to explore the general consensus in the academic community about the potential of social media in citizenship education (e.g. Bennett, 2009; Middaugh, 2012). We are (together with the pupils and teachers who have responded to our questions) extremely positive about the ways in which social media could create new learning spaces for civic engagement. However, we need to know a good deal more about the reality of life in most schools, as opposed to the highly publicised few instances of creativity (and we need to go beyond our small-scale work). We should not ignore those people (teachers and pupils) who deliberately abstain from using the social web. We need to explore with teachers the nature of power relations in learning and teaching situations (Buckingham & Rodríguez-Hoyos, 2013) and we need to do much more to disentangle the complex picture of cause and effect that may be emerging from our work: principally, does social media attract those who are already engaged and could such participation serve to reflect existing or new forms of citizenship education?

## REFERENCES

Beldarrain, Y. (2006). 'Distance education trends: Integrating new technologies to foster student interaction and collaboration', *Distance Education,* 27:2, pp. 139–153.

Bennett, L. (Ed.) (2008). *Civic Life Online: Learning how Digital Media Can Engage Youth.* Cambridge, MA: MIT Press.

Bergman, M. M. (2008). Introduction: Whither mixed methods? In M. M. Bergman, *Advances in Mixed Methods Research. Theories and Applications.* London: Sage.

Biesta, G. (2012). Mixed methods. In J. Arthur, M. Waring, R. Coe & L.V. Hedges (Eds), *Research Methods and Methodologies in Education.* London: Sage.

Buckingham, D. & Rodríguez-Hoyos, C. (2013). Learning about power and citizenship in an online virtual world, *Comunicar,* 20:40, pp.49–57, ISSN: 1134-3478. doi: 10.3916/C40-2013-02-05.

Cohen, L., Manion, L. & Morrison, K. (2011). *Research Methods in Education.* London: Routledge.

Creswell, J. W. (1998). *Qualitative Inquiry and Research Design. Choosing among Five Traditions.* Thousand Oaks, CA: Sage.

Davies, I., Bennett, L., Loader, B., Mellor, S., Vromen, A., Coleman, S., & Xenos, M. (2012). Four questions about the educational potential of social media for promoting civic engagement. In *Citizenship Teaching and Learning,* 7:3, pp. 293–306.

Johnson, R. B., Onwuegbuzie, A. J., & Turner, L. A. (2007). Towards a definition of mixed methods research. *Journal of Mixed Methods Research,* 1:2, pp. 112–133.

Kerr, D., Lopes, J., Nelson, J., White, K., Cleaver, E. & Benton, T. (2007). *Vision versus Pragmatism: Citizenship in the Secondary School Curriculum in England. Citizenship Education Longitudinal Study: Fifth Annual Report (DfES Research Report 845),* London: DfES.

Livingstone, S., Bober, M. & Helsper, E. (2005). Internet literacy among children and young people: Findings from the UK Children Go Online Project. London, LSE Research Online. Available at http://eprints.lse.ac.uk/archive/00000397 (accessed 15 October 2013).

Merien, S., Hooghe, M. & Quintelier, E. (2010). Inequalities in non-institutionalised forms of political participation: A multi level analysis of 25 countries. *Political Studies,* 58, 187–213.

Middaugh, E. (2012). Service and activism in the digital age: Supporting youth engagement in public life. DML, Central Working Papers. www.civicsurvey.org/CERG_Publications.html (accessed 15 October 2013).

Miles, M. B. & Huberman, A.M. (1994). *An Expanded Sourcebook Qualitative Data Analysis.* Thousand Oaks, CA: Sage.

Morozov, E. (2011). *The Net Delusion: How Not to Liberate the Eorld.* London: Allen Lane.

Ofsted (2004). *ICT in Schools. The Impact of Government Initiatives Five Years on (HMI 2050),* London: HMSO.

Selwyn, N. & Gorard, S. (2003). Reality bytes: Examining the rhetoric of widening educational participation via ICT, *British Journal of Educational Technology,* 34:2, pp. 169–181.

Smith, F., Hardman, F. & Higgins, S. (2006). 'The impact of interactive whiteboards on teacher–pupil interaction in the National Literacy and Numeracy Strategies', *British Educational Research Journal,* 32:3, pp. 443–457.

# Part III

# Agency, Mobilization and the Voice of the Young Citizen

# 8 'The Outraged Young'

## Young Europeans, Civic Engagement and the Social Media in a Time of Crisis

*James Sloam*

### INTRODUCTION

Public involvement in traditional political institutions has declined significantly over the past few decades, leading to what some have seen as a crisis in citizenship (Putnam 2000; Macedo *et al.* 2005; Stoker 2006). In Europe, we have witnessed a large decline in voter turnout (Franklin 2004; Fieldhouse *et al.* 2007) and a dramatic fall in the membership of political parties (Van Biezen *et al.* 2012). These trends are most striking amongst young people, who have become alienated from mainstream electoral politics (Sloam 2012, 2013a). In austerity Europe, young people have, furthermore, been forced to bear the brunt of the global financial crisis and sovereign debt crises: from worsening levels of child poverty, to spiralling youth unemployment, to cuts in youth services and education budgets, to increased university tuition fees. Young Europeans' lives have become more precarious and their futures increasingly bleak in the current climate of low growth and falling public spending (OECD 2013). This has led to a second and more dramatic loss of confidence in politicians and political parties to add to the slow-burning participatory crisis in electoral politics.

Nevertheless, there is overwhelming evidence to show that young people are not apathetic about 'politics'—they have their own views and engage in democracy in a wide variety of ways relevant to their everyday lives (Norris 2003; Marsh *et al.* 2007; Spannring *et al.* 2008; Dalton 2009).[1] Thus, the rise and proliferation of protest politics amongst young Europeans in the aftermath of the global financial crisis is hardly surprising (Sloam 2013a). In Europe, the political mobilisation of the 'outraged' young (Hessel 2011) has taken many different forms: from mass demonstrations of the *indignados* against political corruption and youth unemployment in Spain, to the Occupy movement against the excesses of global capitalism, to the growth in support for new political parties (such as the German Pirate Party and the Italian Five-Star Movement) that rail against the elitism of established political parties. Young people's politics has diffused through multiple networks, across borders and continents—from North Africa to Europe to the United States and back again—to demand political change (Bennett and Segerberg 2013; Castells 2012). This chapter focuses on the diversity of youth participation during this current 'cycle of protest' (Tarrow 1998), exploring how young people's politics manifests itself through diverse repertoires of participation across multiple arenas of political action and different civic–political cultures.

In particular, the chapter examines the role that the Internet and new media have played in the political mobilisation of young Europeans. Why have we seen such an explosion of participation through the Internet and the social media in recent years? Bennett and Segerberg (2012: 739, 748) write of the emergence of a new 'logic of connective action . . . based on personalized content sharing across media networks', whereby 'formal organizations are losing their grip on individuals, and group ties are being replaced by large-scale fluid social networks'. These networks form the basis of alternative modes of political participation that match younger citizens' preferences for non-institutionalised, horizontal engagement. For example, it is much more attractive to sign an online petition, forwarded by a friend, on online 'snooping' than to actively support the broad programme of a top-down organisation like a political party.

The point here is that recent crises—of disillusionment with politicians, of anger at corporate greed, of discontent with government cuts in public services and benefits, of frustration with youth unemployment—have created the ideal conditions for *connective action* amongst an ideal target group: young, highly educated, technologically savvy citizens. With these ideal conditions for connective action, we have witnessed a *quickening of political participation,* whereby the new media enables a dramatic speeding up of political mobilisation by: a) acting as a real-time filter for alternative politics, where only the most resonant ideas rise to the surface e.g. 'the outraged young', 'we are the 99%!'; and b) radically reducing communication costs (Bimber *et al.* 2005) for participation in new political movements. These new movements often take on hybrid forms with both an online and an offline presence (Castells 2012; Chadwick 2013). This chapter emphasises the importance of this hybridity (of media systems and arenas of engagement).

Although one can make some general claims about the current wave of youth protest, it is important to put these rich but diverse forms of political engagement into context. The chapter draws upon four case studies: two largely informal and non-institutionalised movements—the Spanish *indignados* (outraged young) or 15 March Movement (M15M) and the Portuguese Geração à Rasca (desperate generation) or 12 March Movement (M12M); and two nascent political parties—Beppe Grillo's Five-Star Movement (5SM) in Italy and the German Pirate Party (Piratenpartei). These case studies have interesting similarities but important differences with regard to the depth of the economic and political crises they were responding to (in Spain, Portugal, Italy and Germany), how the movements came into being and the nature of their political mobilisation (from demonstrations and occupations to political representation). Three common features of the M15M, the M12M, the 5SM and the Pirate Party are their prominent use of the Internet and new media, their attractiveness to highly educated young people and their issue-based (rather than programmatic) appeal.

## CHANNELLING DIVERSITY: EMERGING REPERTOIRES AND ARENAS OF POLITICAL PARTICIPATION

The lives of young Europeans have changed quite considerably over recent decades. Younger citizens are increasingly faced by a 'risk society' (Beck 1992) in which they must negotiate their own way and construct their own identities (social, economic and political) within a network society (Castells 2010). The transition from youth to adulthood has become more staggered (Arnett 2004; Furlong & Cartmel 2007): Europeans on average stay in education longer, leave home, marry and have children later and take longer to acquire 'permanent' (if often precarious) employment (European Commission 2009). The concept of 'risk' is best illustrated by the uncertainty of a changing labour market—even in good times, there is nowadays little prospect of a *job for life*.

These changes have led to the individualisation of young people's lives—the breakdown of traditional social mores and the increasing fluidity of identities defined by social networks. The individualisation of modern society has, in turn, led to the individualisation of politics (Giddens 1991; Bennett 1998)—the growing prominence of 'lifestyle politics', 'identity politics' and (in terms of political participation) personal action frameworks. These changes have important consequences for political participation. Today's young Europeans can be characterised as 'stand-by citizens' (Amnå and Ekman 2013), who have a preference for intermittent, non-institutionalised, horizontal forms of engagement in issues that have relevance to their everyday lives (Bang 2003; Marsh *et al.* 2007).

Voting is still the most common mode of engagement in established European democracies, but youth turnout has declined significantly in recent years (Fieldhouse *et al.* 2007; Sloam 2013a) as repertoires of participation have become more diverse. The existing literature on participation has highlighted increasing public involvement in petitions, boycotts and demonstrations since the 1970s (Norris 2002; Inglehart & Welzel 2005). However, detailed analysis shows that these forms of engagement are just one part of a broader spectrum of participation. Van Deth *et al.* (2007), in their study of 'citizenship and involvement in Europe', employ a much more comprehensive battery of political activities (see also Pattie *et al.* 2004) and find that two less commonly surveyed modes of engagement, 'donating money' and 'buying certain products' ('buycotts'), were the second and fourth most common types of participation (Teorell *et al.* 2007). With declining youth participation in electoral politics and increasing engagement in alternative forms of participation, young people's repertoires of political action have become more heterogeneous than is the case for older generations (Sloam 2013a).

As repertoires of participation have become more diverse, so have the arenas in which they take place. With the growth and proliferation of non-electoral forms of politics, citizens have sought to make their voices heard across many different platforms (beyond formal politics). In this context, non-governmental organisations have become more important channels of participation (Norris 2002), but so too have more individualised forms of political action such as consumer politics (Stolle *et al.* 2005). In reality, individualised forms of political engagement and organised political action can operate in tandem (Bennett & Segerberg 2013). Indeed, a defining feature of the current wave of youth protest has been the use of *hybrid public spaces* (Castells 2012). On the one hand, these movements have focused on the occupation of physical locations of key symbolic value—from Egypt's Tahrir Square to Madrid's Puerta del Sol to Zuccotti Park in Manhattan to Gezi Park in Istanbul. On the other hand, the Internet and the new social media have provided an invaluable tool for connecting and mobilising young people to become active in these movements (Kaldor and Selchow 2013).

In this regard, new technologies have become wedded to (and have often transformed) existing forms of participation across the broad spectrum of political participation (Banaji *et al.* 2009; Pew Research Center 2013). The explosion of online petitions is a good example of where the Internet has enhanced opportunities for political engagement (Earl & Schussman 2008). Banaji and her colleagues (2009), in their study of political websites in Europe, highlight the importance of 'civic sharing' in online youth participation. Civic sharing is central to the recent *quickening* of youth participation, enabling the dramatic sifting through of ideas in real time, whereby the most resonant ideas rapidly rise to the surface. Once again, this process is facilitated by the low cost of online communication.

The following analysis of the four case studies highlights the quickening of political participation in a time of crisis. Young, highly educated 'stand-by citizens' (Amnå & Ekman 2013) have become *activated* by these crises (of youth unemployment, of frustration with politics and public policy, of anger with corporate greed) into 'digitally networked action' utilising new technology platforms (Bennett & Segerberg 2013). The following sections look at how participation takes place in a time crisis—how young people are mobilised and how this manifests itself in political action—across the case studies.

## TAKING THE SQUARE: THE 'OUTRAGED' AND 'DESPERATE' GENERATION

The protests of the 'outraged' and 'desperate' generation that flourished so vividly in the central squares of Madrid and Lisbon in 2011 were the clear expression of frustration and anger with a political and economic class that had led Spain and Portugal to the brink of political and economic collapse. By 2011, it was also obvious that the younger generations would have to bear the brunt of these crises. According to Eurostat (2013) figures, in the four years from 2007 to 2011 youth unemployment (the proportion of young people looking for a job that are unemployed), jumped from 18.2% to 46.4% in Spain and from 20.4% to 30.1% in Portugal. The youth unemployment ratio (the proportion of all young people who are unemployed) rose from 8.7% to 19% in Spain and from 6.9% to 11.7% in Portugal during the same period. Economic crisis was accompanied by political crisis, with the emergence of governments that were fixated on the reduction of public spending. In 2011, the socialist administrations of Spain (Prime Minister Zapatero) and Portugal (Prime Minister Socrates) both fell after trying to implement swingeing austerity measures, but were replaced by governments (under Rajoy in Spain and Coehlo in Portugal) that only deepened planned cuts in public spending.[2] Thus, there appeared to be no political alternative to this economic course. In both countries austerity had a particularly large impact on youth—from falling education budgets, to reduced unemployment benefits, to the closure of many youth leisure facilities. So, in a very immediate sense, the relevance of politics for the everyday lives of young Spaniards and young Portuguese was impossible to ignore (Taibo 2013).

Although the protests of young people in Spain and Portugal sprang from similar political and economic crises, the countries have quite different participatory cultures and traditions of protest. Pooled European Social Survey data from 2002 to 2008 shows that, in comparison to other countries in Western Europe, Spain has a healthy participatory culture (Sloam 2013b). Furthermore, Spaniards participated in demonstrations at higher rates than did the populations of any other 'old EU15' states (before the financial crisis, 27% of young Spaniards had taken part in a demonstration in the previous year). Of particular note were the protests against Spanish involvement in Iraq.[3] By contrast, youth participation in Portugal is relatively low across eight political activities (including voting and protest activities)—lowest of all the EU15 countries and about half the rate of youth participation in Spain (Fernandes 2012; Sloam 2013b).[4] Nevertheless, in both countries the youth protests that emerged in 2011 were united in their rejection of existing civil society groups (Taibo 2013). In Portugal, it could be argued that the digitally networked action of young people filled a void in a country with weak levels of participation in traditional political institutions (Baumgarten 2013). In Spain, however, the protestors made the deliberate choice to work outside the trade unions (and other established groups with whom they shared a similar cause), to horizontally network their own participatory activities rather than fall under the control of existing institutions. The omnipresent crises led to the rise of two significant movements, operating outside of formal networks, that enjoyed the support of activists *and* of the general populations in these two countries.

The largely young and well educated (and mostly female) Spanish and Portuguese protestors (Anduiza *et al.* 2013) sprang to life in real time through social networks in response to the political and economic crises that touched their everyday lives (Estanque *et al.* 2013). In this sense, the new social media acted as a catalyst for the *quickening* (acceleration and intensification) of political participation. The political objectives of the two movements shared many features—the desire for: more transparent forms of politics and greater use of direct democracy; an end to austerity and an investment in measures to boost youth employment; government regulation of 'corporate greed'; and the implementation of measures to address socio-economic inequalities (DRY 2013; Estanque *et al.* 2013; Geração à Rasca 2013; Taibo 2013).

Both M12M and M15M made use of hybrid media systems and public spaces. The movements were founded online, and new technologies provided the main arena for the sharing of information and the mobilisation (through social networks) of participants (Anduiza *et al.* 2013). However, the occupation of real-world spaces—through demonstrations and protest camps—became the key participatory focus of the movements. Here, the relationship between these hybrid systems and forums and the *sequencing* of these participatory acts is of great interest. In these instances, the logic of connective action privileged the online start-up and mobilisation of the protests with a real-world participatory focus that— in turn—was sustained through the new social media.

In Spain, the protests of 15 May 2011 can be traced back to a call from the digital platform Real Democracy Now! (Democracia Real Ya!) for political action. In its manifesto, this group drew upon a common sense of grievance to invoke political action:

> Some of us have clearly defined ideologies, others are apolitical, but we are all concerned and angry about the political, economic and social outlook which we see around us: corruption among politicians, businessmen, bankers leaving us helpless, without a voice . . . For all of the above, I am outraged.
>
> (DRY 2013)

In January 2011, Real Democracy Now! asked social networks and forums to unite and take to the streets, and thus acted as a central node in the protest network.[5] Twenty to fifty thousand mostly young people took to the streets in Madrid on 15 May (alongside demonstrations in many other Spanish cities), marching to the central squares to declare and highlight their grievances. The heavy-handed police response to these mostly peaceful protests escalated the situation, leading to the outbreak of violence. After the demonstrations, hundreds of protestors headed to the Puerta del Sol. Their subsequent eviction by the police, led to the call—via Twitter, Facebook and SMS (moving beyond the DRY platform)—for the mass occupation of the main squares of Spanish cities until 22 May, the date of upcoming national elections. Thus, the elections also provided an important focus. The occupation of the square by thousands of young Spaniards, in Madrid in particular, was supported by the on-the-ground organisation of food and sanitation as well as the use of live webcams (through the website Upstream.tv) to publicise the cause. Although the occupation gradually dispersed over several months, Puerta del Sol remained at the heart of the *indignados* movement. And the M15M channelled its energies into a series of further actions, including a mass march to Madrid in June 2011 and a demonstration of over half a million people in support of the 15 October 2011 global day of protest.

In Portugal, the 2011 protests of the so-called *desperate generation* can be traced back to the performance of a song, 'How silly am I?', by the group Deolinda, that directly addressed the frustrations of young (educated) Portuguese. The singer sang of her experiences:

> I'm lucky just to be an intern . . . what a stupid world, where to be a slave you have to study . . . I'm from the generation living with their parents . . . I'm from the generation 'can't take it any more', the situation has been going on far too long, and I'm not stupid.
> (Deolinda 2013)

Immediately the song struck a chord with young people across Portugal and became a big hit on YouTube. It inspired four young friends to set up a Facebook event calling for a peaceful demonstration to highlight the issues of youth unemployment and precarious job contracts for a generation that felt it had no voice (Geração à Rasca 2013). This call to arms, networked through various online media, led directly to the demonstrations that took place on 12 March 2011 of hundreds and thousands of (mostly young) citizens in Lisbon, Porto and several smaller cities. As in Spain, these protests became intertwined with the political fate of the governing parties. Socrates resigned as prime minister, after failing to achieve parliamentary support for further austerity measures, less than two weeks after the demonstrations. The 12 March protest marked the foundation of a broader M12M movement (formed in April 2011) that became involved in a series of activities—linked to the Spanish *indignados* and the global Occupy movement—such as the occupation of Rossio Square in Lisbon (May 2011) and participation in the 15 October day of global protest.

The logic of connective action appears to have been particularly important in Portugal in filling the relative vacuum in political engagement (Baumgarten 2013). However, in both Spain and Portugal, the M15M and the M12M made a deliberate point of not working with or through established political institutions such as the trade unions, which might otherwise have been seen as natural political allies. Another noticeable feature of the two movements was the almost seamless interaction between the real and virtual worlds (Anduiza *et al.* 2013). Online start-ups fed real-world engagement, which—in turn—fed further networking through the social media, e.g. the creation of the 'Forum of the Generations' in Portugal. However, the *indignados* movement in Spain has been better able to maintain its momentum—perhaps thanks to a healthy indigenous participatory culture. Real Democracy Now! still (in October 2013) maintains a strong following with over half a million Facebook likes and more than quarter of a million Twitter followers. This dwarfs the online audience of any of the M12M platforms in Portugal.

Another important aspect of the M12M and the M15M was the international dimension of the protest movements. This was clear for all to see. The Spanish *indignados* were directly influenced by the initial Portuguese demonstrations, as well as by other recent movements. In reference to the 'Arab Spring', the Egyptian flag could be seen flying in Madrid. And, in turn, the occupation of Puerta del Sol was mimicked by the M12M occupation of Rossio Square—indeed, some of the Portuguese protestors referred to themselves as the *Lisbon indignados* (Baumgarten 2013). In both countries, young people were re-energised by the Occupy movement that spread from the United States across Europe, leading to their mass participation in the 15 October 2011 day of action. The Spanish M15M have played a proactive role in this internationalisation process—the 15 October global day of protest was first called for by Real Democracy Now! and the M15M sought to maintain the international momentum through the creation of the international TaketheSquare.net platform (which aims to connect with similar youth protest movements in Europe, the United States, Brazil, Turkey and so on).

## MARCHING THROUGH THE INSTITUTIONS: FROM POPULISM TO PIRACY

The clamour for young people to vent their frustration with political and economic elites not only found its expression through the socially networked demonstrations, occupations and rallies of the outraged young across Europe (and beyond). The emerging political voice of young Europeans was also felt more directly in the political system through the decline in support for mainstream political parties and the rise in support for smaller parties. One consequence has been a growth in political extremism—from the anti-immigrant National

Front in France, to the neo-fascist Golden Dawn in Greece. Young men from less-privileged backgrounds have been particularly attracted to these far-right groups. Another consequence has been the rise of new anti-system parties that offer to do politics in a different way. In this sense, the Italian Five-Star Movement and the German Pirate Party emerged from the same fertile ground, drawing much of their support from highly educated young people (Bartlett *et al.* 2013; Bordignon & Ceccarini 2013; Niedermayer 2013). These two parties are particularly interesting for the purposes of this chapter because of their use of new technologies and apparent commitment to horizontal, networked forms of democratic participation.

However, the levels of political and economic crisis in Germany and Italy are at opposite ends of the spectrum in the European context. In Italy, young people have for decades been excluded by a closed political elite—a system saturated with corruption and nepotism—whereby the dominant political figure over the past two decades, former prime minister Silvio Berlusconi, has regularly become embroiled in court-room battles and out-of-court controversies. Berlusconi's vast media empire is symbolic not only of highly concentrated press ownership but also of the cosy relationship between political and economic elites. Germany has witnessed some long-term disillusion with electoral politics (*Politikverdrossenheit*)—more specifically, the vote for the two largest parties, the Christian Democrats and Social Democrats, has fallen significantly since re-unification in 1990. This has resulted in a significant growth in support for the three smaller parties—the liberal Free Democrats, the socialist Left Party and the Greens. However, any disillusionment with politics amongst the younger generation seems to have been mollified by the diversity of choice within the political system. Thus, youth support for democracy and trust in the political system remains strong (Albert *et al.* 2010).

Youth participation in Germany is supported by a vibrant participatory culture which can boast above-average (in the EU15) levels of participation in electoral and non-electoral forms of politics (Sloam 2013b). Political protest is a common feature of German political life. A number of mass demonstrations have taken place in recent years, including protests against nuclear power (in the wake of the March 2011 Fukushima nuclear disaster), which led to a reversal of government policy on the closure of Germany's nuclear power stations. Although youth participation in Italy is about average among the EU15, this figure is skewed by high voter turnout amongst young people (Sloam 2013b), which may have something to do with the penalties associated with non-voting (i.e. the restriction of entry to public sector jobs). In fact, general disillusionment with the Italian political, business and media elites (discredited by numerous financial and political scandals) is very common.

In Italy, the perilous state of the economy and state indebtedness (approximately 120% of GDP in 2011) forced the Berlusconi government into a €70 billion package of savings measures. In November 2011, after pressure from the markets, Berlusconi was forced to resign. He was replaced by the technocratic administration of former EU Commissioner Mario Monti, who was charged with restoring the country's debt to sustainable levels. Even before the financial crisis, Italy was dogged by persistently high levels of youth unemployment and low social mobility. The post-2008 sovereign debt crisis made a bad situation worse.[6] According to Eurostat (2013) figures, youth unemployment rose from 20.3% in 2007 to 29.1% in 2011, while the youth unemployment ratio rose from 6.3% to 8.1% during the same period. In Germany, by contrast, the economy bounced back quickly after 2008–9 to deliver export-led growth in 2010.[7] Thus, Germany was the only EU country that managed to significantly *decrease* youth unemployment between 2007 and 2011, from 11.9% to 9.9% (Eurostat 2013). The youth employment ratio also fell, from 6.1% to 4.5%, during this period (ibid.).

The Five Star Movement (5SM) and the German Pirate Party were not founded as a direct consequence of the global financial crisis (even if the crisis was particularly useful in accelerating the emergence of the 5SM). In a sense, both parties were born of the slow-burning crisis in electoral politics—the long-term decline in electoral turnout and support (and membership) for mainstream political parties. Both were able to reach out to young, highly educated (mostly male), technologically savvy citizens (Bartlett *et al.* 2013) who felt alienated or repelled by mainstream parties and politicians—through the new media and social networks. And, in both cases, the parties have also been able to attract many non-voters (Bartlett *et al.* 2013; Niedermayer 2013).

The central aims of the two parties are similar in a number of key features. The aims of the 5SM, articulated in Grillo's blogs and online in his so-called 'non-statute' (5SM) centred on the overturning of the political and media establishment—'the two casts' (Bordignon & Ceccarini 2013). But, as the movement expanded it began to embrace a wider range of issues (articulated by Grillo), from better internet connections, to greater government transparency, to universal healthcare and environmental protection. The *raison d'etre* of the German Pirate Party is clearly established within the realms of new technologies. Niedermayer (2013) emphasises how the party has tried to portray itself as the defender of citizens' rights in the digital age. The Pirate Party advocates a free Internet (free from government restrictions, and cost-free downloads), transparent politics, direct democracy and (more recently) a minimum wage (Neumann and Fritz 2012).

The 5SM (founded in 2009) is centred on the person and personality of Beppe Grillo, a well-known comedian whose stand-up routine highlighted and mocked the corruption and cronyism within the political and business worlds. For Grillo, the use of the new media became central to his organisation to circumnavigate the Berlusconi-dominated *old* media, which he viewed with as much distrust as politicians themselves. As the leader of a major political party, he is distinct in not giving interviews to any of the Italian print and broadcast media. In 2005, Grillo set up a blog, www.beppegrillo.it, to serve as a mouthpiece to discuss political and social problems. This blog soon became one of the most popular sites in Italy and played a central role in the growth of Grillo's movement, acting as 'a shop window to recruit interested passers-by' (McDonnell 2013). However, the key to the success of the 5SM has also been the interaction between the online and the offline (ibid.). Grillo called on followers to meet up to discuss the issues raised in his blog and act on them in their local communities. Working through meetup.com, these groups were a great success, and by the time of writing (October 2013) had expanded to a network of over 150,000 activists—covering almost all major Italian towns and cities.[8] These meet-up groups, in turn, helped to sustain the growth of the movement online. By 2013, Grillo could boast over a million Twitter followers and Facebook likes. These activities were also supported by the organisation of 'V-Days' (literally 'fuck-off days')—'a message directed in particular towards Italy's political class' (Bartlett *et al.* 2013: 21). The first V-Day in 2007 took place across hundreds of squares in Italian towns and cities. In these public events, Grillo demonstrated his undeniable talent for tapping into citizens' sense of everyday politics:

> It is up to us to do politics every day, a little bit more each time . . . when we do the shopping, when we travel by bus . . . when we go to school.
>
> (Grillo, V-Day 2007, cited in Bordignon & Ceccarini 2013: 8)

The scale of Italy's political economic crisis after 2008 proved to be the main catalyst in the foundation (in 2009) and growth of the 5SM, lending Grillo's political message added weight. And this was soon translated into electoral success through the mobilisation of 'friends of Beppe Grillo' groupings in local, regional and national elections. Grillo has tried to remain aloof from the political fray, and refused to run for elected office himself. Nevertheless, he has remained key to the success of the 5SM, supporting electoral campaigns through public events and the use of his blog.[9] A major turning point was achieved in 2012 with the election of four 5SM mayors (including a notable victory in Parma). The crowning glory came in the February 2013 national elections where the party rose from under 5 per cent in the opinion polls (in 2011) to capture over 25 per cent of the vote and 109 seats in the Chamber of Deputies.

The German Pirate Party has been more limited in its electoral achievements. It began life in 2006 as an extension of the international Pirate Party movement with the original goal of shaping the 'digital revolution' through the fight against regulation of the Internet and the championing of direct democracy (Niedermayer 2013). For the Pirate Party, the Internet and the new social media are both a key political issue and an important organisational tool. In October 2013, the Pirate Party had over 120,000 Twitter followers and almost 90,000 Facebook likes in Berlin alone. In contrast to the centralisation of policy making around Grillo in the 5SM, the Pirate Party has advocated the 'co-production' (*Mitmachung*) of party policy (around 20 per cent of its approximately 30,000 members are regularly engaged in policy making) (Neumann & Fritz 2012). Through the system of 'liquid democracy' party members have the right to help draft policies (in forums and wikis), which are then diffused and debated through the social media.

After 2011, the party was able to score some notable electoral successes. The Pirate Party's central message, its criticism of government surveillance through internet snooping, has particular resonance in Germany as a result of its nationalist socialist past and the prevalence of state surveillance in East Germany through the Stasi. This came to a head after 2009, when the federal government tried to push through legislation allowing greater supervision of the Internet so as to (allegedly) deal with the problem of child pornography.[10] The Pirate Party's argument was that the issue of child pornography was being 'instrumentalised' by the government to allow the regulation of a free Internet (Niedermayer 2013: 35–36). In this instance, the Pirate Party could 'claim' to be the only political party on the side of citizens' rights. The party was also able to tap into support for the global protest movement in 2011, capitalising on sentiment against the authority of political and economic elites. At this point in time, the Pirate Party was able to successfully profile itself against the existing political order, offering a new way of doing politics, and move beyond it niche support.

From 2011 onwards, the Pirate Party gained significant ground, moving well beyond its 2 per cent showing in the 2009 federal elections, to pass the 5 per cent threshold needed to enter the regional assemblies of four German states (Berlin in 2011, and Saarland, Schleswig-Holstein and North-Rhine Westphalia in 2012). The great success in the Berlin city elections, where the Pirate Party took just under 9 per cent of the vote, was telling. Berliners were particularly disillusioned with city politics, due to rapidly rising rents, overstretched public services and the spiralling costs of building a new city airport. Berlin also had the right demographic—a relatively large proportion of young, highly educated and social progressive citizens (Niedermayer 2013). And these demographic advantages helped the party to establish a major grass-roots presence (the Pirates made themselves visible on the streets through a poster campaign, rallies and various publicity stunts) that it has been unable to achieve on a national scale. These regional successes helped to create a groundswell of support for the Pirate Party, which was regularly (nationally) polling over 10 per cent in 2012.

However, with increased visibility came increased scrutiny. The Pirate Party was heavily criticised by mainstream politicians and the traditional media for its lack of leadership. This, on its own, was not decisive. But, after its success in regional elections, the party became beset with internal disputes, often over inward-looking matters such as the operation of its *liquid democracy* policy-making procedures. Furthermore, the party's representatives in the regional assemblies came across as naive and lacking direction, and any attempt to assert leadership was met with a backlash by the party faithful. For example, the decision by the party group in the Berlin Senate to hold policy meetings behind closed doors was widely derided for its lack of transparency and exclusivity. Efforts by party chairman Bernd Schlömer to develop a broader programme and 'set out the Pirates' policy positions more clearly' were also met with fierce resistance by 'fundamentalists', who wanted to maintain a strict focus on the issue of internet freedom (Der Spiegel 2013). The political in-fighting, the lack of coherent leadership at the national level, and the *amateurish* behaviour in regional assemblies contributed to a dramatic fall in the opinion polls and the failure of the party in the September 2013 federal election, in which it polled only 2 per cent (well below the 5 per cent threshold needed for representation in the Bundestag). When the story of US surveillance of German nationals through the so-called PRISM system broke in May 2013, the Pirate Party was not even able to take advantage of an open goal in the run-up to the national election.[11]

As much as these two quite different political parties were marked by their use of online and offline media systems and spaces—more successfully in the case of the 5SM—to sustain their political support, the 5SM and Pirate Party were also defined by their organisational structures. In particular, the abundance (in the case of Grillo and the 5SM) or lack (in the case of the German Pirate Party) of hierarchical power structures. Grillo himself held the rights to the name and symbol of the Five-Star Movement (Bartlett *et al.* 2013). And, through his populist appeal, characterised by his blogs and public appearances, he maintains a strong control over the party. Bordignon and Ceccarini (2013: 2) explain that Grillo 'is the mouthpiece of the party from the bottom up, but, at the same time he exercises a total control of the movement's strategic choices'.[12] At the level of the Meetup networks, this was not problematic, as the activities of 5SM activists in their communities did not contradict Grillo's positions on national issues. However, after the 5SM's electoral success in the national elections of 2013, the contradiction between these hierarchical power structures and the populist appeal of Grillo, and the work of 5SM elected representatives became more apparent. After the national elections of 2013, several 5SM representatives, including Senator Adele Gambaro, complained about Grillo's continued assaults on parliament and his failure to engage in the political process in a constructive way after the movement's electoral success. Gambaro and others were subsequently invited to leave the party if they did not like the way it was run.

For the Pirate Party, the lack of a centralised leadership inhibited the work of its representatives in regional assemblies, but also led to political in-fighting and the inability of the party to capitalise on a favourable political climate (i.e. the Snowden/ PRISM Affair) in the run-up to the 2013 federal elections. In comparison to the 5SM, the Pirate Party lacked the leadership, the street presence and a deep sense of political and economic crisis. The diversity of the 5SM hybrid model, with its strong combination of offline and online engagement, has also helped to sustain the movement, despite the problems associated with political success. However, this chapter argues that the rise and fall of the Pirate Party (and, to a lesser extent, the dilemmas facing the 5SM after its electoral success) both illustrate the limits of *connective action* for political parties. For political parties, operating within existing political structures, hierarchies of power continue to be necessary for electoral success: they provide leadership autonomy, allowing parties to appeal beyond niche audiences.

## NEW YOUTH PROTEST: BORN OF CRISES OR THE NEW NORMAL?

This chapter has examined the organisation, communication and mobilisation of youth-oriented movements and parties in the digital age. The case studies shed light on where new forms of participation are successful and what the limits of this success might be within different socioeconomic contexts and operating within different civic–political cultures.

It is clear that Bennett and Segerberg's (2013) *logic of connective action* has a profound relevance for the loosely institutionalised protest movements that developed in Spain and Portugal. The 15 May and 12 March movements deliberately distanced themselves from established political organisations and organised themselves in a networked fashion through the integration of offline and online tools. In these instances, the use of the new media led to a *quickening* of political participation, as the movements were able to share information, recruit and mobilise online (in real time) alongside engagement in offline activities that were of great symbolic value.

Although *connective action* also has relevance for the emergent political parties, the 5SM and the Pirate Party, the interface between loose, horizontal organisational structures and the realities of party politics is clearly problematic. The 5SM demonstrates that, within the framework of a charismatic and populist leadership, connective action and digitally networked action is quite possible.[13] Nevertheless, the danger is that, by trying to be everything, you become nothing. This is the lesson shown by the rise and fall of the German Pirate Party. However, the Pirate Party was not boosted to nearly the same extent as the M12M, M15M and 5SM by an urgent sense of political and economic crisis. The re-election of Chancellor Merkel in 2013—with an 8 percentage point gain from 2009—was indicative of general satisfaction with how the country was being run.

What these four cases studies also show is the importance of *hybridity*— of media systems and public spaces (Castells 2012; Chadwick 2013). The most successful of the case studies, the Spanish *indignados* and the Italian 5SM, have used different media platforms and online and offline spaces to reinforce one another and sustain the momentum of the movements. The new media also provided a central tool to directly appeal to citizens (particularly the young and highly educated) without having to play by the rules of the old media or channel their energies through established political institutions.

The social movements and political parties examined in this chapter all had a particular appeal to young and highly educated citizens. In Spain, Portugal and Italy, the M15M, the M12M and the 5SM all managed to tap into a broader sense of crisis felt by large sections of society. These crises have proved so effective in mobilising young people because they operate on both a personal (micro) and a societal (macro) level, connecting young people's individual experiences of youth unemployment, high university tuition fees etc. to broader economic and political issues such as economic inequality. In Germany, that broader sense of crisis simply did not exist, and so the Pirate Party found it hard to move beyond its rather niche political constituency. In Spain, Portugal and Italy, the concerns of citizens and the (negative) impact of political and economic elites on young people's everyday lives were tangible.

However, if these movements are dependent upon crises, how sustainable are they likely to be over the longer term? The first point to make is that, if they are supported by a vibrant civic–political culture (as in the Spanish case), their impact can be more enduring. The second point to make is that the influence of these kinds of movements is always likely to be diffuse, as their ideas permeate through the political system—and maybe become adopted or adapted by the political establishment—over time.

Finally, is political engagement through connective action the new normal? In the future, we may not have the ideal conditions for digitally networked political action: young, highly educated citizens with a deep sense of grievance. Many authors have pointed to the tendency of the Internet to reinforce participation amongst people who are already engaged, and the limited ability to connect with the socially excluded. Schlozman, Verba and Brady (2010) go further—in their work, they characterise the Internet as 'the weapon of the strong'. The prominence of highly educated young people—the frustrated middle class—in these protests certainly raises questions about inequality and political voice amongst the younger generations, and further research on this subject is needed. But, in some sense, we may have already crossed that bridge.

The youth protest movements and nascent political parties that emerged in 2011 have shown what can be done, and others—from a broader set of social backgrounds—will follow.

## NOTES

1 The emergence of self-reflexive forms of participation was evident long before the recent financial crisis began in 2007 and 2008 (Giddens 1991). Norris (2002), for example, charts the decline in participation in electoral politics alongside the rebirth of political engagement in issue-based forms of activism (e.g. the environmental movement) since the 1970s.

2 In Portugal, the dire economic situation led to the acceptance of an EU/IMF financial bailout (of €78 billion) in May 2011 under the condition of further austerity. Spain did not accept a financial bailout—under similar terms—until 2012 (a €100 billion bailout for Spanish banks), but large public spending cuts had already been put in place by 2011.

3 Another recent example of youth protest in Spain was the exposure of the Aznar government's manipulation of the facts (by thousands of young Spaniards on their mobile phones) regarding the Madrid train bombings of 11 March 2004 for political purposes. This contributed directly to the fall of the Conservative government in national elections a few days later.

4 There was a conspicuous lack of mass demonstrations in Portugal between the Carnation Revolution in 1974 and the protests that followed the global financial crisis.

5 The 15 May demonstrations were preceded by several smaller ones, including a demonstration in Madrid on 7 April by the student group Youth Without a Future (Juventud Sin Futuro).

6 For example, one of the Monti government's first measures was to freeze recruitment in the public sector.

7 Through it social policies—in particular the state subsidies for employment during this period—the German government thus managed to forestall significant increases in unemployment.

8 The network also extended to a number of cities outside Italy with large Italian communities, including a large Meetup group in Washington, DC.

9 One such public event was Grillo's swim from Calabria to Sicily in the run-up to the Sicilian election in 2012. These elections proved to be an important success, as the 5SM candidate for the regional presidency achieved and an impressive 15 per cent of the vote.

10 The German Pirate Party again seemed to be on the right side of the public debate regarding the publishing of leaked US intelligence documents through WikiLeaks (from April 2011), unequivocally supporting the position of the organisation and its founder, Julian Assange.

11 German public opinion was generally supportive of Edward Snowden, so the Pirate Party's position—unlike that of the two main parties—had clear public backing.

12 Grillo was not afraid to exert his authority over party representatives. For example, Bologna city councillor Frederica Salsi was publicly condemned by Grillo (on his blog) for holding a TV interview. This went against Grillo's own position on non-engagement with the established media (although the rules for 5SM representatives had been far from clear) (Bartlett *et al.* 2013).

13 Indeed, Grillo supporters have a particular distrust for traditional political and social institutions, including politicians, political parties and big business, and also the Church and trade unions (Bartlett *et al.* 2013: 40).

# REFERENCES

5SM (Movimento Cinque Stelle) (2013). *Non-Statute*, www.movimentocinquestelle. eu/documenti/non-statuto-en.pdf (last accessed 1 October 2013).

Albert, M., Hurrelmann, K., & Quenzel, G. (eds) (2010) *Shell Jugendstudie 2010* (Frankfurt: Fischer).

Amnå, E., & Ekman, J. (2013). 'Standby Citizens. Faces of Political Passivity', *European Political Science Review*, online first (17 June), doi: 10.1017.S1755 773913400009X.

Anduiza, E., Cristancho, C., & Sabucedo, J. M. (2013). 'Mobilization through Online Social Networks: The Political Protest of the *indignados* in Spain', *Information Communication & Society* [online first], www.tandfonline.com/ doi/abs/10.1080/1369118X.2013.808360.

Arnett, J. (2004). *Emerging Adulthood: The Winding Road from Late Teens through the Twenties* (Oxford: Oxford University Press).

Banaji, S., Buckingham, D., van Zoonan, L., & Hirzalla, F. (2009). *CivicWeb Report: Sythesis of Results and Policy Outcomes*, CivicWeb, www.civicweb.eu/ images/stories/reports/civicweb%20wp11%20final.pdf (last accessed 1 September 2013).

Bang, H. (2003). 'A New Ruler Meeting a New Citizen: Culture, Governance and Everyday Making', in H. Bang (ed.) *Governance as Social and Political Communication* (Manchester: Manchester University Press), pp. 241–267.

Bartlett, J., Froio, C., Littler, M., & McDonnell, D. (2013). *New Political Actors in Europe: Beppe Grillo and the M5S* (London: Demos).

Baumgarten, B. (2013). '*Geração à Rasca* and beyond: Mobilizations in Portugal after 12 March 2011', *Current Sociology* 61(4), pp. 457–473.

Beck, U. (1992). *Risk Society: Towards a New Modernity* (London: Sage).

Bennett, W. L. (1998). 'The UnCivic Culture: Communication, Identity, and the Rise of Lifestyle Politics', *P.S.: Political Science and Politics* 31, pp. 41–61.

Bennett, W. L., & Segerberg, A. (2012). 'The Logic of Connective Action: Digital Media and the Personalization of Contentious Politics', *Information, Communication and Society* 15(5), pp. 739–768.

Bennett, W. L., & Segerberg, A. (2013). *The Logic of Connective Action: Digital Media and the Personalization of Contentious Politics* (New York: Cambridge University Press).

Bimber, B., Flanagin, A. J., & Stohl, C. (2005). 'Reconceptualizing Collective Action in the Contemporary Media Environment', *Communication Theory* 15(4), pp. 365–388.

Bordignon, F., & Ceccarini, L. (2013). 'Five Stars and a Cricket. Beppe Grillo Shakes Italian Politics', *South European Society and Politics* [online first], www.tandfonline.com/doi/pdf/10.1080/13608746.2013.775720.

Castells, M. (2010). *The Rise of the Network Society*, 2nd edn (Oxford: Wiley-Blackwell).

Castells, M. (2012). *Networks of Outrage and Hope* (Cambridge: Polity).

Chadwick, A. (2013). *The Hybrid Media System: Politics and Power* (Oxford: Oxford University Press).

Dalton, R. (2009). *The Good Citizen: How a Younger Generation is Reshaping American Politics* (revised edition) (Washington: CQ Press).

DRY (Democracia Real Ya!) (2013). *Manifesto*, www.democraciarealya.es/ manifiesto-comun/manifiesto-english/ (last accessed 1 September 2013).

Deolinda (2013). *Parve Que Non,* www.youtube.com/watch?v=CtBUeuiYY1M (last accessed 1 September 2013).

Der Spiegel (2013). 'Piraten zereissen Schömer's Profilpläne', *Spiegel Online,* 13 January, www.spiegel.de/politik/deutschland/piraten-schloemer-plan-fuer-mehr-profil-loest-debatte-aus-a-877267.html (last accessed 1 October 2013).

Earl, J., & Schussman, A. (2008). 'Contesting Cultural Control: Youth Culture and Online Petitioning', in W. L. Bennett (ed.) *How Digital Media Can Engage Youth* (Cambridge, MA: MIT Press), pp. 71–96.

Estanque, E., Costa, H. A., & Soeiro, J. (2013). 'The New Global Cycle of Protest and the Portuguese Case', *Journal of Social Science Education,* http://pirate.24nieuwe.nl/http://www.jsse.org/index.php/jsse/issue/view/7 (last accessed 1 September 2013).

European Commission (2009). *Youth in Europe: A Statistical Portrait,* European Commission, http://epp.eurostat.ec.europa.eu/cache/ITY_OFFPUB/KS-78-09-920/EN/KS-78-09-920-EN.PDF (last accessed 1 March 2012).

Eurostat (2013). 'Dashboard on EU Youth', http://epp.eurostat.ec.europa.eu/portal/page/portal/employment_social_policy_equality/youth/indicators (last accessed 1 September 2013).

Fernandes, T. (2012). 'Civil Society after Dictatorship: a Comparison of Portugal and Spain, 1970s–1990s', *Kellog Institute for International Relations Working Paper 384,* http://kellogg.nd.edu/publications/workingpapers/WPS/384.pdf (last accessed 1 October 2013).

Fieldhouse, E., Tranmer, M., & Russell, A. (2007). 'Something about Young People or Something about Elections? Electoral Participation of Young People in Europe: Evidence from a Multilevel Analysis of the European Social Survey', *European Journal of Political Research* 46, pp. 797–822.

Franklin, M. (2004). *Voter Turnout and the Dynamics of Electoral Competition since 1945* (Cambridge: Cambridge University Press).

Furlong, A., & Cartmel, F. (2007). *Young People and Social Change* (Maidenhead: Open University Press).

Geração à Rasca (2013). *Manifesto,* http://geracaoenrascada.wordpress.com/manifesto/english/ (last accessed 1 October 2013).

Giddens, A. (1991). *Modernity and Self Identity: Self and Society in the Late Modern Age* (Cambridge: Polity).

Hessel, S. (2011). *Time for Outrage* (London: Quartet Books).

Inglehart, R. & Welzel, C. (2005). *Modernization, Cultural Change and Democracy: the Human Development Sequence* (Cambridge: Cambridge University Press).

Kaldor, M., & Selchow, S. (2013). 'The "Bubbling Up" of Subterranean Politics in Europe', *Journal of Civil Society* 9(1), pp. 78–99.

McDonnell, D. (2013). 'The Real Innovation in Beppe Grillo's Campaigning Is not His Use of Social Media, but His Success In Using the Internet to Bring together Activists at the Grassroots Level', *LSE Europe Blog,* 23 April, http://blogs.lse.ac.uk/europpblog/2013/04/23/innovation-beppe-grillo-internet-campaigning-m5s-social-media-meetup/ (last accessed 1 September 2013).

Macedo, S., Alex-Assensoh, Y., & Berry, J. (2005). *Democracy at Risk: How Political Choices Undermine Citizen Participation, and What We Can Do about It* (Washington, DC: Brookings Institution).

Marsh, D., O'Toole, T., & Jones, S. (2007). *Young People and Politics in the UK: Apathy or Alienation?* (Basingstoke: Palgrave).

Neumann, T. & Fritz, J. (2012). 'Die Piratenpartei – ein neues Demokratieverständnis', *Gesellschaft, Wirtschaft, Politik* 3/2012, pp. 327–337.

Niedermayer, O. (2013). *Die Piratenpartei* (Wiesbaden: Springer).

Norris, P. (2002). *Democratic Phoenix: Reinventing Political Activism* (New York: Cambridge University Press).

Norris, P. (2003). 'Young People and Political Activism: From the Politics of Loyalties to the Politics of Choice?' Report for the Council of Europe Symposium: 'Young people and democratic institutions: from disillusionment to participation', Strasbourg, 27–28 November 2003, www.hks.harvard.edu/fs/pnorris/Acrobat/COE%20Young%20People%20and%20Political%20Activism.pdf (last accessed 1 July 2011).

OECD (2013). 'Income Distribution Database', www.oecd.org/social/income-distribution-database.htm (accessed 1 July 2013).

Pattie, C., Seyd, P., & Whiteley, P. (2004). *Citizenship in Britain: Values, Participation and Democracy* (Cambridge: Cambridge University Press).

Pew Research Center (2013). *Civic Engagement in the Digital Age,* www.pewinternet.org/Reports/2013/Civic-Engagement.aspx (last accessed 1 September 2013).

Putnam, R. (2000). *Bowling Alone: The Collapse and Revival of American Community,* (New York: Simon & Schuster).

Schlozman, K., Verba, S., & Brady, H. (2010). 'Weapon of the Strong? Participatory Inequality and the Internet', *Perspectives on Politics* 8(2), pp. 487–509.

Sloam, J. (Ed.) (2012). 'Youth, Citizenship and Politics', *Parliamentary Affairs* 65(1) special issue, pp. 4–194.

Sloam, J. (2013a). '"Voice and Equality": Young People's Politics in the European Union', *West European Politics* 36(4), pp. 836–858.

Sloam, J. (2013b). 'The "Outraged Young": How Young Europeans are Reshaping the Political Landscape', *Political Insight* 4(1), pp. 4–7.

Spannring, R., Ogris, G., & Gaiser, W. (eds) (2008). *Youth and Political Participation in Europe. Results of the Comparative Study of EUYOUPART* (Opladen: Barbara Budrich).

Stoker, G. (2006). *Why Politics Matters: Making Democracy Work* (Basingstoke: Palgrave).

Stolle, D., Hooghe, M., & Micheletti, M. (2005). 'Politics in the Supermarket: Political Consumerism as a Form of Political Participation', *International Political Science Review* 26(3), pp. 245–269.

Taibo, C. (2013). 'The Spanish *indignados*: A Movement with Two Souls', *European Urban and Regional Studies* 20(1), pp. 155–158.

Tarrow, S. (1998). *Power in Movement: Collective Action, Social Movements and Politics* (New York: Cambridge University Press).

Teorell, J., Torcal, M., & Montero, J. R. (2007). 'Political Participation: Mapping the Terrain', in van Deth *et al.* (eds) *Citizenship and Involvement in European Democracies: A Comparative Analysis* (London: Routledge), pp. 334–357.

Van Biezen, I., Mair, P., & Poguntke, T. (2012). 'Going, going, . . . Gone? The Decline of Party Membership in Contemporary Europe', *European Journal of Political Research* 51, pp. 24–56.

van Deth, J., Ramón Montero, J., & Westholm, A. (2007). *Citizenship and Involvement in European Democracies: A Comparative Analysis* (London: Routledge).

# 9 The Contribution of Websites and Blogs to the Students' Protest Communication Tactics during the 2010 UK University Occupations

*Yannis Theocharis*

## INTRODUCTION

In November 2010 more than 50,000 people marched through central London in opposition to the Conservative–Liberal Democrat coalition government's plans to raise the tuition fee cap while cutting state funding for education by £4.2bn. The proposed budget reduction, which followed a review into higher education funding in UK universities led by Lord Browne that proposed radical changes to the system of university funding—including removing the cap on the level of fees that universities can charge—was perceived by the students as excessive. Students criticized the cuts as an attack on education that would deter the majority of poorer students from applying, and a break of campaign promises, especially on the part of the Liberal Democrats (Williams & Vasagar 2010). Ministers, protesters and the media acknowledged that the demonstration, which was at that time the largest and most dramatic in response to a series of austerity measures planned by the British government, gained significant public support and was followed by even more intense mobilizations that lasted for months (Rusbridger 2010; for an overview see Ibrahim 2011).

Following the mass demonstrations in early November, groups of students occupied over thirty-eight UK universities for more than two weeks in a symbolic act of opposition to government plans. A major characteristic of the students' mobilizations was their informational nature; students deployed an arsenal of electronic and multimedia tools from the first hours of the occupation. The occupation network used the online realm as an informational space where students could formulate, develop and distribute the demands that they made of their universities and the government without any external interference from the authorities or the mainstream media. Research on this case shows that social networking sites (SNS) such as Facebook and Twitter were used extensively (Theocharis 2012). The Twitter accounts employed by all occupations attracted more than 15,000 followers in fewer than five days during the first week of the occupations, which triggered intense media attention (see Lewis & Walker 2010).

Yet the young activists' protest tactics were not limited to social media: thirty-three occupation groups created websites and blogs using free blog-hosting platforms, some of which received more than 70,000 hits fewer than five days into the occupation (University College London, UCL occupation blog 2010). The use of blogs and websites attracted much less attention in the mainstream media debate (see, for instance, Singer 2011) on online political activism, which tends to focus more on the assumed political impact of social media (see, for example Gladwell 2010; Houn-shell 2011; Morozov 2011; Shirky 2011).

Although websites have been found to be indispensable tools for pro-test activism (Vegh 2003; Bennett 2003; Van Aelst & Walgrave 2004; Stein 2009), the literature has focused primarily on social movement organization (SMO) websites and has overlooked their use by spontaneously formed, short-lived, loosely organized protest groups. This study analyses the thirty-three UK occupation websites to assess which of the standard SMO website features they incorporated and how they differed from SMO websites. Spe-cifically, it explores the amount and nature of information included in those websites and their relevance to the protesters' cause, the variety of tools visi-tors could use to interact with the content and engage in debate or simply post their opinion, and the ways in which these websites mobilized support. The study builds on the literature of social movements' web strategies and uses a modified version of the website content analysis model proposed by Van Aelst and Walgrave (2004), which has helped to examine other web-sites built by groups engaged in collective action (see Stein 2009). It contex-tualizes these findings with information derived from analysing the content of all posts on the occupation websites until the night of the government vote. In this way, the study contributes empirical evidence to the ongoing body of literature concerned with the adoption of digital tools to mobilize political protests and finds that informational, interactive and mobilization features were not equally prominent in all occupation websites. Although all standard SMO website features could, to some extent, also be found on the students' websites, the features were emphasized differently. Mobilizing (and some interactive) features played a more central role in the occupa-tion websites, while a blend between websites and social media was also detected. To place the findings in context, previous research on the use and potential of the internet and websites for protest purposes is reviewed.

## ONLINE POLITICAL ACTIVISM

Since the late 1990s, the literature has explored how a variety of social movements effectively use new information and communication technol-ogies (Kahn & Kellner 2004; Pickerill 2004; Chadwick 2006; Gillan *et al.* 2011; Gillan 2009; della Porta & Mosca 2009). This research suggests that the internet can serve multiple functions for social organizations, including email lobbying of elected representatives, public officials and policy elites. Online lobbying organizations such as Avaaz and 38 Degrees, for example, pressure governments on behalf of citizens who are willing to support certain causes by signing online petitions, donating online and emailing. Lobbying efforts to familiarize and influence worldwide public opinion about local struggles (i.e., influencing governments, and also private corporations—see McCaughey & Ayers 2003) have also significantly benefited from internet communication capabilities (Vegh 2003). Early research in Australia, for instance, found that manifestations such as 'Woomera 2002' contributed to the refugee debate within that country (and internationally), enabling several hundred citizens to communicate their opinions using websites (Pickerill 2004). Likewise, recent research has found that, during the 'Arab Spring', social media platforms significantly helped to communicate real-time developments in Tunisia and Egypt: an extensive network of bloggers, activists and journalists co-constructed news on Twitter, which amplified and spread timely information around the world to familiarize the mainstream media public with the efforts of the revolutionary movement (Lotan *et al.* 2011).

Social movement scholars have argued that the internet's real-time, global reach makes it particularly useful for transnational advocacy networks (Van Aelst & Walgrave 2004; Bennett 2003, 2005). The 1994 Zapatista uprising in Mexico is a case in point (Olesen 2004): what began as a local struggle for the rights and autonomy of the indigenous people of the Mexican region of Chiapas rapidly attracted global attention. The internet facilitated a growing network of international support by quickly and successfully linking the local Zapatista rebellion with many other local and international struggles against neoliberal globalization (Kahn & Kellner 2004; Garrido & Halavais 2003). Given its potential to make a variety of group activities easier, scholars have argued that the internet now plays a key role in helping groups to better organize and coordinate their actions (Chadwick 2007; Bimber *et al.* 2009; Shirky 2008). Indeed, as research on the Anti-war movement has demonstrated, the internet's ability to facilitate weak ties between diverse networks of activist groups and social movements has been decisive for the effective coordination and global diffusion of protest and solidarity (Gillan *et al.* 2011; Wright 2004). Successful examples, such as the 'Battle of Seattle' (Van Aelst & Walgrave 2004) and the Zapatista movement, marked the beginning of online activism; recent studies also highlight the internet's role in organizing millions of protesters against the 2003 Iraq war (Gillan *et al.* 2011). Although the internet can facilitate, support and complement traditional offline collective actions—such as organization, mobilization and transnationalization—Van Laer and Van Aelst (2010) argue that it has not replaced traditional forms of political action. Rather, since the participation costs for groups and activists seeking to organize and mobilize in collective action have been considerably reduced, the internet has reinforced some forms of engagement by making them easier to carry out online, and has made them more widespread. Most importantly, it has created new, solely internet-based forms of collective action that complement activists' offline and online toolset of repertoires.

## ORGANIZATION AND MOVEMENT WEBSITES AS INFORMATION, INTERACTION AND MOBILIZATION TOOLS

Organization websites have been reported to contribute to conditions that assist in the establishment of movement formation, by mobilizing collective identities and establishing networks with other organizations (Van Aelst & Walgrave 2004; Mercea 2012). The late 1990s anti-World Trade Organization (WTO) mobilizations in Seattle, for example, used the International Civil Society's website as the hub, transmitting hourly updates about the major demonstrations in Seattle to a network of almost 700 non-governmental organizations in approximately eighty countries, including environmental, student, religious, human rights and other related movements, as well as trade unions (Chadwick 2006; Kahn & Kellner 2004). Similar website features have been studied by Stein (2009), who used a large sampling of environmental, lesbian/gay, anti-corporate, human rights, media reform and US-based women's movement organizations to examine whether the websites: provided information; assisted in action and mobilization; promoted interaction and dialogue; made lateral linkages; served as an outlet for creative expression; or promoted fundraising. Further research on movement organizations' use of websites maintains that they can facilitate communication between organizations that deal with the same general issues by combining greater speed; reduced costs through the use of free online actions such as emails, online petitions, action alerts, newsletters and RSS feeds (Gurak & Logie 2003; Chadwick 2006; della Porta & Mosca 2009); transnational reach; and by providing virtually unlimited content (Van Aelst & Walgrave 2004).[1]

Previous research has explored the use of websites by social movement and issue-oriented organizations (Van Aelst & Walgrave 2004; della Porta & Mosca 2009; Gillan *et al.* 2011; Coleman 2008). However, less is known about whether the same communication practices used by major and long-established activist organizations and movements—and the informational, interactive and mobilizing features that can be found on their websites—can also be found on the websites or blogs of loosely organized groups like those of the occupying students (see Maireder & Schwarzenegger 2012). The major informational functions of organization websites, for example, have been deemed to be their capacity to help interested individuals to subscribe to (or follow) advocacy and lobbying groups, receive emailed policy newsletters and action alerts and learn about forthcoming street demonstrations and protest events. As Van Aelst and Walgrave (2004: 115) show in their study of the anti-globalization movement, almost all the organization websites they examined hosted calendars with upcoming protest activities; visitors were encouraged and given detailed information (e.g., transport, sleeping, accommodation, etc.) on how to participate. Research has also shown that SMOs use websites to facilitate lateral linkages with other organizations in order to acknowledge their presence, build a network of support and make each other aware of common views and interests (Stein 2009; Van Aelst & Walgrave 2004; Van Laer & Van Aelst 2010). In addition, in their study of the use of new media during the build-up and the duration of the 2003 Iraq war protests in the UK, Gillan and colleagues (2011) found that the majority of anti-war groups and organizations had websites that were relatively cheap and easy to set up and maintain, which contained varying amounts and qualities of information, but typically provided a statement of principles, news and comments as well as links to like-minded organizations and groups. Maireder and Schwarzenegger (2012), who explore a short protest by Austrian students with very similar characteristics of self-organization and interaction with the public and media to that of the UK students, found that both individual and institutional protest websites and weblogs were mainly focused on providing information and communication. They note, however, that the discourse was communicated not only by websites but also within a wider portfolio of digital media that included the interconnection of websites with social media platforms such as Facebook and Twitter. Finally, a consistent finding in the literature has been that although they successfully provide information, SMO websites include few opportunities for interaction and dialog (Van Aelst & Walgrave 2004; della Porta & Mosca 2009; Stein 2009)—which has also been observed in political campaign websites (Gibson & Ward, 2000; Foot & Schneider 2006).

Could this often cheap-and-easy model, which emphasizes information provision rather than interaction, better describe the development of websites by loosely organized groups? Research on the living wage campaign that took place in the US in 2001 confirms that loosely organized groups of students used websites to build quick and efficient low-cost campaigns that developed into long-lasting networked campaigns, and attracted significant attention from political elites, celebrities and the media (Biddix & Park 2008). Maireder and Schwarzenegger (2012) found that even though in the Web 2.0 era social media can provide faster communication and content distribution between interconnected, loosely organized groups of students, do-it-yourself websites and weblogs are still a part of activists' online toolsets, albeit one whose role is now limited to information provision rather than interactivity. The variety of online strategies that characterized the student occupations in the UK provides fertile ground to observe the role and development of these trends, and demonstrates the functions, similarities and differences that websites created by loosely organized groups can have with those of SMOs in the Web 2.0 era of digital media abundance.

## WEBSITE CONSTRUCTION BY LOOSELY ORGANIZED GROUPS: THE CASE OF THE STUDENT OCCUPATIONS

### Case Selection

As noted by Garrett (2006) and Stein (2009), few studies investigate the exact communication practices of SMOs. Yet, given the diversity and different functions of organization websites discussed in recent studies, perhaps loosely organized groups that spontaneously come together for potentially short protest events cannot be expected to have a comparable capacity to develop websites with a similar sophistication, or even similar features, to long-established SMO websites. The students' reaction to the government's proposed cuts was not the result of a coordinated effort by an already established and well-organized group or SMO but, rather, a spontaneous, loosely organized and leaderless collective outburst of young and well-educated people that grew into the UK's 'Anti-cuts' movement (Lewis & Taylor 2010; Penny 2011). With no financial support for their e-tactics, students developed and maintained their online strategy with the help of their 'techie' fellow students (Penny 2011) rather than by hiring professional website developers.[2] These features made the students' protest act a suitable case for evaluating the way loosely organized groups build and use protest websites, and comparing the websites with those of large SMOs.

### Theoretical Framework and Research Questions

Contrary to the perception disseminated by the mainstream media debate, which focused on how the protest events were transformed by student-activists' use of social media such as Facebook and Twitter (Singer 2011), members of the occupations actually used a number of different e-tactics, platforms and devices. Their function, however, was not independent but, rather, interlinked in order to share and distribute content across the entire media infrastructure, which ranged from social media platforms and video-sharing sites to websites and smartphones (for a review of the students' media infrastructure see Penny 2011).

Students' protest repertoires of action conform to those observed in recent internet-supported mobilizations (Mercea 2012; Maireder & Schwarzenegger 2012), which reinforces theoretical conceptualizations about the changing nature of protest repertoires and protest action dynamics (Van Laer & Van Aelst 2010; Bennett & Segerberg 2012). Repertoires can be divided into three categories: (a) solely virtual activities, such as linking with other occupations, responding to real-time enquiries from professional journalists using Twitter, and posting aims and demands, signing petitions or accepting monetary contributions through websites; (b) solely offline activities, such as organizing flash mobs or lobbying members of the university management; or (c) a mix of internet-supported, internet-organized and coordinated offline activities such as demonstrations or acceptance of material donations such as food and clothing that were requested online (specific cases are discussed below). These activities are consistent with what has been classified in Van Laer and Van Aelst's (2010) typology of SMOs as 'online action repertoires'.[3] The typology distinguishes 'real' offline actions that are supported and facilitated by the internet from 'virtual' activities, which are solely internet based. It further differentiates internet-*based* and internet-*supported* tactics, with low and high thresholds, to show how the internet may have lowered action-related barriers. Van Laer and Van Aelst point out that action groups almost never use only one tactic, but instead draw on a myriad of offline and online tactics;[4] this was exemplified in the student protests.

This study builds on Van Aelst and Walgrave's (2004) model, which examined the internet's role in shaping the anti-globalization movement. Their study examined 17 (out of a network of at least 600) organization websites and created an experimental coding scheme to quantify and analyse the depth of information, interactivity and mobilization that they provided to their visitors. This model was later used by others (Stein 2009). The occupation students, however, especially at the beginning of the mobilizations, had neither the time to build sophisticated websites, nor the institutional or financial support and specialized technical equipment that activist groups during the anti-WTO mobilizations had at their disposal (Chadwick 2006). This study explores the websites' capacity to nevertheless successfully uphold the discourse, communicate the students' aims, interact with the public and activists by gathering feedback and support and offer content to mobilize others in a period in which young activists increasingly rely on social media for political communication (Maireder & Schwarzenegger 2012; Mercea 2012; Valenzuela *et al.* 2012). It does that by comparing the websites of thirty-three occupations to evaluate their informational, interactive and mobilizing aspects and their relevance to the rising, more interactive protest media ecology through the following research questions:

1   What sort of information did the occupation groups include on their websites, and to what extent was this information related to their cause?
2   Which methods of interacting with visitors did the websites employ, and what features did the websites use?
3   Were websites used to mobilize? If yes, in what ways?

An additional research question aims to assess which of the features typically found on SMO websites can also be found in those built by loosely organized groups:

4 Which of the above features (information, interaction, mobilization) were more predominant in the occupation websites? Where there any differences or similarities with features that normally appear on SMO websites?

## METHODOLOGY

### The Sample

The study analysed the web pages of all student groups that staged occupations, and therefore provides a reliable picture of the students' website strategies. To track the number of occupation websites, we conducted daily searches on Google, Indymedia and Twitter, and read messages posted on the web pages about new protest activities and occupations taking place in universities across the UK. This research yielded thirty-three sites out of a total of thirty-eight universities that staged occupations at one time or another (including four occupations that lasted fewer than two days but kept updating their web pages with news until at least the night of the vote). Some occupation websites were excluded, such as the University of Sussex, which posted information about its five-day occupation on an existing website that was maintained by the local anti-education cuts movement, which began in 2009.

The survey ended on 9 December, when the British parliament passed the proposed plan for cuts in education. All occupation websites were first saved as complete web pages to a hard drive so that all essential files could be stored for analysis even if the websites went offline.[5] The websites were first screened by an undergraduate assistant; the author then confirmed that they provided information about the occupation's cause and included interaction capabilities and/or calls for mobilization. All thirty-three websites met at least two of these criteria.

The content was mapped in two stages. First, the author previewed the websites and developed an adapted version of the Van Aelst and Walgrave coding scheme (adding new web functions such as RSS feeds and Twitter flow incorporated on the homepage). Second, Discovertext (discovertext.com)—a text analytic software that can be programmed to harvest content from various online platforms such as social media, wikis, blogs, news aggregators, websites, etc.—was used to gain more in-depth insight into each web page's content. After the website content was gathered and archived, the main topics of concern were identified, and the way in which the discourse unfolded was analysed in order to better understand why the website was important for framing the discourse and narrative. Given that nearly all the occupations used free blog-hosting platforms (e.g., WordPress) that provided an RSS or Atom feed service, occupation feeds were 'followed' through subscription using Google Reader, a web-based aggregator that can read and store RSS and Atom feeds. The home page content of each website was then harvested in its entirety and archived for analysis. Content posted between 22 November, when students started occupying universities and the first websites or weblogs came online, and 9 December,[6] the evening of the vote and the biggest demonstration in response to it, was examined individually for each occupation group and in aggregate, in order to identify similarities and differences in the posted content.

## Stages of Coding and Intercoder Reliability

In the first stage of coding, the author and an experienced coder (graduate student) separately ascribed codes to various aspects of information, interaction and mobilization ranging from 0 (feature was absent) to 2 (the most extended version of the feature was present) using the modified coding scheme developed by the author (Table 9.1). We compared all websites for intercoder reliability. Across the three main categories (information, interaction and mobilization) agreement was high (88 per cent on average), which is consistent with acceptable standards (Bachen *et al.* 2008; Bennett *et al.* 2011).

In the second stage, analysis with the text-analysis software returned 773 units[7] during the designated period. A random preview of 200 units led to the formation of eleven coding classification categories: occupation positions/negotiations, opinion article, newspaper article/press, multimedia content, moral encouragement, report from inside the occupation, field experience, schedule of events, call for action/invitation to occupation, appropriate preparations for action and live correspondence. Two undergraduate student assistants classified all posts into one of these categories. We used the software to validate codes[8] by selecting a random sample of 200 coded posts. Across all eleven codes, agreement averaged 84.6 per cent. Eight of the codes reached 80 per cent agreement or above; preparation for action, inside report, and opinion article earned 72.7 per cent 65 per cent and 63 per cent, respectively. This was partly expected because inside reports, which often involved descriptions of the issues discussed in meetings, included political commentary and opinion, and the coders had been instructed to assign only one code per post, which resulted in different interpretations.

A methodological problem arose when analysing the websites of occupations that ended before the vote—because of eviction (Oxford occupation), because students took a collective decision to end the occupation (Edinburgh, Royal Holloway), or because they reached an agreement with the university management (London South Bank, Nottingham University)—but kept updating their web pages until the evening of the vote (well after the occupation had ended, in some cases). As a general rule, all websites that were initiated and run by occupation students were included in the study until the evening of the vote—regardless of whether their occupation continued until this time. It is important to note that students from

*Table 9.1* Method of coding occupation websites' communication, interactivity and mobilisation capacities

| Features | Scores | | |
|---|---|---|---|
| | 0 | 1 | 2 |
| *Information* | | | |
| Self-presentation | No information | Minimal info about the group and the occupation | Extensive info on the origins of the group, the acts so far, the goals of the occupation, its structure, its members, and the statement and the reasons behind it |
| Views and demands | No views/ demands | Minimal or unclear info on the views and demands of the occupation | Extensive explanations of the views and demands of the occupation and downloadable content. |
| External information (links) | No links | Minimal info on other organizations and few links | Extensive info about other occupations and links to several groups |
| Background information | No background info | The issue at stake is briefly placed in context and other ideas and arguments are refereed to | There is an extensive overview about the debate on education cuts with elaboration on different views, exemplified by links to newspaper articles, academic studies, reports |
| *Interactivity* | | | |
| Feedback opportunities | No opportunities | There is an email address for further info, suggestions or complaints | Visitors are encouraged to react by email, the email button is not placed only in the homepage |
| Information distribution | No distribution | Occasional info via email or RSS feed (provided by the platform) | Regular info via newsletter, or 'subscribe' option |
| Online debate | No opportunities | A general forum for discussion or a chat | Numerous debate opportunities on different issues and posts |
| Personal contribution | No opportunities | Visitors can react to specific info on the website (for example reply to a post) | Visitors can make their own contribution to the site (e.g., post a message of solidarity or an opinion) |
| New Media interactivity | No interactivity | Link to YouTube/ Vimeo/Flickr | Videos and pictures incorporated on the website, Twitter feed |

(*Continued*)

*Table 9.1* (Continued)

| Features | Scores | | |
|---|---|---|---|
| | 0 | 1 | 2 |
| *Mobilization* | | | |
| Donation | No option | Option for donation | — |
| Action calendar | No calendar | Calendar with an overview of activities | Calendar with an overview of activities accompanied by call of participation or more detailed info such as venue, duration, participants |
| Call for online action | No calls | Online petition | Extensive online actions such as lobbying, emailing, politicians online or more aggressive acts such as denial or service attacks and email flooding |
| Call for offline action | No calls | Call for participation in demonstrations | Call for participation in demonstrations, invitation to events organized by the occupation such as talks/musical events/training and lessons by specialized lawyers on protest behavior and rights |

occupations that ended earlier often joined other occupations and kept updating their own web page with protest material about forthcoming events and essays about their experiences during the occupation. Since this content had the potential to contribute to the general discourse against the cuts until the end of the mobilization, it was considered worthwhile and was included in the analysis. Treating all the websites as if all the occupations ended at the same time is a limitation of this study, as, despite the valuable additional information about the discourse, it introduces a conceptual problem: occupations that ended early but kept updating their web pages with content about the debate were pooled alongside those that kept posting content about their occupation's activities and plans.

The minimum requirements were: (1) clear and unambiguous information that an occupation had taken place and (2) a new web page exclusively built by students for the occupation. There was no way to verify whether the websites were actually built by students and not by paid professionals. Some websites clearly stated that members of the occupation (the 'techies') created and maintained the online voice of the occupations (website/blog, Twitter and Facebook accounts). Even for those who did not state it clearly, however, the ease of creating a blog or a basic website that uses a blog format (such as those of UCL and Cambridge[9]) makes it unlikely that students paid website developers. It can be argued that student-created websites may, by definition, lack the complex content, layout and communicative potential of large, professionally designed organization and protest movement websites (e.g., Global Justice Movement, Stop The War Coalition or Amnesty International).

## RESULTS

Findings on the study's three main parameters (information, interactivity, mobilization) are presented in Table 9.2, and are contextualized by findings from the second-level analysis and discussed separately below.

*Table 9.2* Codes and scores of the 33 occupation webpages based on their information, interactivity and mobilisation functions

|  | Code 0 | Code 1 | Code 2 | Score | Standardised 100-point sum score |
|---|---|---|---|---|---|
| *Information* |  |  |  |  |  |
| Self-presentation | 0 | 19 | 14 | 47 | 71 |
| Views and demands | 0 | 12 | 21 | 54 | 81 |
| External information (links) | 9 | 9 | 15 | 39 | 59 |
| Background information | 2 | 14 | 17 | 46 | 69 |
| *Average category score* |  |  |  | 140 | 70/100 |
| *Interactivity* |  |  |  |  |  |
| Feedback opportunities | 1 | 15 | 17 | 49 | 74 |
| Information distribution | 0 | 0 | 22 | 66 | 100 |
| Online debate | 0 | 0 | 0 | 0 | 0 |
| Personal contribution | 0 | 22 | 11 | 44 | 66 |
| New Media interactivity | 1 | 11 | 21 | 53 | 80 |
| *Average category score* |  |  |  | 212 | 64/100 |
| *Mobilisation* |  |  |  |  |  |
| Donation | 27 | 6 | 0 | 6 | 18* |
| Action calendar | 10 | 10 | 13 | 36 | 54 |
| Call for online action | 11 | 10 | 12 | 34 | 51 |
| Call for offline action | 4 | 6 | 23 | 52 | 79 |
| *Average category score* |  |  |  | 128 | 50/100 |

*This feature could be coded from 0 to 1.

## Information

The first research question addressed the kind of information that was found on the websites and the extent to which it was related to the cause. Table 9.2 demonstrates that websites scored higher on the information function than in any other category. Nine websites topped the information category's score (8) with posts ranging from simple occupation statements to long articles about university and equality in education, while only three received the minimum score (2). Overall, however, fewer than 50 per cent of the websites provided extensive information about their occupation. This information ranged from a brief note about how students took over the occupied spaces, a list of demands or the outcome of meetings with the university management, to extensive overviews of the debate, long opinion articles, protest field reports and detailed schedules of events.

Twenty-two sites included elaborate 'occupation statements' or 'manifestos' that clearly stated the students' demands, which were mainly focused on lobbying the university management to release statements formally opposing the cuts, protecting protesters from punishment or urging MPs to vote against the cuts. For instance, UCL students demanded that their university 'issue a statement condemning all cuts to higher education and the rise in tuition fees', and 'ensure no victimisation or repercussions for anyone participating in the occupation'. These demands, which are directly related to the cause, were consistent across universities. Similar demands included:

> Calling on the uni to pledge not to increase fees/not to implement the cuts and issue a statement saying that uni is opposed to both above things; no victimisation of students involved here, at Milbank or on Oxford Road.
>
> (Manchester occupation)

> That the University completely oppose the increase in fees, fight against it and fight against all cuts to education, and use its influence to oppose the spending review's threat to education, welfare, health, and other public services; That the University ensure that no students who take part in any form of peaceful protest will face disciplinary action.
>
> (Cambridge occupation)

> We call for MPs to vote against the rise in tuition fees on Thursday 9 December.
>
> (Exeter occupation)

Some occupations (fewer than 15 per cent)[10] also took the opportunity to express a number of other concerns and demand changes to various university policies considered to be unfair. UCL's students, for example, stated among their demands that their university should 'implement the full living wage package for all cleaning, catering and security staff with no cuts to hours and jobs', while Cambridge students demanded that 'the University acknowledge and take steps to combat the systemic inequality of access to this elitist institution and the danger of its intensification posed by the scrapping of the education maintenance allowance (EMA), a rise in tuition fees and removal of programs such as Aim Higher'.

Figure 9.1 displays the breakdown of content in the second level of analysis. Information regarding the occupations' positions, narrative and their negotiations with the university management (often tagged by the students as a 'press release') was found to be the most predominant informative feature, accounting for 17.5 per cent of all content posted on protest websites. An example of such content is as follows:

### Current Action at Newcastle University

Students from the Occupation at Newcastle University are currently in the newly built Kings Gate building peacefully demonstrating. This is in response to the Vice Chancellors refusal to meet with the members of the Occupation to discuss our demands. The protesters are laid on the floor in the entrance of the building with their mouths taped up, symbolizing the frustration and anger we feel at being excluded from talks about the impact that cuts to higher education will have on Newcastle University and the country.

(Wednesday, 1 December, Press release of
Newcastle University occupation)

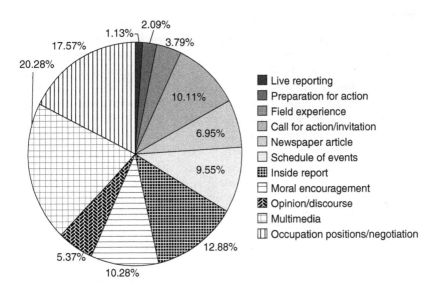

*Figure 9.1* Breakdown of overall website content

Fewer than half of the occupation websites included links to other occupations, either on separate sections of the page or in the form of solidarity posts to groups that had just occupied spaces and come online.

Fewer than half of the websites included an opinion article that elaborated on the education cuts debate; these either were written eponymously by a member of the occupation or were sent to the occupation website via email. Opinion articles were more common and longer on web pages with higher scores in the information category, and accounted for 5.37 per cent of all website content. They were often accompanied by newspaper articles (or links to articles), which accounted for 6.95 per cent of content, and mostly related to the pre-election assurances, the debate of what became known as the 'Browne proposals'[11] and press reports about the occupations. Other web pages also emphasized the opinions against the education cuts, which were often voiced in the mainstream press by economists, education specialists and university officials. Descriptions of life in the occupations were found on 12.88 per cent of the websites, and 3.79 per cent described recent experiences in the protest field.

The information category scored 70 out of a possible 100 (see Table 9.1), which indicates that providing information to support the reasons for the occupations was important to the students. Based on these findings, we can address both components of the first research question to conclude that websites provided diverse information in order to frame the debate, popularize the students' aims, negotiations and actions across the occupations, put forward their demands and project their unity.

## Interactivity

The second research question concerned the ways and methods visitors could use to interact with the content (Table 9.2). Many websites included opportunities for feedback, and all could in some way or another disseminate information. All except one website, for example, provided an email address for feedback accompanied by a message such as 'Anything missing? Comment below or contact occupiedessex@gmail.com'. About half of the web pages explicitly encouraged visitors to react to the posted content with prompts such as 'email us!' or 'submit more agenda items to [email]', while some web pages encouraged visitors to send commentary about the cause via email and promised to read and post responses on the website.

Eight websites offered newsletters, asking visitors to provide their email address in a form so they could be notified about the latest developments in the occupation, and thirty websites prompted visitors to follow their respective Facebook and Twitter accounts. All websites could be followed via RSS or Atom feed. Eight websites achieved a score of 8 out of 10 for interactivity, and only one website received the lowest score (4).

Notably, none of the websites featured a dedicated forum or chat for online debate.

All thirty-three websites gave visitors the opportunity to comment on messages posted by website administrators. The integrated 'comment-below-post' function was enabled in all cases, and responses to posted content were found on as many as twenty-eight websites. Reaction to content was observed in posts that addressed ideas about and counter-arguments to the Browne review, protest tactics, police behaviour and, most extensively, moral encouragement (the latter accounting for 10.28 per cent of all content analysed. Indeed, almost 30 per cent of the websites included a dedicated space to submit messages of solidarity, which arrived by the dozen from diverse sources such as journalists, actors, singers, university teaching staff, activists, politicians, trade unions and the public. Since individual messages were posted in the solidarity section, however, these messages were not sent to our Google Reader as part of the RSS/Atom feeds that the text-analysis software captured. The software captured only those solidarity messages (coded as 'moral encouragement') that were posted on the home page of the websites/blogs. Thirteen websites had integrated Twitter feed on their home page that could direct visitors to their Twitter page. Overall, live reporting accounted for a little more than 1 per cent of web postings.

More than 50 per cent of the websites featured integrated multimedia content taken by the students or media outlets, including video or photos from YouTube, Vimeo or Flickr or links to photo/video collections on other websites. This content amounted to about 20 per cent, making it the most predominant content on the websites (see Figure 9.1). The themes of videos and photos varied, but mainly focused on life in the occupations, including music, poetry gigs and dancing; talks delivered by key visitors; video-recorded instructions about protester rights delivered by lawyers or experienced activists; and calls for action. There was also a significant amount of content taken from the demonstrations. For example, a coalition of London-based universities that carried out 'flash mobs' and anti-consumerist protests in the commercial centre of the city included videos of those activities, alongside others showing riot police reactions and the experience of 'kettling' (crowd-containment method) from the protest battlefield.

Even without live online debate features on their web pages, students emphasized interacting with website visitors by keeping their posts open to comments, integrating multimedia content into the web pages and allowing personal contributions on separate solidarity sections. The total standardized score of the interactivity category was 64 (see Table 9.2), but it should be noted that all websites lost 2 points because of the absence of an online forum or chat feature for instant debate. These functions appear to have been incorporated, to some extent, in the 'comment-below-post' facility.

## Mobilization

The third research question assesses whether, and in what ways, the websites were used for mobilization. Calls for mobilization mostly promoted offline action, such as calls for students to attend preparations for action (such as protest training) or petition signing. Fewer than half of the web pages included calls for online action, for example by posting elected representatives' Twitter accounts, emails, addresses and telephone numbers for lobbying. No calls for 'denial of service attacks' or any other form of aggressive online activism were detected on any of the websites.

Only six web pages had a 'donation' option, with varying types of donations. The Newcastle occupation, for example, which according to its website received 'an overwhelming amount of donations from individuals, lecturers, political parties, friends and families' simply posted a message that it was running out of 'plates' and 'savoury non-perishable food items'. Students of the UCL occupation incorporated a PayPal link that led directly to a form to transfer money in support of students who were deemed liable for the costs of the occupation. Goldsmiths University occupiers included a separate email address to allow website visitors to contact students about monetary support to cover court fees (to overturn the university management's High Court possession order). Calls for offline action were often accompanied by solicitors' phone numbers and legal advice to inform students of their rights in case of arrest, but most of these pleas encouraged visitors to participate in forthcoming demonstrations and 'come down' to the occupation; 2 per cent of the posted content provided detailed information about how to adequately prepare for upcoming protest actions. The following messages reflect the common format of such calls:

### Direct Action Workshop

Wanna avoid police kettles?? Tired of spending 8 hours in the cold? Want to know your rights inside an occupation?

Come to SOAS occupation,
Brunei Gallery
Thornhaught St
Russel Sq

Friday,
3 December
7PM

for direct action training!

(3 December, SOAS occupation website)

### Vote on Tuition Fees—March on Parliament!

This is IT people! The day has come!

The date for the parliamentary vote on fee increases has been announced!

9 DECEMBER 2010

We all need to start mobilizing, organizing, publicizing . . . the works!

I would urge everyone to come to the meeting on Friday at 6pm in the Arts building to discuss actions, building for the march etc, really important to bring everyone together - www.facebook.com/event.php?eid=132098420181499

text, call 07847736758, 07723396279 if you can't make it etc.

www.facebook.com/event.php?eid=136567579732280

We are certainly going to encourage the SU to organise coaches or support people to go down to London.

SU general meeting tomorrow, 8pm, need people there www.facebook.com/event.php?eid=135786923142154

See you soon

(1 December, Royal Holloway<br>Anti-Cuts Alliance website)

Almost all websites featured an online calendar of important dates. Although fewer than half of them included extensive notes about the events on the calendar itself, most of the events—such as meetings with the university management, demonstrations or protest gigs—were posted on the main page on the same day, or one day in advance, and were accompanied by a paragraph outlining the details (venue, time, etc. Detailed information about the time and nature of the scheduled events accounted for 9.55 per cent of the content posted on occupation websites (see Figure 9.1). Overall, calls for action, which were more often short messages like 'COME DOWN AND MARCH WITH US!! STAND UP AND BE COUNTED!!', and less often long, argumentative paragraphs, accounted for 10 per cent of the website content—although sometimes such calls were integrated into longer texts about occupation positions or schedules of events.

The findings show that mobilization was less prominent in the websites' content than information and interaction. Table 9.2 illustrates that calls for mobilization were the least predominant feature of the occupation websites, receiving a score of 50. Very few websites featured donation buttons, while protest calendars were empty on most web pages, as events were adequately advertised on the home page. The Royal Holloway Anti-Cuts Alliance call for action shown above demonstrates the new way that protesters frame mobilization calls on their websites. Web page content intertwined with Facebook links was a consistent feature of calls for action, and was found on twenty-six websites. The links advertised Facebook events, to which people could sign up to attend and, literally, be counted.

## DISCUSSION AND SUGGESTIONS FOR FURTHER RESEARCH

None of the web pages accumulated a top score of 25, but nine scored higher than 20. The top-scoring websites were constantly updated; the posts were clearly organized into categories depending on their content, and their Twitter feed appeared on the home page. Some websites, such as that of Royal Holloway, included comprehensive maps of the protests, while on 9 December, UCL's website integrated a link to an interactive Google map that was streaming the current position of protesters and policemen, accompanied by short comments about the number of protesters, police crowd-containment methods and other information. Eleven websites accumulated scores of between 15 and 20, while the content of the rest of the websites was of average utility; some were used purely as a diary of the occupation or, in the case of some Fine Arts schools such as Camberwell College of Fine Arts, were strongly focused on visual and artistic contributions rather than on long posts or an emphasis on the discourse.

Based on these findings, a number of comparisons can be made between the informational, interactive and mobilizing features of loosely organized protest group websites and those of SMOs. In their evaluation of movement websites, Van Aelst and Walgrave (2004: 120) found that large organization websites were used during the anti-globalization protests against the WTO in Seattle to provide information about the cause, frame positions and provide detailed guidelines to actively mobilize people to demonstrate or join the cause. However, Van Aelst and Walgrave (2004) concluded that there were few opportunities for interaction and dialogue. Likewise, della Porta and Mosca (2009) found that only 10 per cent of the SMOs they examined had interactive mechanisms, while Stein's (2009) examination of SMO websites showed that, with the exception of providing information, the majority of SMOs exhibited low or no interactivity. To answer the fourth research question, this study observed both similarities with and differences from previous research about predominant features in SMO websites. It also shows that not all website features were developed to the same extent in the occupation websites. Consistent with previous findings in the literature, information, interaction and mobilization features were found to exist to some extent in all occupation websites. As previous studies have suggested, information provision was found to be the most predominant feature of the websites. As Van Aelst and Walgrave (2004) observed in their study of anti-globalization mobilizations, this included not only general information on the issue (cuts in the educational sector), but also the framing of its origins and consequences in opinion articles.

Previous research has reported that features of interaction, dialogue and creative expression are usually lacking, not just from movement websites (Stein 2009), but from political campaign websites too (Foot & Schneider 2006). The occupation websites were somewhat different, since they did emphasize interactivity; they gave visitors the opportunity to comment on the posted content, provided possibilities for feedback and published visitors' commentary on their home page. Some even had a dedicated section for messages of solidarity and support. Nevertheless, more interactive possibilities for online debate—specifically, forums or chats[12]—were nowhere to be found. Previous research on youth (especially student) mobilizations has described e-strategies based on the extensive use of social media (and less use of websites) that are characterized by rich interconnectivity, opportunities for discussion and debate, and interaction with individuals and groups both within (participating protest groups or individuals) and outside (mass media, political sphere, citizens) the activist circle (Mercea 2012; Maireder & Schwarzenegger 2012). In this context, the absence of interactive discussion opportunities on the occupation websites may indicate that such features will continue to receive less attention in such groups' mobilization websites in the future.

At the same time, it remains to be investigated whether social media such as Twitter, which were used by all occupations,[13] made up for the lack of interactivity on the websites. The presence of a Twitter feed in thirteen websites might be one such indication, while the fact that some occupations used just Twitter and Facebook and no website might signal a turn towards a more interactive way of protest organization that needs to be studied further. Research has shown that social media can play an important interactive role for activists, due to its built-in capabilities that enable the fast and easy exchange of messages and the rapid transition of information from different types of sources located in strategically different physical spaces (Lotan *et al.* 2011). The diversity of the pre-existing contacts of participating 'networked individuals' (each of whom has their own loosely connected personal network) and the type of personalized communication that helps protest messages to spread within these networks can be a significant source of further interactivity (boyd 2008; Maireder & Schwarzenegger 2012; Bennett & Segerberg, 2012). At the same time, blending social media with live journalistic correspondence, which has been reported in previous studies and was also observed in the student occupations (Theocharis 2012), not only quickly attracts the attention of the public and the political elite, but gives the protester/social media user the opportunity to shape the news agenda (Chadwick, 2012; Anstead & O'Loughlin 2010).

Calls for action with integrated links for people to join the advertised event on Facebook, such as that posted by the Royal Holloway Anti-Cuts Alliance shown above, may also suggest that such groups employ a hybrid e-tactic that involves the use of websites and blogs that are intertwined or linked with recruitment through Facebook events and Twitter discussions. This method of recruitment has not been reported in the previous literature on online protest activism, but has gained attention in the Occupy Wall Street movement (Caren & Gaby 2011). Further research should investigate whether such a tactic could have provided the protest organizers with valuable information regarding the attendance at demonstrations and other protest activities, allowing for better organization and coordination. Given the low overall levels of opportunities for interaction and dialogue that previous studies have repeatedly detected on movement websites, using social media as a complement to websites is likely to have a positive effect on recruitment and offline participation in future mobilizations.

Mobilization features appeared to be less predominant in the occupation websites than in their SMO counterparts. Very few websites, for example, had a donation option, which might be explained by the relatively short duration of the protest action and the limited time students had to organize and execute a protest strategy that required funding. Protest calendars, although present, did not include much information; however, important event information was usually provided on the home page. SMO websites generally contain calls for action that, like those reported by Van Aelst and Walgrave (2004), are accompanied by a variety of information about ways to participate, information about the protest venue and the time of the planned demonstration, training, clothing and legal lessons about protesters' rights in case of arrest.

Establishing links with other occupation websites through hyperlinks was another feature that appeared on only a few occupation websites. This study's findings show that fewer than half of the occupation websites included links to other occupations. SMOs, however, establish lateral linkages with one another through hyperlinks to acknowledge, connect with and support the presence of other groups (Stein 2009; Foot & Schneider 2006; Van Laer & Van Aelst 2010). Was this feature given lesser emphasis because all occupations were already loosely connected through social media? We cannot be sure, but research has found that there was indeed a 'Twitter occupations network' through which university occupation Twitter accounts established electronic ties with one another and acted as organising agents (Theocharis 2012). Future research should explore whether establishing links with like-minded organizations, a fundamental element of social movement mobilization, is now better—or exclusively—facilitated by communication tools other than websites. Given the visibility of profiles, and followers, in social media such as Facebook and Twitter, further research should explore the importance and impact of *visibly* building strong networks of followers and online alliances (attracting 'followers' from other mainstream media, the political elite, the public and being supported by other organizations) for the recruitment and mobilization of protest groups.

Overall, this study demonstrates that, despite differences with regard to the extent to which they use various features, occupation websites share common elements with those of large SMOs—especially in terms of information provision and calls for mobilization. Being able to, quickly and without financial support or specialized knowledge, develop websites or blogs that can have similar effects to those of large SMOs, in terms of mobilizing support, can be a great benefit for loosely organized groups. The relatively stronger presence of interactive features in the occupation websites, mainly in the form of 'comment-below-post' features and solidarity sections, was nevertheless marked by the absence of more interactive tools such as forums or chats. The absence of these features—alongside the appearance of Twitter feeds on the home pages, the linking of occupations via Twitter and the fact that all occupations used Twitter—may mean that spontaneously organized and short-lived protest groups use websites for interactivity and public engagement to a certain degree, while these functions also simultaneously migrate to, or become more intertwined with, more interactive platforms like social media. There are indications that one such process might be at work, at least as far as loosely organized groups with low resources are concerned. In their research on the Austrian student protests, Maireder and Schwarzenegger describe a similar type of mobilization organized by loosely connected individuals in which websites and social media played different roles (some undertook the role of interaction, while others were used mainly as announcement platforms, depending on the circumstances) but at the same time intertwined, linking content to each other and allowing information to be diffused across media (2012: 175). Although, based on this analysis, it cannot be established whether people visited the UK student occupation websites on a regular basis or were redirected by Facebook or Twitter, the presence of particular features (such as integrated news feeds and posts redirecting readers to Facebook groups) indicates that websites and social media were elements of a wider media portfolio that allowed them to synergize and distribute content in different ways (see also Theocharis 2012: 181). Despite the flexibility that these developments provided in terms of communicating the discourse, there are also important caveats. Future research on the relationship between websites and social media might reveal more about the extent of protest groups' use of these platforms in future mobilizations and help to better understand the consequences of migrating the discourse from websites to social media.

## NOTES

1 It has been argued that this differentiates them from ? and gives them significant advantages over ? the micro-blogging format of social media (see Java *et al.* 2007).

2 As eloquently described by Penny (2011: 26), 'Amid tangled blankets and computer tables, students are sending out press releases, updating the group's Twitter feed and liaising with fellow dissidents about keeping the younger contingent safe on tomorrow's day of direct action against the tuition fees.'

3 It should be noted here that, despite past efforts to compile a list of the most frequently used repertoires of online mobilization (Vegh 2003; Van Laer & Van Aelst 2010), which sometimes extended street-theatre protest action repertoires into the online realm, the speed with which the internet offers new opportunities for internet-based or internet-supported action makes compiling a definitive list impossible. Therefore, this study considers action-mobilizing website functions to be those that broadly ask (or give the opportunity to) visitors to join or support the cause (see also Van Aelst & Walgrave 2004).

4 The three types of activities unavoidably prompts a question regarding the direction of causality in terms of offline/online participation; that is, whether students' e-tactics preceded offline mobilization, or whether they resulted from offline mobilization that demanded a web presence to support the offline cause. The relationship between online and offline participation has been the subject of a long-lasting debate in the internet literature; it remains to be seen whether the relationship implies a form of causality (see, for example, Boulianne 2009; Quintelier & Vissers 2008). A definitive answer cannot be given based on the approach (or findings) of this study. Although it is likely that some people mobilized as a result of online calls for action, the widespread and intense reaction that the government's plans for education cuts provoked would have been opposed by students with or without the assistance of internet technology, making the internet a way of effectively complementing the inevitable offline reaction.

5 As happened, for example, with www.bristoluniresistance.org.uk.

6 It is worth noting that after the vote passed, most of the occupations ended the next day or up to ten days later. Some of the occupation websites went offline or were completely abandoned, while others kept posting information, albeit less frequently, about the larger Anti-cuts movement.

7 The text-analysis software harvested all 1,187 occupation blog/website posts that appeared on the Google Reader RSS/Atom feed from 22 November to 22 December. 'Units' are defined as *all* blog/website posts (articles, video, pictures, etc.) on the home pages of all occupation websites from 22 November to 9 December.

8 The text-analytic tool offers a 'validate dataset' option that compares the codes given to each unit by individual coders (in this case, the graduate students) and provides a percentage of coding agreement between the coders.

9 See: www.ucloccupation.com/ and www.defendeducation.co.uk/.

10 Although the students of all occupations received hundreds of messages of solidarity from both students and members of staff, which demonstrated that their cause and demands received widespread acceptance, it should not be assumed that the opinions and requests presented on the occupation websites necessarily represented the views of the entire student body/staff of the occupied universities.

11 Named after Lord Browne, who chaired the review of higher education funding.

12 Embedding a forum or a chat is an option that features in all of the website/blog platforms used by the students; their absence marks an obvious choice on the students' part not to use them.

13 Some acquired and interacted with thousands of followers (based on the number of tweets produced) in just a couple of days (Theocharis 2012).

# REFERENCES

Anstead, N. & O'Loughlin, B. (2010). 'The emerging viewertariat and BBC Question Time television debate and real-time commenting online', *International Journal of Press/Politics*, Vol. 16, No. 4, pp. 440–462.

Bachen, C., Raphael, C., Lynn, K. M., McKee, K., & Philippi, J. (2008). 'Civic engagement, pedagogy, and information technology on web sites for youth', *Political Communication*, Vol. 25, No. 3, pp. 290–310.

Bennett, L. W. (2003). 'Communicating global activism: Strengths and vulnerabilities of networked politics', *Information, Communication, & Society*, Vol. 6, No. 2, pp. 143–168.

Bennett, L. W. (2005). Social movements beyond borders: understanding two eras of transnational activism', in *Transnational Protest and Global Activism*, ed. D. della Porta & S. Tarrow, Lanham, MD: Rowman & Littlefield.

Bennett, L.W. & Segerberg, A. (2012). 'The logic of connective action: Digital media and the personalization of contentious politics', *Information, Communication & Society*, [online, iFirst article], Available at: www.tandfonline.com/doi/full/10.1080/1369118X.2012.670661.

Biddix, J. P. & Park, H. W. (2008). 'Online networks of student protest: The case of the living wage campaign', *New Media & Society*, Vol. 10, No. 6, pp. 871–891.

Bimber, B., Stohl, C., & Flanagin, A. J. (2009). 'Technological change and the shifting nature of political organization', in *Routledge Handbook of Internet Politics*, ed. A. Chadwick & P. Howard, London: Routledge.

Boulianne, S. (2009). 'Does internet use affect engagement? A meta-analysis of research', *Political Communication*, Vol. 26, No. 3, pp. 193–211.

Caren, N. & Gaby, S. (2011). 'Occupy online: Facebook and the spread of Occupy Wall Street', [online], Available at SSRN: http://ssrn.com/abstract=1943168 or http://dx.doi.org/10.2139/ssrn.1943168.

Chadwick, A. (2006). *Internet Politics: States, Citizens and New Communication Technologies*, New York: Oxford University Press.

Chadwick, A. (2007). 'Digital network repertoires and organizational hybridity', *Political Communication*, Vol. 24, pp. 283–301.

Chadwick, A. (2012). 'Recent shifts in the relationship between the internet and democratic engagement in Britain and the United States: Granularity, informational exuberance and political learning', in *Digital Media and Political Engagement Worldwide*, ed. E. Anduiza, M. Jensen & L. Jorba, Cambridge: Cambridge University Press.

Coleman, S. (2008). 'Doing IT for themselves: Management versus autonomy in youth e-citizenship', in *Civic Life Online: Learning How Digital Media can Engage Youth*, ed. L. W. Bennett, Cambridge, MA: MIT Press.

Della Porta, D., & Mosca, L. (2009). 'Searching the net: Web sites' qualities in the global justice movement', *Information, Communication & Society*, 12, Vol. 6, pp. 771–792.

Foot, K. A., & Schneider, S. M. (2006). *Web Campaigning*, Cambridge, MA: MIT Press.

Garrett, R. K. (2006). 'Protest in an information society: A review of literature on social movements and new ICTs', *Information, Communication & Society*, Vol. 9, No. 2, pp. 202–224.

Garrido, M., & Halavais, A. (2003). 'Mapping networks of support for the Zapatista movement: Applying social-networks analysis to study contemporary social movements', in *Cyberactivism: Online Activism in Theory and Practice,* ed. M. McCaughey & M. Ayers, New York: Routledge.

Gibson, R., & Ward, S. (2000). 'A proposed methodology for studying the function and effectiveness of party and candidate websites', *Social Science Computer Review,* Vol. 18, No. 3, 301–319.

Gillan, K. (2009). 'The UK anti-war movement online: Uses and limitations of internet technologies for contemporary activism', *Information, Communication & Society,* Vol. 12, No. 1, 25–43.

Gillan, K., Pickerill, J., & Webster, F. (2011). *Anti-war Activism: New Media and Protest in the Information Age,* Basingstoke: Palgrave Macmillan.

Gladwell, M. (2010). 'Why the revolution will not be twitted', *New Yorker,* 4 October, [online], Available at: www.newyorker.com/reporting/2010/10/04/101004 fa_fact_gladwell.

Gurak, L., & Logie, J. (2003). 'Internet protests, from text to web', in *Cyberactivism: Online Activism in Theory and Practice,* eds M. McCaughey & M. Ayers, New York: Routledge.

Hounshell, B. (2011). 'The revolution will be tweeted', *Foreign Policy,* [online], Available at: www.foreignpolicy.com/articles/2011/06/20/the_revolution_will_be_tweeted.

Ibrahim, J. (2011). 'The new toll on higher education and the UK student revolts of 2010–2011', *Social Movement Studies,* Vol. 10, No. 4, pp. 415–421.

Java, A., Finin, T., Song, X. *et al.* (2007). 'Why we Twitter: Understanding microblogging usage and communities'. Paper presented at the 9th WEBKDD and 1st SNA-KDD Workshop '07, 12 August 2007, San Jose, California, US.

Kahn, R. & Kellner, D. (2004). 'New media and internet activism: From the "Battle of Seattle" to blogging', *New Media and Society,* Vol. 6, No. 1, pp. 87–95.

Lewis, P. & Taylor, M. (2010). 'Student demos in Twitter age: No leaders, only chatter', *Guardian,* [online], Available at: www.guardian.co.uk/education/2010/nov/24/student-demos-in-twitter-age (24 December).

Lewis, P. & Walker, P. (2010). 'Twitter did not suppress student protesters' accounts', *Guardian,* [online], Available at: www.guardian.co.uk/technology/2010/dec/01/twitter-student-protesters-accounts (1 December).

Lotan, G., Graeff, E., Ananny, M., Gaffney, D., Pearce, I., & boyd, d. (2011). 'The revolutions were tweeted: Information flows during the 2011 Tunisian and Egyptian revolutions', *International Journal of Communication,* Vol. 5, [online], Available at: http://ijoc.org/ojs/index.php/ijoc/article/view/1246.

Maireder, A., & Schwarzenegger, C. (2012). 'A movement of connected individuals: Social media in the Austrian student protests 2009', *Information, Communication & Society,* Vol. 15, No. 2, pp. 171–195.

McCaughey, M. & Ayres, M. (2003). *Cyberactivism, Online Activism in Theory and Practice,* New York: Routledge.

Mercea, D. (2012). 'Digital prefigurative participation: The entwinement of online communication and offline participation in protest events', *New Media & Society,* Vol. 14, No. 1, pp. 153–169.

Morozov, E. (2011). 'Picking a fight with Clay Shirky', *Foreign Policy,* [online], Available at: http://neteffect.foreignpolicy.com/posts/2011/01/15/picking_a_fight_with_clay_shirky.

Olesen, T. (2004). 'Globalizing the Zapatistas: from third world solidarity to global solidarity?', *Third World Quarterly,* Vol. 25, No. 1, pp. 255–267.

Penny, L. (2011). 'No drugs. No sex. And no leaders', *New Statesman,* 31 January, pp. 24–29.

Pickerill, J. (2004). 'Rethinking political participation: Experiments in internet activism in Australia and Britain', in *Electronic Democracy: Mobilisation, Organisation and Participation Via New ICTs,* eds R. Gibson, A. Rommele & S. Ward, London: Routledge.

Quintelier, E. & Vissers, S. (2008). 'The effect of internet use on political participation: An analysis of survey results for 16-year olds in Belgium', *Social Science Computer Review,* Vol. 26, No. 4, pp. 411–427.

Rusbridger, A. (2010). 'Student protests: Demonstration effect', *Guardian,* [online], Available at: www.guardian.co.uk/commentisfree/2010/nov/11/student-protests-demonstration-editorial?intcmp=239.

Shirky, C. (2008). *Here Comes Everybody: How Change Happens when People Come Together,* New York: Penguin.

Shirky, C. (2011). 'The political power of social media', *Foreign Affairs,* Vol. 90, No. 1, pp. 28–41.

Singer, C. (2011). 'Social media has transformed protests—and the Daily Mail', *The Guardian,* [online], Available at: www.guardian.co.uk/commentisfree/2011/jan/08/social-media-student-protest-topshop-mail.

Stein, L. (2009). 'Social movement web use in theory and practice: A content analysis of US movement websites', *New Media & Society,* Vol. 11, No. 5, pp. 749–771.

Theocharis, Y. (2012). 'Cuts, tweets, solidarity and mobilisation: how the internet shaped the student occupations", *Parliamentary Affairs,* Vol. 65, No. 1, pp. 162–194.

UCLOccupation blog (2010). *UCL occupation blog,* [online] Available at: http://blog.ucloccupation.com/.

Valenzuela, S., Arriagada, A., & Scherman, A. (2012). 'The social media basis of youth protest behaviour: The case of Chile', *Journal of Communication,* Vol. 62, No. 2, pp. 299–314.

Van Aelst, P., & Walgrave, S. (2004). 'New media, new movements? The role of the internet in shaping the anti-globalization movement', *Information, Communication & Society,* Vol. 5, No.4., pp. 465–493.

Van Laer, J. & Van Aelst, P. (2010). 'Internet and social movement action repertoires: Opportunities and limitations', *Information, Communication & Society,* Vol. 14, No. 8, pp. 1146–1171.

Vegh, S. (2003). 'Classifying forms of online activism: The case of cyberprotest against the World Bank', in *Cyberactivism: Online Activism in Theory and Practice,* ed. M. McCaughey & M. Ayres, New York: Routledge.

Williams, J. & Vasagar, J. (2010). 'University tuition fees hike "will deter most poorer students"—poll', *Guardian,* [online], Available at: www.guardian.co.uk/education/2010/nov/18/ipsos-mori-poll-tuition-fees-cuts

Wright, S. (2004). 'Informing, communicating and ICTs in contemporary anti-capitalist movements', in *Cyberprotest: New media, citizens and social movements,* e., W. van de Donk, B. D. Loader, P. G. Nixon *et al.,* London: Routledge.

# Index

Page numbers in *italics* denotes a table/figure

For Product Safety Concerns and Information please contact our EU
representative  GPSR@taylorandfrancis.com
Taylor & Francis Verlag GmbH, Kaufingerstraße 24, 80331 München, Germany

www.ingramcontent.com/pod-product-compliance
Lightning Source LLC
Chambersburg PA
CBHW071422050326
40689CB00010B/1945